Foreign Policy Making
and the American
Political System

Foreign Policy Making and the American Political System

James A. Nathan
James K. Oliver
University of Delaware

Little, Brown and Company

Boston   Toronto

Library of Congress Cataloging in Publication Data

Nathan, James A.
  Foreign policy making and the American political system.

  1. United States—Foreign relations—1945–
I. Oliver, James K.   II. Title.
JX1417.N295   1983   353.0089   81-83819
ISBN 0-316-59852-6

Copyright © 1983 by James A. Nathan and James K. Oliver

Library of Congress Catalog Card Number 81-83819

ISBN 0-316-59852-6

9 8 7 6 5 4 3 2 1

MV

Published simultaneously in Canada
by Little, Brown & Company (Canada) Limited

Printed in the United States of America

Acknowledgments
  Extracts from *The New York Times* © 1972, © 1973, © 1974, © 1975, © 1977, © 1980, © 1981 by The New York Times Company. Reprinted by permission.
  Portions of Chapter 6 appeared originally, in slightly different form, in "The Roots of the Imperial Presidency" by James Nathan, *Presidential Studies Quarterly*, January 1975, and are used here by permission.
  Extract from *The Washington Post*, 30 November 1980, © The Washington Post. Reprinted by permission.

Preface

The formulation and administration of United States foreign policy have long been matters of concern to observers of American society and politics. Early in the nineteenth century, Alexis de Tocqueville concluded that American democracy, with its institutional fragmentation and increasingly democratized politics, constituted a "decidely inferior" system for making and carrying out foreign policy. Reflecting similar concerns, the architects of American foreign policy after World War II tried to modify the institutions and processes of national security and foreign policy making. In an effort to make the executive establishment more responsive to the demands of the cold war, the National Security Act of 1947 sought to strengthen the hand of the President. Simultaneously, the notion of "bipartisanship" was developed to mute foreign policy conflict among Democrats and Republicans and was then extended to encompass executive-legislative conflict itself.

Again in the 1970s, as American foreign policy encountered the frustrating limitations of an international system in which military capability was widely diffused and the very nature of power itself seemed transformed, institutional changes assumed prominence. A presidency, now characterized as "imperial" in form, saw its authority undercut by failure in Vietnam and scandal at home. A new congressional assertiveness emerged as reformers in both the House and Senate searched—not always successfully—for ways to increase the foreign policy role of Congress as an institution while at the same time strengthening the influence of the individual legislator in the policy making process.

The relationship of the ruled and the rulers has proved no less difficult. Throughout the postwar decades of cold war activism, retrenchment, détente, and then return to Soviet-American tension, the capacity of the American people to recognize their national interests and the extent to which they would allow policy elites to define those interests have been matters of uncertainty. For their part, most Americans seem to have maintained attitudes of mixed indifference and pragmatism toward things foreign. However, the resulting latitude for foreign policy makers has not been unlimited, and in both the early 1950s and 1970s was curtailed as the costs of Korea and then Vietnam mounted. Indeed, in the latter case, popular disaffection was manifested in a marked decline in the vague "internationalism" characteristic of public opinion during the preceding decades. Thus on the threshold of the 1980s, and following the jarring onset of complex political and economic interdependence in the mid- and late 1970s, a far more complicated and less predictable amalgam of attitudes seemed to have taken hold; and with it returned all the old questions about the inherent capacity and incapacity of a democracy for dealing with the world.

This book seeks to define and illuminate the many dimensions of the relationship between foreign policy making and the American political system. Because many dimensions are to be dealt with—e.g. the executive establishment, executive-legislative relations, public opinion, the role of private power—our approach involves many styles and levels of analysis. Where complex and extended institutional relationships and policy making processes are involved, a mix of institutional description and more abstract conceptual frameworks, such as the perspectives and insights of bureaucratic politics, have been used. In other instances, constitutional issues are explored by means of the review and exposition of legal questions and, where necessary, case law. A survey of public opinion necessarily requires attention to poll data—and the problems associated with its use. And where we have found analysis and theory as yet undefined as, for example, in the analysis of private power and foreign policy, we have advanced our own tentative framework.

In addition, we have tried to place our analysis in a context of policy and the development of the foreign and national security policy making institutions and processes during the postwar period. Underlying this approach is our conviction that "officials," institutions, processes, and the relationship of them to the larger political system reflect as well as shape policy and its demands. Moreover, institutions, processes and the broader political relationships exist in a legal, organizational, and temporal matrix. The structure and dynamics of policy making processes are therefore constrained by previous political and institutional developments and policy commitments. Accordingly, analysis must incorporate these factors no less fully than it does institutional description and the latest social scientific models and frameworks of analysis.

Finally, we would note that this volume has emerged from its own context of previous development. Though this is essentially a new book, users of the first edition of our *United States Foreign Policy and World Order* will recognize that the coverage of *Foreign Policy Making and the American Political System* is similar to Part II of the earlier book. As we noted in the preface to the second edition of *United States Foreign Policy and World Order*, we have developed the present book in order to provide greater pedagogical flexibility and a more detailed survey and analysis of the foreign policy making process than the original format of *United States Foreign Policy and World Order* allowed.

ACKNOWLEDGMENTS

In addition to those acknowledged in the endnotes in the text, a small group of scholars read part or all of the text and provided critiques. The efforts of David Ziegler, Western Washington University, John Keeler at the University of Washington, and Reid Reading of the University of Pittsburg were especially helpful. Though we have not always agreed with their criticism, their evaluations were important in clarifying our analysis and sharpening the presentation. The results of this dialogue are, of course, solely the responsibility of the authors.

Finally, Will Ethridge of Little, Brown served, as on other projects, as a patient editorial presence. His task was doubly difficult, for the present book had not only to be extracted from the two authors but also to be coordinated with the production of the second edition of *United States Foreign Policy and World Order*. We are most appreciative of his forbearance, editorial judgment, good humor, and encouragement.

Contents

*Foreign Policy Making
and the American
Political System*

Chapter 1
Introduction

A nation's foreign policy encompasses more than its behavior in the world. Since it both proceeds from and purportedly serves the interests of a nation, foreign policy also embraces institutions, policy making processes, and people. For the last 200 years, both foreign and American observers of American government have remarked and worried about the difficulties the American system faces in fashioning a coherent and effective foreign policy. This book is about the American governmental process and the society in which it is embedded. Most important, it is about the relationship between those two and America's foreign policy.

In this introduction we will briefly survey some of the policy making dilemmas that have arisen within the American political system as the result of America's world role since World War II. These policy making problems are rooted in the tension between the demands imposed by the constitutional framework and its evolution, and the development and working of American democracy, on the one hand, and the exigencies of an activist and globalist foreign policy on the other. Finally, we suggest how these problems can serve as the basis for useful levels of analysis for an understanding of foreign policy making in the American political system.

THE FOREIGN POLICY CONTEXT

Since World War II, American policy makers, whatever their partisan identification, have felt that securing American international interests requires an activist foreign policy. They have sometimes strongly disagreed over the most appropriate means to be employed. Nonetheless, since at least 1947, they have acted on the premise that

1

American security is inextricably tied to the structure and dynamics of world order. They consider American security to be a function of world order and believe that deep and long-term American involvement in the development and maintenance of world order is essential.[1]

For two decades after World War II the pursuit of these interests and the world political context within which American policy was defined and implemented seemed simple. The presence of the Soviet Union, which possessed a similarly globalist view of its interests and also represented the only other power in the international system with even an approximation of American strategic capability, meant that world politics tended towards bipolarity.[2] The possibility of nuclear war compounded the tensions inherent in the Soviet-American ideological confrontation. Moreover, the emergence from colonial domination of scores of new non-Western nations toward the end of the period blurred somewhat the structural simplicity of world politics. Nonetheless, a combination of American strategic and economic superiority contributed to a generally successful pursuit of unambiguous American objectives.

The United States, however, faced in the late 1960s and early 1970s a much more complex international system than the one that had been dominated by the Soviet-American confrontation of the cold war. In addition to the inability of the United States to win the Vietnam War and the severe disruption of domestic politics and society that accompanied that failure, the 1970s saw the emergence of new international conditions that seem likely to constrain the process of defining, making, and administering American foreign policy throughout the remainder of the century.

First, military capability has become increasingly diffused. Although the United States and the Soviet Union remain superpowers, others now possess significant military arsenals. At the beginning of the 1980s, almost a dozen states either had nuclear weapons or the capacity to acquire or develop them within a matter of months or at most, a few years. Second, the Soviet Union has achieved military parity with the United States. These two new conditions mean that threats of force or the actual use of military force by the United States have become less credible options than they had been in the earlier years of undoubted American superiority.

But more has changed than the stark and terrifyingly simple

bipolar strategic structure of world politics. Indeed, some analysts of world politics maintain that the economic interdependence and relationships that emerged and occupied so much attention during the 1970s are equally significant developments.[3] Thanks in part to American foreign policy, Western Europe and Japan had fully recovered from the effects of World War II by the 1960s and had become centers of economic power competitive with the United States. Moreover, the Arab oil exporting countries dramatically demonstrated and took advantage of the industrialized world's dependence on imported oil in 1973 and 1974 and continued to increase the price of oil, in league with the other oil exporting countries in the Organization of Petroleum Exporting Countries, throughout the 1970s. These developments in the international economy are an indication that the very structure, dynamics, and nature of power and influence in world politics have changed.[4] Some observers are dubious, however,[5] arguing that whatever difficulties the United States has experienced in maintaining its former position are more the product of poor leadership and a misunderstanding of the traditional and unchanged interaction of power and interests in world politics than the result of any basic changes in international relations.[6]

Whether the web of interdependence in which the United States finds itself in the 1980s constitutes a new world politics or not, the diffusion of military power, the onset of strategic parity, and the salience of political economics make for a more complex world in which the operational meaning of security is not self-evident. The traditional problems of managing military power remain central to American policy makers, but additional new military actors and new world relationships now command an equal amount of their attention. And precisely because the demands of global involvement have become both more complex and intense, the constraints imposed by the American domestic political framework have become more important.

THE DOMESTIC CONTEXT OF FOREIGN POLICY MAKING

In comparison with other political systems the American constitutional framework has proved remarkably stable, resilient, and long-lived. Yet throughout American history, foreign and domestic observers have tended to concur with Alexis de Tocqueville's judgment that in matters pertaining to the conduct of foreign affairs, the American democracy—indeed, all democracies—constituted a "decidedly inferior" form of government.[7] The concern has been that the constitutional framework and the modalities of democratic politics would combine to produce a policy making milieu and process that, although perfectly appropriate to the needs of American domestic politics, would prove disastrously inappropriate to the demands imposed by international politics. The paradoxical dilemma of American democracy was summarized by a group of American textbook writers in the late 1960s:

> . . . the more civilized and non-violent a democratic nation becomes in its internal institutions and behavior, the more peaceful and frank the outlook and conduct of its people, the more it may find it difficult, as a nation, to survive and prosper in the semi-anarchy of international affairs, in which secrecy, suspicion, and violence always lurk in the background.[8]

There are at least three complex dimensions of this dilemma that warrant elaboration because they are so fundamental to the operation of the American foreign and national security policy making process. They are, first, the constitutional and institutional framework of American government, especially what Madison referred to as the "partial mixture of powers" between Congress and President.[9] Second, there is the foreign and national security policy bureaucracy that developed as a corollary to America's expanding world role in the post–World War II era. Finally, one must be concerned with the character and role of public opinion and those groups in American society that possess significant foreign affairs weight either in tandem with or independent of the United States government.

The Constitutional and Institutional Framework

The limits and obstacles imposed by the constitutional and institutional framework are perhaps the most frequently lamented characteristics of the foreign and national security policy making processes. In an effort to establish a governmental framework that was stronger than the Articles of Confederation, that is, provided for greater capacity in the national government, but not so strong as to threaten liberty, the framers of the Constitution established the now familiar fragmented institutional structure of the American national government. Policy making authority and responsibility was to be shared among three branches of government, with the Congress and the Executive assuming the most important roles in the formulation and conduct of foreign affairs.

The men who drafted the Constitution were in no way insensitive to the complexities and dangers of international relations. They understood fully that the quasi-anarchy of world politics in the late eighteenth century required an executive fully able to respond to security threats and conduct diplomacy with dispatch. But although the Executive was given the authority and responsibility to conduct war and diplomacy, the authority to commence war and commit the nation to significant foreign undertakings was reserved to the Congress. The President was Commander-in-Chief and responsible for the negotiation of treaties and the day-to-day conduct of diplomacy, but the Congress maintained the Army and Navy, declared war, authorized the undertaking of limited—or in the argot of eighteenth century international law, "imperfect wars"[10]—and had to tender its advice and consent to treaties before they became the law of the land. The system was understood to be complex, even inefficient, but as Madison argued in Federalist 48:

> Unless these departments be so far connected and blended as to give to each a constitutional control over the others, the degree of separation which the maxim requires, as essential to a free government, can never in practice be duly maintained.[11]

Or as he put it in a later paper:

> But the great security against a gradual concentration of the several powers in the same department consists in giving to those who administer each department the necessary constitutional means and personal motives to resist encroachments of the others. The provision for defense must in this, as in all other cases, be made commensurate to the danger of attack. Ambition must be made to counteract ambition.[12]

But the well-being and prosperity of the Republic vis-a-vis the world were ultimately to be secured by Washington's axiom concerning the content of America's international relations: "The great rule of conduct for us in regard to foreign nations is, in extending our commercial relations to have with them as little political connection as possible."[13] Insofar as this axiom could be followed, the policy making dilemmas and dangers inherent in shared policy making authority could be avoided. In the first place, constitutional authority and responsibility for the regulation of commercial relations among nations was clearly set forth in the Constitution: it belonged to the Congress. Thus foreign relations so defined remained in conformity with the Madisonian assertion that "in republican government, the legislative authority necessarily predominates."[14] Furthermore, inasmuch as the actual conduct of commercial relations was undertaken not by the government but by private individuals, worry about the efficiency of foreign relations was unwarranted.

In sum, Washington and the founding fathers understood full well the problems posed by the institutional structure that they had created. They anticipated the dilemmas and inadequacies of that system in the face of deep political involvement in world affairs. They hoped, however, that America's geographic isolation, combined with a concentration on what was assumed to be the greatest international asset of the United States, its commercial relations, would save the American system from the agonies of European systems perpetually locked in intimate political relations with their neighbors. The European system led inevitably to conflict, the necessity for military preparedness, the threat and use of military force, and, concomitantly, a political regime in which necessities of executive efficiency predominated at the expense of individual liberty if the national security was to be realized; they were, in short, the very forms of government the Americans had left behind and rebelled against.

These hopes were frustrated from the very outset. Commercial relations required open seas, and the new republic soon discovered that these could be secured only by force, often at considerable distance from American waters. Moreover, the international politics of Napoleonic Europe would not leave North America alone, notwithstanding American assertions of neutrality. War came within the lifetimes of the founding fathers, followed in the early nineteenth century by the acquisition and opening up of the continent itself. And at every turn the question of executive-legislative relations in the conduct of American foreign and military relations became more complex.

By the mid-twentieth century, however, they were increasingly acute. Global depression and world war left the United States a world power. Within 2 years after the close of the Second World War, the Truman administration had begun the process of defining and executing a globally activist role for the United States. Washington's "great rule of conduct for us in regard to foreign nations" was stood on its head. America's "political connection" with the world was now paramount. But in so transforming the conception of the national interest, a transformation or at least a significant adaptation of the institutional relationships at the heart of the constitutional framework seemed a compelling necessity.

The process of adaptation has not involved formal constitutional modification. Rather, Presidents beginning with Truman have pursued a course of claiming inherent prerogatives for their office as the purported demands of American internationalism increased throughout the cold war. Often, as with the Vandenberg Resolution, Marshall Plan, or military assistance programs, Presidents would seek congressional support and approval. In other instances, such as in Korea or Vietnam, Presidents have acted first and then sought congressional approval. In virtually every instance, however, there was either an implicit or explicit claim of inherent presidential power based on the often unarticulated assumption that the demands of the cold war extended to nothing less than the survival of the Republic itself. Under such circumstances, this argument went, the initiative for the exercise of the foreign and national security powers that were the "joint possession"[15] of Congress and President under the constitutional design, must shift to the Executive if the national interest was to be advanced.

Although there were partisan disagreements, Congress by and large acceded to this logic. Especially during the 1950s and early 1960s, when American power and political economic reach were nearly hegemonial, the accession was easy. Indeed, it could be readily rationalized as the only responsible course to follow. Thus the largely informal and incremental circumventing of the institutional constraints of the constitutional framework had the apparent virtue of leaving the constitutional forms intact even as their operation was modified to confront exigencies only dimly perceived by the framers of the Constitution.

The solvent of the institutional dilemmas posed by the constitutional framework was, however, success and American hegemony. And when the latter became more problematic in Vietnam in the late 1960s and with the onset of complex interdependence in the early 1970s, the executive-legislative modus vivendi of the cold war years disintegrated rapidly and rancorously. The "Vietnam Revolution" in Congress and the wound inflicted on the presidency by Richard Nixon through Watergate culminated in a reassertion of the congressional presence in the foreign and national security policy making processes.

But by the late 1970s the impetus behind this congressional renascence seemed spent. The membership of Congress had been renewed by a generational change; the institution had reformed its budgetary processes and internal governance through a diffusion of power within the institution; and had asserted more active involvement in program oversight. However, the inherent fragmentation of Congress was, if anything, exacerbated by the diffusion of power within and democratizing of the institution. The reassertion of program oversight and a new activism in the policy making process—evident in the ratification fights over the Panama Canal treaties, SALT II, and disruption of the delicate balance of Greek and Turkish sensitivities resulting from a congressionally mandated cutoff of military aid to Turkey at the time of the Turkish invasion of Cyprus—raised anew all the difficult questions about the efficacy of the congressional role in the foreign policy making process. If the "new executive-legislative relationship" amounted to little more than the old constitutionally mandated inefficiency, was this sufficient in an international system characterized by fragile Soviet-American parity, and greater American economic interdependence but also vulnerability to international economic vagaries?

Bureaucratic Power and Politics

The onset of a global role for the United States has had other important consequences for the policy making processes beyond executive-legislative relations. Within the Executive itself, the establishment and pursuit of an internationalist foreign and national security policy has led to major institutional change. By 1947, President Truman was asking Congress through the National Security Act of that year to reorganize the executive branch by establishing a new Department of Defense, a more centralized intelligence establishment under a new Central Intelligence Agency, and a new National Security Council to serve as a means for facilitating the integration of American foreign and defense policy. Throughout the succeeding 3 decades the executive establishment making foreign and national security policy has grown enormously as the American world role has expanded. In one sense, of course, this bureaucratic establishment augments the capacity of the President to formulate and conduct American foreign policy, in that it represents organized and mobilized expertise. At the same time, however, these tens of thousands of people organized within scores of departments, agencies, bureaus, and other bureaucratic structures serve as an important constraint on the policy making process that they are ostensibly serving.

An examination of the development and character of these bureaucratic constraints follows in subsequent chapters. For now it is sufficient to note that the existence of numerous bureaucracies responsible for bringing their particular expertise and experience to bear on the formulation and implementation of foreign policy inevitably means that within the United States government, many perspectives coexist on international realities, American interests, and the appropriate policies for achieving American objectives. Thus, for example, members of the Department of State are likely to possess a view of what ought to be emphasized in U.S.–West European relations somewhat different from the Department of Defense. Whereas the latter, given their organization's responsibilities, are likely to emphasize the necessity for military preparedness and a strong NATO alliance, a State Department official may well stress the necessity of sensitivity to diverse political currents within Europe in formulating U.S. policy. For example, early in the Reagan administration the Secretaries of State and Defense found themselves recommending contradictory approaches to the decision to deploy a new American nuclear warhead—the "neutron bomb"—in Europe. The Secretary of State urged that the United States proceed cautiously in view of strong antinuclear feeling among several of America's European allies. In contrast, the Secretary of Defense recommended that the defense of the United States required immediate deployment of the weapons and that the United States should not allow the Europeans to influence American decision making unduly.

The problem of multiple and conflicting policy perspectives is often extended by disagreements within these very large bureaucracies. Thus in developing American policy with respect to a dispute between two American allies such as Greece and Turkey over Cyprus, one can expect to find those responsible for monitoring events and representing American interests in Greece and Turkey becoming advocates of the primacy of American interests vis-a-vis the country or countries for which they are responsible.

In addition, personal ambitions for dominance within the policy making process, such as have arisen in virtually every administration between members of a President's personal staff and cabinet officers such as the Secretaries of State and Defense, inevitably compound the problem of organizational fragmentation. In these instances substantive policy disputes sometimes become indistinguishable from an individual's desire to control the flow of information to a President or the implementation of decisions reached by a President. Finally, how a member of the bureaucracy perceives reality and American interests is colored by the desire to protect the bureaucrat's organization. Here threats to American interests or opportunities for the United States tend to be defined in a manner that can be most effectively dealt with by one's own agency, thereby enhancing the organization's resources, that is, its budget, personnel, and mission.

To the extent that the members of the foreign and national security policy making establishment respond to these diverse organizational and personal perspectives and interests, which are not necessarily the same as those of the President, the President faces a significant obstacle in the policy making process.[16] The problem has at least two dimensions. First, a President must draw out of this conflictual bureaucratic process analysis and advice relevant to the policy making problem of the moment and fashion policy with the help of his closest advisers (who will themselves be influenced by these conditions, given that most of them will in some measure represent their respective organizational bases—State, Defense, Central Intelligence Agency, etc.). Having done so, however, a President is then faced with a second difficulty: having policy carried out; for the implementation of policy will be no less subject to the interplay of personal and organizational interests than the policy formulation phase.

In sum, the relative preponderance of the presidency in the executive-legislative relationship throughout most of the post–World War II era of American global activism has not alleviated the structural fragmentation that is fundamental to the American constitutional design. Even were it true that the struggle between President and Congress for control of the policy making process has been resolved—and this is arguable—the dilemma of bureaucratic power and politics remains. The problem is one of communicating the President's sense of priorities and objectives to the bureaucracy and having it accepted—a seemingly essential concomitant of an activist and globalist foreign policy.[17]

Democracy and the Policy Process

The relationship between those who govern and those who are governed is one of the most important elements of any political system. One of the distinguishing characteristics of democratic forms of government is the presumption that those who rule should be accountable to those who are ruled. Moreover, people are assumed to have a fundamental right to participate, either directly or through representatives chosen by and accountable to them, in those decisions that affect their lives. Clearly decisions concerning foreign and national security policy affect the lives of Americans, people who regard themselves as citizens of a representative democracy. Yet in perhaps no other area of public policy has the joining of democratic ideal and perceived governmental realities proved more troublesome.

The democratic norms of accountability, participation, and representation do not assume that the people are omniscient. Rather, the presumption is that through the course of open and public debate, facilitated by an unencumbered press, media, and expression of opinion, a more or less wise and prudent course of action can be set. However, the domain of international politics, especially in a nuclear age, is commonly viewed as uniquely dangerous. Moreover, the sheer quantity of information necessary to understand, the subtlety of the judgments that must be made, and the delicacy of the relationships that must be sustained in this domain are frequently viewed as beyond the capacities of ordinary people caught up in the day-to-day course of raising families and earning a living. Under such circumstances, the making and implementation of foreign and national security policy decisions is seen as necessarily devolving to a specialized governmental establishment with the training, experience, and wisdom necessary to the ultimate task of advancing the national interest and security.

Clearly, therefore, we are in the presence of a major dilemma for a democratic society. Granting that the exigencies of international politics are sometimes acutely demanding, should those who must make decisions and policy regarding this domain be subjected to the full measure of constraint demanded by democratic theory? Might not full and open debate endanger the country? Might not the demands of periodic elections prove disruptive and debilitating and contribute to gross inconsistencies in policy? And given the need for a free press and free media in a democracy, what are their responsibilities in dealing with issues that involve the security of the country?

These are not easy questions that can be subjected to simple remedies. Furthermore, they are made all the more difficult because of important disagreements as to the character and capabilities of mass publics in the United States. Most policy makers during the post–World War II period have been impressed by what they view as the fundamental and often profound ignorance of the American people about public affairs in general and foreign affairs in particular. This ignorance has been seen as leading in turn to a dangerous volatility in the American public which, if not contained, can stampede and crush laboriously constructed and delicately balanced international relations.[18] On the other hand, some students of American public opinion have concluded that although the public is by no means as well informed as one might like, levels of public information about foreign affairs have increased during the last decade. Moreover, the people can be seen as having developed reasonably sophisticated conceptions of the problems confronting the United States in its foreign relations. And above all, there is no evidence to support the view that the people are incapable of forming coherent and generally prudent judgments about frustratingly complex foreign policy questions when provided information and a full and responsible public debate on the issues.[19]

Yet, undeniably, the dilemma remains. Indeed, to the extent that policy makers, especially elected policy makers, believe that the people are ignorant, even dangerous, the relationship between leadership and the people becomes more problematical. If Presidents, for example, believe that policy departures must be sold to an ignorant, uncomprehending, and resistant populace, the danger exists that threats will be overstated and dangers magnified in order to mobilize popular support. The reverse may also prove to be true: if one believes that one is facing, or that previous efforts at public education have produced, a public convinced of the necessity for confrontation with the Soviet Union, then efforts to improve relations must be similarly oversold. Thus John Kennedy's Test Ban Treaty in 1963, or detente and SALT in the early 1970s, were accompanied by massive public relations campaigns. On the other hand, if the public comes to view the process of public debate as having degenerated into a demagogic manipulation of information, then one may well be confronted with growing public cynicism concerning not only the issues at hand but the entire policy process.[20]

Finally, the onset of economic interdependence seems to have added yet another element to the relationship between democracy and the foreign policy making process. Interdependence and the decline of American hegemony during the late 1960s and 1970s have contributed to greater economic vulnerabilities for the American people. Escalating energy prices were symptomatic of numerous other points where international effects had penetrated American society and now exact high economic and social costs from the American people. These circumstances seem likely to call forth more public demands, more interest groups, and in general, more constraints on public officials responsible for American foreign and especially for international economic relations. Indeed, some observers[21] now fear that increased public demands and mobilization have resulted in an American society characterized by an excess or "distemper of democracy" that seriously threatens the ability of American leadership to fashion any coherent international role for the United States.

POLICY MAKING DILEMMAS AND
APPROACHES TO ANALYSIS

Understanding the structure and operation of such complex and overlapping policy making institutions, processes, and problems is sometimes facilitated by the use of analytical frameworks. The purpose of such frameworks is to suggest a set of questions or domains of inquiry to guide one's analysis. Such frameworks may also provide a conceptual structure comprised of levels of analysis that suggest relationships—perhaps causal—between subsets of a phenomenon. It is conceivable that such frameworks can form the basis for or lead to theories of policy making that possess comprehensive explanatory capacity and predictive power.

This book does not aspire to the development of a comprehensive theoretical framework. However, the survey and discussion that follow are developed in response to a set of questions or concerns that are substantive and normative. Specifically, the inquiry proceeds from de Tocqueville's concern about the adequacy of the American policy making structures and processes for simultaneously formulating and sustaining a cogent foreign policy and serving the ideals of a respresentative and accountable democratic republic. As we have noted in the preceding discussion, this large question implies a number of subsidiary questions in two areas: (1) the implications of the fragmentation of foreign policy making and administrative authority in American constitutional theory, institutional design, and development; and (2) the demands of democratic theory for the representation of public opinion and accountability. These sets of issues broadly define the levels of analysis that frame the chapters to follow.

First, we take up the policy making institutions and the relationships between them. Here American constitutional theory has mandated—in the interests of limited governmental power—a pattern of institutional fragmentation, that is, the separation and sharing of foreign and national security policy making authority between executive and legislative branches of government. But institutional fragmentation has been compounded by the development of a large executive branch establishment—in response to the demands of global activism—that gives rise to its own constraints on the policy making process and its Chief Executive.

The approach to understanding the nature and implications of these two kinds of policy making fragmentation is to proceed from the center of foreign policy making in the post–World War II period—the presidency and the executive establishment—out to the domain of executive-legislative relations. Initially, therefore (in Chapters 2 and 3), we explore the nature and effects of institutional fragmentation within the executive foreign and national security policy making establishment. A survey and analysis of the growth of presidential power as an administrative necessity in the face of a growing world role and expanding bureaucracy makes up the focus of the analysis. The growth of presidential power also provides a framework for analyzing the emergence and rise to prominence of the Special Assistant for National Security Affairs and the National Security Council staff as the focus of presidential efforts to cope with the policy making fragmentation of the executive domain.

Next (in Chapters 4 and 5), we turn our attention to the second aspect of policy making fragmentation: an assessment of the nature and effects of the constitutionally mandated executive-legislative relationship. The decline of Congress as a locus of policy making after World War II is traced, as well as its renascence in the wake of the "Vietnam Revolution" in executive-legislative relations in the early and mid-1970s. A detailed analysis of the potential and limits of Congress in the 1980s is undertaken with special emphasis on the prospects for the development of a new executive-legislative relationship built around congressional capability in two areas: (1) program development and oversight, such as control of the military budget, economic and military assistance programs, and CIA/intelligence establishment oversight; and (2) policy formulation, such as the attempt of the Congress to reclaim the war making powers through the War Powers Resolution.

Our second level of analysis focuses on questions rooted in the problematic relationship between foreign and national security policy making at the presidential and executive-legislative center and the demands of democratic representation and accountability. Attention is focused on the outer sphere of the American system: the public and its relationship to the policy making sector. Thus we examine (in Chapters 6 and 7) the complex character of public opinion, the images of the public held by policy makers and vice versa, and also the effort by the Executive to control and condition the terms of public debate on foreign policy. We also devote attention (Chapter 8) to the operation of private power in American foreign policy. That is, we survey the activities of interest groups as well as other forms of private power in the policy process. Specifically, through examination of the close relationship between the government and the arms industry, we develop a concept of private power existing in a kind of symbiotic relationship with government. By considering multinational corporations, we explore a form of private power that can act somewhat independently of the government and thereby can take on some attributes of a private government.

In sum, this analysis seeks an overview of the dimensions, performance, strengths, and weaknesses of the American political system as a context for foreign and national security policy making. Simultaneously, however, the approach taken here relates the development and operation of foreign policy making institutions to the normative demands of democratic accountability. Such a framework necessarily excludes detailed attention to many other questions. Thus this analysis does not devote explicit attention to the interaction of the external environment with these internal institutions and processes. Implicit throughout the analysis, however, is the assumption that the expansion of America's role in an international system—itself a complex mix of anarchical fragmentation and interdependence—is the source of the developments and dilemmas that constitute the focus of this analysis of the domestic sources of American foreign and national security policy. In the final analysis, therefore, the approach of this survey turns attention inward to the contemporary state of the balance between institutional capacity for policy making and the demands of democratic accountability, while recogizing that this balance must be understood within a context of American global activism.[22]

NOTES

1. For a detailed review of the American foreign policy that grew out of this framework, see James A. Nathan and James K. Oliver, *United States Foreign Policy and World Order*, 2nd ed. (Boston: Little, Brown, 1981).

2. For the earliest authoritative statement of this view, see Harry S. Truman, "The Truman Doctrine: Special Message to the Congress on Greece and Turkey, March 12, 1947," *Public Papers of the Presidents, Harry S Truman, 1947* (Washington, D.C.: U.S. Government Printing Office, 1948), pp. 177–178.

3. For an enumeration and discussion of the "new forces" see Robert Keohane and Joseph Nye, eds., *Transnational Forces and World Politics* (Cambridge, Mass.: Harvard University Press, 1972); Seyom Brown, *New Forces in World Politics* (Washington, D.C.: The Brookings Institution, 1974); C. Fred Bergsten and Lawrence Krause, eds., *World Politics and International Economics* (Washington, D.C.: The Brookings Institution, 1975); and Robert Keohane and Joseph Nye, *Power and Interdependence: World Politics in Transition* (Boston: Little, Brown, 1977).

4. See Seyom Brown, "The Changing Essence of Power," *Foreign Affairs* 51, no. 2 (January 1973): 286–299.

5. See Kenneth Waltz, *Theory of International Politics* (Reading, Mass.: Addison-Wesley, 1979), esp. pp. 138–160; and Robert W. Tucker, *The Inequality of Nations* (New York: Basic Books, 1977).

6. Robert W. Tucker, "America in Decline: The Foreign Policy of 'Maturity'," *Foreign Affairs* 58, no. 3 (1980): 449–484.

7. Alexis de Tocqueville, *Democracy in America*, vol. 1 (New York: Vintage Books, 1945), p. 243.

8. W. Ebenstein, C. H. Pritchett, H. A. Turner, and D. Mann, *American Democracy in World Perspective* (New York: Harper and Row, 1967), pp. 645–646.

9. Quoted in Arthur Schlesinger, Jr., *The Imperial Presidency* (Boston: Houghton-Mifflin Co., 1973), p. 3. Schlesinger's book is an invaluable historical account of the development of the foreign policy making relationship between the presidency and Congress.

10. This power can be inferred from the constitutional grant of authority to Congress to "grant letters of Marque and Reprisal." See Article I, Sec. 8 of the Constitution and Schlesinger's discussion, op. cit.

11. "Federalist No. 48" in *The Federalist Papers*, ed. Clinton Rossiter (New York: Mentor, 1961), p. 308.

12. "Federalist No. 51," pp. 321–322.

13. Washington's "Farewell Address," quoted in Schlesinger, op. cit.

14. "Federalist No. 51," p. 322.

15. The term is Hamilton's from "Federalist No. 75."

16. The literature on bureaucratic politics has grown enormously in the last few years. Perhaps the most important works are Graham T. Allison, *Essence of Decision: Explaining the Cuban Missile Crisis* (Boston: Little, Brown, 1971); Morton H. Halperin, *Bureaucratic Politics and Foreign Policy* (Washington, D.C.: The Brookings Institution, 1974); Graham T. Allison and Morton Halperin, "Bureaucratic Politics: A Paradigm and Some Policy Implications," *World Politics*, vol. 24 (Supplement, Spring 1972), pp. 40–79; Morton Halperin and Arnold Kanter, eds., *Readings in American Foreign Policy: A Bureaucratic Perspective* (Boston: Little, Brown, 1973), esp. the "Introduction," pp. 1–42; Richard

Neustadt, *Alliance Politics* (New York: Columbia University Press, 1970); and the critiques of the perspective by Stephen D. Krasner, "Are Bureaucracies Important? (Or Allison Wonderland)," *Foreign Policy* 17 (Summer 1971); Robert Art, "Bureaucratic Politics and American Foreign Policy: A Critique," *Policy Sciences* 40 (1973); and James A. Nathan and James K. Oliver, "Bureaucratic Politics: Academic Windfalls and Intellectual Pitfalls," *Journal of Political and Military Sociology* 6, no. 1 (Spring 1978): 81–91.

17. For development of this concept of administration see Richard E. Neustadt, *Presidential Power: The Politics of Leadership from FDR to Carter* (New York: Wiley, 1980) and Neustadt's testimony in U.S., Congress, Senate, Hearings before the Subcommittee on National Security Staffing and Operations of the Committee on Government Operations, *Administration of National Security*, 88th Congress, 1962–1963.

18. Perhaps the most straightforward expression of these concerns has been that of George Kennan. See his *American Diplomacy 1900–1950* (New York: New American World Library, 1959), esp. p. 59. See also Leslie Gelb, "The Essential Domino: American Politics and Vietnam," *Foreign Affairs* 50, no. 3 (April 1972): 459–475.

19. For a recent statement of this view see Daniel Yankelovich, "Farewell to 'President Knows Best'," *Foreign Affairs* 57, no. 3 (1979). See also John Immerwahr, Jean Johnson, and John Doble, *The Speaker and the Listener: A Public Perspective on Freedom of Expression* (New York: The Public Agenda Foundation, 1980).

20. See Yankelovich for a discussion of these possibilities, esp. pp. 687–688.

21. See Samuel Huntington's contribution to *The Crisis of Democracy: Report on the Governability of Democracies*, Trilateral Commission (New York: New York University Press, 1975). See also Lester Thurow, *The Zero-Sum Society* (New York: Basic Books, 1980).

22. For the author's assessment of the development of American global activism, see Nathan and Oliver, *United States Foreign Policy and World Order*, 2nd ed.

Chapter 2

The National Security Policy Making System and the Onset of White House Dominance

Harry Truman once observed that the President as national security policy maker had powers that "would have made Caesar, Genghis Khan or Napoleon bite his nails with envy." [1] Two decades later a succession of Presidents complained about the hobbling limitations placed upon their power by Congress and the courts. Whereas the late 1960s and early 1970s saw great concern about a swollen and imperial presidency, the 1970s closed with worried reflections on the state of a diminished and "imperiled" presidency. [2] For Truman the powers of a presidency that took on imperial proportions were necessary for the prosecution of World War II followed by global cold war. Twenty years later, however, policies and powers framed during Truman's administration, institutionalized during Eisenhower's, and reinvigorated and extended under Kennedy and Johnson had culminated in Vietnam and Watergate. Presidents Ford and Carter chafed under restrictions placed on the office in reaction to a presidency and a foreign policy seen as having become too strong and activist. Yet, on the threshold of the 1980s, Carter was swept from office because he and his policies, if not the office he held, were thought to be too weak. Moreover, the man who defeated him was applauded for the strong leadership he showed in pushing his economic program through Congress even as he was being criticized for his lack of an equally well-defined and forceful foreign policy.

The presidency that has developed around post–World War II

national security policy would seem, therefore, to be the epitome of what Thomas Cronin has called the ultimate paradox of a paradox-ridden modern presidency:

> It is always too powerful and yet it is always inadequate. Always too powerful because it is contrary to our ideals of a "government by the people" and always too powerful, as well, because it now possesses the capacity to wage nuclear war (a capacity that unfortunately doesn't permit much in the way of checks and balances and deliberative, participatory government). Yet always inadequate because it seldom achieves our highest hopes for it, not to mention its own stated intentions.[3]

Undoubtedly much of this paradox can be explained in terms of the policy and ideological predispositions of the observer. A President is a political leader when policy conforms to our preferences; a dangerous threat to the constitutional balance when acting in a manner that offends our values. Moreover, Presidents themselves always seem sensititive to the limitations of their position as national security policy maker precisely because they may have to use their capacity to wage nuclear war and must, on a day-to-day basis, make and administer policies in an international environment increasingly less responsive to their perspective.

But there is more to the paradox-ridden domain of the President's national security policy than is revealed by the sometimes self-serving arguments made by observers and occupants of the office. Notwithstanding enormous institutional capability, there are real constraints on the presidency. Most fundamental, of course, is the constitutionally mandated sharing of foreign and national security policy making authority with Congress. We return to this relationship subsequently as well as to the constraints imposed by public opinion and the domestic political environment within which an American President must make foreign and national security policy. In this and the succeeding chapter, we examine the limits resulting from the structure and dynamics of the policy making institutions that make up the modern national security policy presidency itself, that is, the executive foreign policy establishment and the managerial response to it by the succession of post–World War II Presidents.

THE POSTWAR FOREIGN POLICY BUREAUCRACY

The close of hostilities following World War II initiated a period of unparalleled U.S. world involvement. At the center of this global activity were the tensions of the Soviet-American relationship in which military force and global commitments became more and more salient as instrumentalities of American foreign policy. The emergence, expansion, and evolution of powerful new bureaucratic actors within the executive branch, side by side with the traditional foreign policy units such as the Department of State, contribututed to new policy making and administrative problems.

The expansion of the foreign affairs bureaucracy has had two manifestations: a much larger number of people in the processes of making and administering policy, and the organization of these people into an expanded number of departments, agencies, and bureaus charged with separate but often overlapping responsibilities.

Whereas before World War II fewer than 1,000 people comprised the Department of State's staff in Washington, the number exceeded 7,000 in the 1970s. Overseas representation before World War II was handled by fewer than 2,000 people, but during the 1970s, though staffing fewer diplomatic posts, the State Department required more than 23,000 Americans. In addition to the Secretary of State, the department is headed by the Undersecretary of State, the Undersecretary for Political Affairs, the Deputy Undersecretary for Economic Affairs, and the Deputy Undersecretary for Administration. In 1938 the staff of the secretary's office numbered 21; in the 1970s it exceeded 350. Below this top level, the department has become a mix of geographic and functional bureaus, each headed by an Assistant Secretary of State. The five geographic bureaus (African, Inter-American, East Asian and Pacific, European, and Near Eastern and South Asian) are made up of scores of country desks responsible for the daily monitoring of events around the world. The functional bureaus (Congressional Relations, Intelligence and Research, International Organization Affairs, International Scientific and Technological Affairs, Consular Affairs, and Politico-Military Affairs) are responsible for specialized policy areas that stretch across not only countries and regions but also the many other departments and agencies involved in foreign policy. Thus, for example, the Bureau of Politico-Military Affairs attempts to insure that the Department of State's concerns are represented in military decision making. Finally, by some estimates, at least 25 percent of the 2,000 or so people employed in these geographic and functional bureaus are administrative personnel involved in such matters as budgeting, personnel assignments, selection of supplies, processing travel, and so forth.

No less important and illustrative of the organizational and bureaucratic implications of the shift in American foreign policy after World War II, however, is the development of parallel and often competing foreign policy bureaucracies throughout the government. Even as President Truman was announcing the global mission of the United States in his Truman Doctrine speech, legislation for a significant modification of the national security policy establishment was being prepared and submitted to Congress as the National Security Act of 1947. The act, which was approved by Congress, led to the establishment of a Department of Defense responsible, under civilian leadership, for the defense policy of the United States. In addition, an intelligence establishment was set up that included the Central Intelligence Agency as well as military and cryptographic intelligence operations. By the 1970s these intelligence agencies employed more than 10 times the people at State and had a combined budget at least 12 times larger than that of the Department of State.

Within the Department of Defense there had developed by the 1970s three separate staffs: those of the Joint Chiefs of Staff, the Defense Intelligence Agency, and the Office of the Secretary of Defense. Within the Office of the Secretary of Defense is the Assistant Secretary of Defense for International Security Affairs responsible for assessing the national security implications of American foreign policy. In addition, there are the Secretaries of the Army, Navy, and Air Force, as well as eight military commands, and organizations responsible for manpower, logistics, program analysis and evaluation, research and engineering, communications, atomic energy, mapping, and other specialized functions.

American activism in the post–World War II years has of course involved much more than military and intelligence operations. There were large economic and technical assistance programs as well as food assistance and propaganda operations. In addition, large numbers of ostensibly domestic agencies became involved in some aspects of foreign policy and, therefore, required specialized bureaucracies of their own to carry out their foreign operations. The American economic assistance program went through several bureaucratic incarnations during the late 1940s and 1950s, but emerged in its present form, the Agency for International Development (AID), in the early 1960s. By the 1970s AID employed more than 15,000 people, more than half of whom were aliens. AID's Washington staff consisted of well over 3,000 people, and the more than 5,200 Americans posted overseas by AID constituted a foreign representation larger than that of the Department of State. Informational, educational, and cultural exchange as well as propaganda programs are conducted by the United States Information Agency, employing more than 10,000 people with representation in each American embassy. The Arms Control and Disarmament Agency, established in the early 1960s, has had responsibility for some arms control negotiations during the 1960s and 1970s. The Peace Corps has been responsible for sending thousands of Americans abroad to represent the United States during the same period.

Finally, more than a half dozen other departments and agencies maintain significant overseas representation, including the Departments of Agriculture, Energy, Interior, Health and Human Resources, Labor, Transportation, Commerce, Justice, and Treasury, and the National Science Foundation. The intrusion of economic issues onto the agenda of American policy during the last decade has meant that especially the Treasury Department but also the Departments of Commerce and Agriculture have emerged as truly important and powerful foreign policy bureaucracies. Indeed, the negotiations involving the heads and senior officials of these departments have assumed an importance equal to virtually any other set of international interactions and representations of the United States government. The persistence of international trade, financial, and other technical issues ensures that these agencies will be no less active and prominent in the future.

Presumably all of this foreign activity and representation is coordinated by the Department of State, the agency charged with primary responsibility for the conduct of American foreign policy. This institutional position would imply that the various elements of the foreign policy establishment are in some sense aware of one another's activities and are operating within some consistent framework of policy. However, so vast a government establishment, comprising so many agencies and, in some instances, with departmental representation and resources dwarfing those of the Department of State, has proved rather consistently to be beyond the control and coordinating capacity of the Secretary of State and the Secretary's representatives.

The department has not even been successful in controlling the expansion of the overseas presence of these several agencies within its own preserve—the embassies abroad. Thus in 1958, the Ambassador to Brazil, Ellis Briggs, one of the most caustic critics of the swollen foreign affairs establishment, responded to news from Washington that he was about to be the recipient of a new science attaché with a cable informing the State Department that "the American embassy in Rio de Janeiro needs a science attaché the way a cigar-store Indian needs a brassiere." John Franklin Campbell reported that Briggs's response was to no avail; within 10 years the embassy had two science attachés. Campbell, himself a former foreign service officer, commented:

> Each separate agency that sends representatives to foreign missions argues that it has a job to do that relates in some way, however indirectly, to the interests and welfare of the American people. It is hard to challenge the sincerity of this claim. . . . But the extra jobs thus created, and the free-wheeling mandate that accompanies them, swell embassy staffs, confuse foreign governments, and tend to undercut ambassadors, who cannot possibly control all the extra specialists. . . . As a result the United States is the world's only nation that includes as many as forty to fifty separate agency representations on its embassy roles.[4]

Bureaucratic Power . . . and Problems

In some ways a President's position is not unlike that of the Ambassador surrounded by expertise mobilized and organized to make foreign policy and policy making more effective. Clearly this policy machinery provides a President with considerable potential power insofar as each unit of the foreign affairs bureaucracy contains a cumulation of expertise, information, and experience in virtually every aspect of America's international affairs. However, the President does not sit atop this bureaucracy as if it were a pyramid of power, commanding bureaucratic units to do his bidding. Rather, a President is confronted with an ongoing stream of foreign policy, and much of the context and direction is provided by the members of the foreign policy bureaucracy.

Of course Presidents come to office with their own priorities, their own vision of international reality and American interests. Moreover, their appointments to key policy making positions within the bureaucracy are designed to implant representatives of their image of reality and priorities within the bureaucratic structure. Nonetheless, it is rare that Presidents or their representatives bring to their tasks the kind of accumulated experience that is represented by the foreign and national security affairs bureaucracy. Moreoover, Presidents enter into a stream of policies and commitments that antedate them and their closest advisers and that will under most circumstances continue long after a particular individual leaves office. There are, of course, moments when a particular personality or a particular vision of American interests can work to redefine policy in some fundamental way. Truman and Acheson, for example, brought to their offices an inclination for toughness during a period in which the fundamental structure of American policy was being redefined. Their conception of the structure and dynamics of world politics—the Soviet-American bipolar confrontation—gave shape to American policy throughout the succeeding decades of cold war and fragile detente.

The late 1940s were, however, extraordinary times, in that the old European center of world politics had given way catastrophically after 3 decades of war and economic disruption. Most of the time, foreign policy is not developed and conducted in such an environment. Most of the time foreign policy is developed within an existing framework of practice and commitment. And in the face of such prior constraints those responsible for interpreting and conducting relations within the previously developed framework of policy objectives and means will usually prevail. Within that framework, however, considerable political struggle can and does occur as individuals seek personal and organizational advantage in the conduct of policy. It is this process that constitutes the operational crux of the policy making process; and it is this process that a President must confront and come to terms with if presidential priorities are to prevail.

The expertise, information, and experience within the foreign affairs bureaucracy are held by men and women whose loyalties are inevitably divided between their particular programs or agencies and the individual in the White House. Furthermore, the officials staffing these bureaucratic units do not all see the world in the same way. Instead their perception of the world and what to do about it—that is to say, their sense of the national interest—is colored by their bureaucratic perspective. Given the range and disparity of bureaucratic units that now make up the foreign and defense policy establishment, it is not surprising to find that there are often conflicting views concerning how the national interest of the United States might best be achieved.

Until fairly recently, a consensus concerning a broad outline of American policy has been possible, namely, the necessity of global U.S. involvement in the quest of some overarching international order. But within these limits the definition of specific policy options and their attendant allocations of resources has frequently involved bureaucratic conflict. The prevalence of security considerations in the world view of American policy makers has meant that those options centering on the production and use of force have been given more than equal weight. Nevertheless, these options are themselves the product of often intense struggle within the Department of Defense or the Department of State, and Presidents have frequently found themselves caught up in and not on top of such inter- and intrabureaucratic struggles.

In sum, the protection and furtherance of organizational interests becomes a crucial factor in the policy making process. Thus policy itself, especially on the operational level, comes to reflect a great deal more than the simple calculation of the national interest and mobilizing of resources in pursuit of objectives. These steps may be ultimately taken, but their character and content will be shaped by a bureaucratic political struggle for position and control of the policy making agenda and process as well as the implementation of decisions once reached.

Bureaucratic actors recognize and accept the central position of the President in this process. But in practical terms this means a

President becomes as much the object of the bureaucratic political process as the controller of it. Given that a President has the ultimate authority to make foreign and national security policy, subordinate bureaucratic actors contend for control of the flow of information and policy options from which the President must choose. Similarly, once a decision is made, the process of carrying out policy is the subject of the same process, as agencies seek to protect their respective interests or advance their claims on the resources available for the conduct of policy.

The Need for Control

A President's needs are, therefore, twofold. On the one hand, a President confronts an extant framework of policy and commitment that constrains presidential latitude. In many instances, however, Presidents do not come to office with any intention of challenging the basic framework of policy. In fact most American Presidents of the post–World War II period have come to office in basic agreement with the overall objective of global containment of the Soviet Union. Campaign rhetoric gives the impression, upon occasion, that major shifts in the direction of policy are imminent. In most instances, however, these "great debates" have not been over objectives. Rather, they have concerned means. Thus Eisenhower, Kennedy, Nixon, Carter, and Reagan have attacked their predecessors because of inadequacies in their implementation of American policy, not fundamental goals, for by and large these have not changed since 1947–1950.

At the same time, however, one must be impressed with the implications of this history of policy continuity. It suggests that if a President were to come to office with the intent of radically redirecting American policy, the task would be daunting. It suggests that the opportunities for such change are infrequent and that when they are present they may well be more the result of circumstance than the inclination of the individual. That is to say, though a presidential inclination to redirect policy is clearly a necessary condition for such change, it may not be sufficient. At least two conditions would seem necessary as well. First, there must be a demonstrable need to change, which implies that the circumstances that made the old policy cogent and viable have now changed. Thus, for example, the end of World War II saw such a radical transformation of the structure of world power that American interests could no longer be secured via minimal American strategic involvement. But second, leadership inclined to change the direction of policy in terms of means, whether fundamentally or marginally, must gain control of the government itself.

Thus we are brought back to the second great need of the President: gaining control of the foreign and national security policy bureaucracies and their bureaucratic politics. The President does possess means for channeling and redirecting these often complex and extended policy making struggles. But every President since World War II has found it necessary to interject himself into this policy making milieu rather than stand totally outside it. Policy making in the executive branch, therefore, has been a magisterial orchestration of presidential power only in the broadest sense. For within successive presidencies, each Chief Executive, in line with his own administrative style, has sought to exploit those measures of influence and institutional power available to him for the resolution of the dilemma summarized by Senator Henry M. Jackson's Subcommittee on National Security Staffing and Operations:

> The needs of a President and the needs of the departments and agencies are not identical—and herein lies a source of administrative difficulties and misunderstanding. . . .
>
> Essentially he [the President] wants to keep control of the situation—to get early warning of items for his agenda before his options are foreclosed, to pick his issues and lift these out of normal channels, to obtain priority support for his initiatives, and to keep other matters on a smooth course, with his lines of information open, so that he can intervene if a need arises. . . .
>
> Essentially they [the bureaucracy] want orderly, deliberate, familiar procedures—accustomed forums in which to air their interests, a top-level umpire to blow the whistle when the time has come to end debate, and written records of the decisions by which they should be governed. . . .
>
> It is not surprising that the departments often find a President's way of doing business unsettling—or that Presidents sometimes view the departments almost as adversaries.[5]

The approaches adopted by Presidents in dealing with this problem of leading and managing the foreign policy process have differed in detail. Especially during the 1960s and 1970s, however, Presidents, whether Democrat or Republican, have come to rely more and more on the Special Assistant for National Security Affairs and the staff of the National Security Council as their primary means for getting on top of the foreign, national security, and intelligence establishments. Indeed, during the Nixon and Carter administrations, the security adviser, first Henry Kissinger and then Zbigniew Brzezinski, became the focal point for the development of policy options for presidential decision, the primary adviser to the President on those decisions, and the overseer of the implementation of policy once decisions had been taken. In fact, by the end of the Carter administration, Brzezinski had all but replaced the Secretary of State as not only primary adviser to the President but also as the most visible and authoritative public interpreter of policy.

On the threshold of the 1980s, however, serious questions were being raised about the role and prominence of the security adviser. There were concerns about the lack of accountability of the security adviser, but the more persistent criticism centered on the increasingly public role that the Special Assistant had played in the Carter administration. If the security adviser was to be regarded as an authoritative interpreter of foreign and national security policy, how was the role of the Secretary of State to be understood? If the security adviser and Secretary of State disagreed in their interpretations and emphases in their public utterances, whose word was to be taken as final? In sum, even as the energy and visibility of the security adviser seemed to be reaching a peak in the late 1970s, the old problems of imposing coherence on the vast policy establishment seemed pardoxically more intense. For not only did the old bureaucratic perspectives and interests persist, but now there was a babble of authoritative voices at the top. Order and coherence in the making and administering of foreign policy seemed a more distant goal than in 1947.

ESTABLISHMENT OF THE NATIONAL SECURITY COUNCIL SYSTEM

The same congressional action that initiated the expansion of the foreign and national security establishment also sought to provide the

President through the National Security Council (NSC) with the means to coordinate its activity. The NSC was to consist of the President, the Vice President, the Secretaries of State and Defense, the Chairman of the Joint Chiefs of Staff, and the Director of the Office of Emergency Preparedness. The President could invite any other officials to participate whom he desired, and throughout the last 25 years such officials as the Director of the Central Intelligence Agency, the directors of the various foreign aid agencies, and officials from the Treasury Department and the Bureau of the Budget (renamed the Office of Management and Budget during the Nixon administration) have been invited to participate.

The purpose of the NSC was the coordination and integration of the foreign and defense policy of the United States. In point of fact, however, the actual use of the NSC has been left up to the President. Although the NSC system has always been a part of presidential efforts to coordinate and control foreign policy formulation and administration, its precise role has depended upon the President in question and the context of events within which his administration operates. The Truman and Eisenhower administrations provide excellent examples of the extremes to which the use and nonuse of the NSC system can run.

The Truman Administration

Truman, who was partially responsible for the legislation that led to the creation of the NSC, used the council sparingly. His own view was that presidential power in the area of foreign and defense policy could not be shared with a cabinetlike institution such as the NSC. Truman emphasized this point in his memoirs:

> There is much to this idea—in some ways a Cabinet government is more efficient—but under the British system there is a group responsibility of the Cabinet. Under our system the responsibility rests with one man—the President.[6]

Thus at the very outset, Truman sought to establish a principle of policy formulation and administration that emphasized the centrality of presidential authority, responsibility and control.

As if to underscore this principle, Truman seldom met with his

NSC. This has been explained upon occasion as reflecting Truman's desire not to stifle debate within the NSC. On the other hand, Truman made clear his distaste for trends that he saw emerging from the beginning of the NSC:

> There were times during the early days of the National Security Council when one or two of its members tried to change it into an operating supercabinet on the British model . . . [by giving it] the authority of supervising other agencies of the government and seeing that the approved decisions of the Council were carried out.[7]

It is not unreasonable to conclude therefore, that Truman's refusal to meet with the NSC stemmed from his desire not to reinforce and legitimize these trends by his presence at the meetings.[8] Instead, Truman relied on his own personal contacts with his cabinet officers, his own staff, and particularly, the Department of State and Secretaries of State Marshall and Acheson to effect the policy making control he desired. The NSC was originally placed in an institutionally ambiguous position by Congress, and the Truman administration's use of the NSC seemed to confirm this rather marginal status.

The Eisenhower Administration

Notwithstanding the establishment of a more elaborate NSC structure during 1953 and 1954, it is not clear that the NSC system was deeply involved in the primary decision making of the Eisenhower administration. As with Truman, Eisenhower seems to have leaned heavily on his Secretary of State, John Foster Dulles, during periods of crisis or when far-reaching policy decisions were required. Unlike the Truman years, however, the Department of State was not prominent in any of these activities, for domestic political developments during the early 1950s drastically debilitated the department as a primary policy making actor.

Participants and observers of the Eisenhower administration all underscore Eisenhower's desire for comprehensive and extensive staff work, which was followed through well-defined procedures.[9] He preferred full representation of all points of view in the bureaucracy; but, at the same time, he wanted differences of opinion resolved before the statement of policy options reached him. In short, he did not want to become overly involved in lower-level inter- and intra-bureaucratic squabbling.

This view of policy making was reflected in an enlarged NSC system. Frequent and expanded meetings of the NSC were held (sometimes there were forty to fifty people in attendance), with the President a regular participant. Position papers were developed at the departmental and agency level and passed on to the NSC through a planning board whose responsibility was the coordinating and, in many instances, compromising of divergent positions. Presidential and/or NSC decisions were in turn passed to the agencies through an operations coordinating board (OCB), which was responsible for overseeing the implementation of policy. In addition, tens of committees and subcommittees were spawned by the system, each responsible for some issue or group of issues that may have come up through the NSC system.

Structurally, at least, the Eisenhower NSC was quite distinct from its predecessor. The activity of the council was more extensive, in that it met, particularly during the first Eisenhower administration, quite frequently and dealt with a broad range of policy questions.[10] What is somewhat less clear, however, is the exact nature of the decisional role played by the council.

Eisenhower's security advisers have testified to the active participation by Eisenhower in the NSC meetings, even to the point of resolving some questions during the meetings themselves. In other instances, he apparently deferred decision until later or after a series of meetings.[11] Their testimony tells us little, however, about the nature of these decisions, their magnitude and importance to American foreign policy during the 1950s. Other observers, some of them intimate associates of Eisenhower,[12] emphasize a different element of Eisenhower's policy making style—his relationship with John Foster Dulles. Sherman Adams refers, for example, to Eisenhower as having given Dulles "the responsibility for initiating foreign policy."[13] But Emmet Hughes recalls that Eisenhower always qualified such a grant of authority:

I know a lot of people have been saying all along that I should have been out front more. I'm supposed to have left too much to Dulles. Well . . . he has never done a *thing* that I did not approve beforehand.[14]

In short, a much more complex relationship of President, Secretary of State, and the NSC system emerges than is usually drawn of Eisenhower's decisional style. The President had established an elaborate complex of committees and subcommittees and embedded them in a set of procedures that would guarantee that position papers would touch all bureaucratic bases. On the other hand, it appears that the parameters of policy were developed through the interaction of Eisenhower and his Secretary of State.[15]

The Decline of the Department of State

It should be emphasized that it was the Secretary of State and not the Department of State that was central to the Eisenhower administration's decision making process. For by the time the Eisenhower administration was firmly established in the mid-1950s, the Department of State had lost almost all vestiges of its historic role as the primary executive agent of American international relations. The eclipse of the Department of State as a policy making institution can be traced to the interaction of a set of long-term developments in American foreign policy, developments within the department itself, and finally, the domestic political developments during the early 1950s.

The increasing emphasis on the use or threat of force as the primary instrument of American foreign policy meant that those agencies responsible for the making and administration of policy concerning the overt or clandestine uses of force grew in importance in the foreign affairs establishment. By the time of the Eisenhower administration, the upheavals that had marked the military establishment at the time of the formation of the Department of Defense had begun to subside somewhat, although the department was still marked by important cleavages between the service departments and the still-evolving Office of the Secretary of Defense. Administrative and management control of the Department of Defense was increasingly centralized in the Office of the Secretary of Defense, and the Chairman of the Joint Chiefs of Staff, Admiral Arthur W. Radford, emerged as a forceful advocate of the administration's position in a frequently balky Joint Chiefs of Staff.[16] In contrast to a problematic Department of Defense, the use of the CIA, headed by John Foster Dulles's brother Allen, not only as an intelligence gathering agency but also as an operational unit involved in the carrying out of clandestine intervention throughout the world, increased the agency's weight in the policy process.

On balance, however, new institutional powers were emerging in the policy making establishment. These shifts were simultaneously reflected and reinforced by the dominant events of American policy at this time. The remobilization required by the Korean War, the adoption of a defense posture based on the threat of massive nuclear retaliation against communist aggression, the extension of the American alliance system, and clandestine operations in Guatemala, Iran, and Asia, and, of course, the major portions of the budget being absorbed by the Defense Department—all pointed to the new salience of these agencies. Thus, it was probably inevitable that the relative weight of the DOD and the CIA would increase. It does not necessarily follow, however, that the State Department would enter into the kind of precipitate decline that in fact occurred—a decline that is particularly paradoxical in view of the exalted position of the Secretary of State during the Eisenhower years. To resolve this paradox we must examine conditions that were at work within the department itself and, more important, the domestic politics of the 1950s.

The department was confronted throughout the late 1940s and into the 1950s with a nagging and debilitating problem of two personnel systems. The department was made up of an elite officer corps, the Foreign Service Officers (FSO), who were conceived of as diplomatic "generalists" involved with the traditional diplomatic tasks of political and economic analysis and reporting and diplomatic activity. At the same time the department relied on a substantial number of civil service employees who were responsible for the more specialized and technical tasks of administration, economic aid, and some intelligence work. The FSO corps perceived themselves as policy oriented and responsible for overseas diplomatic representation and policy making positions in Washington. Civil service employees, on the other hand, were seen as having primarily technical and administrative functions—important, but nonetheless supportive of FSO personnel and on the periphery of policy making. Much tension marked the relationship between the two groups, and from 1946 to 1954 a series of internal and external analyses of the situation all pointed to the eventual goal of a merger of the two personnel systems.

Beginning in 1954 Secretary of State Dulles vigorously undertook this amalgamation in the wake of yet another report on the State Department, this time by Henry M. Wriston.[17] The rapid merger of the two personnel systems is viewed by some observers as probably having done more harm than good, at least in the short run.[18] The upheaval produced by "Wristonization" exacerbated tensions in the department and undercut the effectiveness of both personnel tracks. Career civil servants who never had any desire for foreign service were sent to specialized posts in remote places. Career diplomats were shifted to technical jobs for which they were frequently ill-prepared and were often located in Washington, which cost them grievously in terms of salary and opportunity to show political skills—which remained the basis of promotion.

The internal difficulties growing out of the personnel problems of the 1950s certainly undercut the effectiveness and morale of the department. The glut of Foreign Service Officers created by Wristonization had two effects. First, it watered down the esprit de corps of the original officer group, who considered themselves, with some justification, a part of a last great aristocracy. Second, it created more officers in search of the old, esteemed, political jobs. Promotions were jammed up. With the Foreign Service promotion system emphasizing promotion or resignation after a few years in each grade, the pressure for conformity and good jobs became excruciating. In a longer view, however, these are important but secondary factors in the decline of the Department of State. More significant were the series of attacks directed at the department during the 1950s by members of Congress. During the campaign of 1952 the Republican candidate for President and the man he was to appoint as Secretary of State joined these assaults on the State Department. The point of the lance, however, was Senator Joseph McCarthy of Wisconsin.

The McCarthy Era and the Department of State

The Department of State became the focus of popular frustrations with American foreign policy as the Russians consolidated control in Eastern Europe and China was "lost" to Mao Zedong in 1949. The policies of the Truman administration were viewed as suspect, and millions of Americans came around to the explanation of American failure advanced by many conservative Republicans. The argument was disarmingly simple: the apparent failures of U.S. policy were not the products of political and historical developments beyond American control. Rather, they came about as a result of communist influence and infiltration within the Democratic administration of Harry S. Truman, an influence that stretched back to the New Deal of Franklin Roosevelt. In January 1950 Alger Hiss, a former high-level member of the Department of State, was convicted of perjury in a controversial case involving the purported passing of State Department papers to the communists. Three weeks later Senator McCarthy, then a little-known freshman Senator, charged in a speech delivered in Wheeling, West Virginia:

> The reason why we find ourselves in a position of impotency [in international affairs] is not because our only powerful potential enemy has sent men to invade our shores, but rather because of the traitorous actions of those who have been treated so well by this Nation. . . . The bright young men who are born with silver spoons in their mouths are the ones who have been the worst. . . . In my opinion the State Department . . . is thoroughly infested with Communists.[19]

These charges were to be the grounds of congressional attack on the Truman administration by way of the Department of State and Secretary of State Dean Acheson. The onslaught was pressed with increasing intensity throughout the remainder of the Truman presidency, into the campaign for President in 1952, and up through the early months of the Eisenhower administration. McCarthy's charges subsequently extended into the Army, and, especially within the policy making establishment, the fear of a persuasive conspiracy grew to hysterical proportions. But no people of policy making significance were ever connnected with the Communist party by McCarthy, and in time the Senator's charges became patently transparent. Finally, after weeks of televised hearings in the spring of 1954 dealing with proported communist infiltration of the U.S. Army and a dramatic confrontation with Army Counsel Joseph Welch, McCarthy's drive was spent. A year later the U.S. Senate censured McCarthy.[20] Truman and Acheson reacted to the Senator's charges with denials and a defense of the department and their foreign policy. The Republicans, on the other hand, played on the unease and fear unleashed by McCarthy and rode the resulting wave into the White House.[21]

After he took office, President Eisenhower's reaction to McCarthyism was one of ambivalence. On the one hand, he needed the support of conservative Republicans, and on the other, it was not *his* administration that was being implicated in McCarthy's attacks. The new Secretary, for his part, showed great reluctance to take on the Senator or, for that matter, anyone in Congress. This may have been a reflection of an overall administrative strategy of passivity in dealing with McCarthy, a reflection of the President's refusal "to get into the gutter with that guy."[22] Rather than take McCarthy on frontally, Eisenhower seemed to hope that McCarthy would hang himself through overextension of his charges and claims.[23]

This is, of course, exactly what happened. But as Emmet Hughes has observed, the "strategy, for all its sensible elements, could hardly be swift, and its slow working exacted a high price in the mutilation of reputations and careers."[24] Nowhere was this more in evidence than in the Department of State, where Dulles was avoiding conflict with McCarthy. Hughes, an Eisenhower intimate, is of the view that "the Secretary of State would have done no violence to Eisenhower's general concept if he had forthrightly met almost any of McCarthy's initial charges with the cold dismissal they deserved."[25]

The consequences of all of this for American foreign policy stretch beyond any single agency. But within the Department of State the consequences were both immediate and long run.

> As Dulles seemed to reel back before the onslaught, the professional officers charged with conduct of America's foreign affairs felt more than a loss of morale: they felt an estrangement from the Administration— edged with an intellectual aversion—that would endure, subtly but stubbornly, throughout the 1950s.[26]

In a more immediate sense, a group of ex-diplomats warned that "a premium has been put upon reporting and upon recommendations which are ambiguously stated or so cautiously set forth as to be deceiving. . . . The ultimate result is a threat to national security."[27]

In summary, perhaps the most serious impact of the McCarthy era was the implanting of a "play safe" attitude. Men and women who saw their colleagues coming under attack for their policy advice during the late 1940s and early 1950s instinctively pulled back from a forceful and forthright presentation of their views—particularly if in so doing one might be challenging the prevailing orthodoxy concerning America's interests and policies. A State Department shibboleth was repeated to each freshman class of entering FSOs: "There are old Foreign Service Officers, and there are bold Foreign Service Officers, but there are no old, bold Foreign Service Officers." This sentiment was not confined to the 1950s. Perceptions of the bureaucratic environment formed during this traumatic period followed young and middle-level FSOs into their later years and into higher policy making positions in the middle and late 1960s. The comments of Ambassador Averell Harriman in 1963 attest to this:

> The Foreign Service Officer has been subjected to the most unfair criticism. I have seen men's careers set back and in fact busted because they held the right views at the wrong time, or for reporting accurately facts which were not popular at the time or some later time.
>
> Furthermore, the job of a Foreign Service Officer throughout his career is to report the facts as he sees them and as he interprets them. If to survive it is necessary to be always right, then the officer must always play safe.[28]

In conclusion: the policy making system of the Eisenhower years was built around an elaborate and highly institutionalized system designed to funnel policy positions and options up to the presidential level. It would be a mistake to view this structure as the crux of the policy making process, however. Eisenhower, with his penchant for thorough staffwork and orderly follow-up to decisions, undoubtedly relied upon this structure to coordinate the activities of the bureaucracy. But the close relationship between Eisenhower and his Secretary of State suggests that fundamental policy decisions were the product of their more informal interaction rather than the structured procedures of the NSC system. Finally, it is important to emphasize the demise of the Department of State as a major participant in these processes. By the end of the 1950s, the combination of internal upheaval growing out of its own personnel problems, but even more important, the morale-shattering impact of Senator McCarthy's attacks, had all culminated in the gutting of the department. McCarthy had a kind of eidetic effect on the collective mind of the department—like a flash bulb witnessed close up but seen much later when one's eyes are closed. And the terrible damage his name came to symbolize still haunts the department's institutional memory. Of course, the department did not slide beneath the waters of the Potomac. FSOs continued to man diplomatic posts, serve on interdepartmental groups, and carry out their traditional functions. But the department was increasingly viewed as a problem for rather than a part of the policy making process—a kind of eccentric and once stylish maiden aunt who must be invited to the party, but is seldom asked to dance.

The Department of Defense [29]

Compounding the diminished position of the Department of State was the emergence of new and potentially powerful bureaucratic actors whose responsibilities extended to the development and administration of policies associated with the Eisenhower administration's militarization of containment. Most important, of course, was the Department of Defense, which by the mid-1950s encompassed not only the budgetary resources comprising the basis of American foreign and defense policy but also increasingly the bureaucratic center of power and policy.

The department was not, however, without its problems, for the evolution of the Department of Defense had been marked by considerable conflict. The residue of this institutional strife was very much in evidence in the Department of Defense of the 1950s, especially in the bifurcation of the department between its civilian and military officials; and, more specifically, in the tension between the military core of the service departments, the Departments of the Navy, Army, and Air Force, and the Office of the Secretary of

Defense and its attendant cadre of Assistant Secretaries. Complicating the picture even more was the ambiguous position of the Joint Chiefs of Staff.

The military establishment that had emerged out of the National Security Act of 1947 was a decentralized institutionalization of service department autonomy. The Secretary of Defense possessed little or no institutional authority over the respective services, and the first Secretary of Defense, James Forrestal, found that he could do little more than serve as mediator in the arrangement of service department consensus and compromise. Forrestal, who as Secretary of the Navy had been in some measure responsible for this decentralized structure so as to protect the autonomy of the Department of the Navy, set about changing the situation once he was Secretary of Defense. In 1949 he successfully advocated establishment of the Office of the Secretary of Defense and the first Assistant Secretary of Defense positions. In so doing Forrestal took the first step in the development of a centralized civilian counterweight to the military service departments and the Joint Chiefs of Staff, but on the eve of the Korean War, the Department of Defense remained basically decentralized.

In 1953 the Eisenhower administration undertook the first of two major reorganizations of the Department of Defense that would occur during its tenure in office. As with the 1949 reorganization, the thrust of the effort was to strengthen the hand of the Secretary of Defense by expanding his management control of the service departments. At the heart of this effort was concentration of budgetary control in the hands of the Assistant Secretary of Defense Comptroller and general management responsibilities under Assistant Secretaries whose functional responsibilities included logistics, research and development of new weapons systems, politico-military affairs, and bases and other installations.

At the same time, however, this increase in the management capability of the Secretary of Defense and his Assistant Secretaries did not result in expanded control over the military planning of the Department of Defense. Here the Joint Chiefs of Staff, serving in large measure as advocates of their respective service departments, remained outside the orbit of the Office of the Secretary of Defense. From 1953 through 1957 the White House was successful in establishing the broad parameters of the new look with its emphasis on tactical and strategic nuclear war and reduction in the size of the army. Within these limits, however, the Joint Chiefs behaved very much as they had during the Truman years, as a kind of trading post at which their respective service interests were bargained, protected, and where possible, advanced.[30]

The crisis of American defense policy brought on by the Soviets' apparent acquisition of significant strategic capability and expanded activity in the Third World provided Eisenhower with an opportunity to strike at this "loose federalism" within the Department of Defense.[31] In the reorganization of 1958 Eisenhower sought to break the linkage between the Joint Chiefs and the services and strengthen further the Office of the Secretary of Defense. Regarding the Joint Chiefs, command responsibilities were redefined in terms of a series of unified geographic and special commands (e.g., Europe, the Pacific, and/or the Strategic Air Command) rather than their respective services. Indeed, the reorganization attempted to submerge the identities of the services by subordinating them to the new unified commands: the Joint Chiefs were made directly responsible to the Secretary of Defense, whose personal authority was now extended to the abolition or consolidation of service missions and roles, control over production, procurement, operational control of new weapons systems; and finally, increased authority over the activities of service secretaries and their departments.[32] By late 1959 the Secretary of Defense had begun to sit in on Joint Chiefs of Staff meetings in order that strategic plans could be debated and resolved in his presence and with his active participation. In addition, command, staffing, and procedural changes were instituted that accentuated the unification of service and Joint Chiefs' activities and functions under the control of the Secretary of Defense.

Thus by the end of the Eisenhower administration the institutional bases for centralized control of the Department of Defense in the hands of the Secretary of Defense were firmly in place. Whereas the decentralization of the department throughout the late 1940s and 1950s may have mitigated somewhat the bureaucratic preponderance of DOD, it was nonetheless the beneficiary of a foreign policy that emphasized the threat of force—that instrumentality of policy that constituted the raison d'être of the organization. The Defense

Department was therefore a growing if troubled institution rising to ascendancy within the executive policy making establishment. Similarly, the Central Intelligence Agency and especially its covert operations element assumed more and more organizational prominence as it proved itself extraordinarily useful to a policy that sought to minimize the costs of containment through destabilizing activities or clandestine intervention in the Third World. In contrast, the Department of State, its morale shattered and its mission preempted by other agencies as well as the personal diplomacy of the President, slid into frustrated impotence.

THE KENNEDY AND JOHNSON ADMINISTRATIONS

The administrations of John F. Kennedy and his successor, Lyndon B. Johnson, reflected the personalized style of the Truman years. In so doing, they confirmed the trend toward centralization of decisional processes in the White House.

The Kennedy Years

Kennedy's approach to policy making and administration stood in clear contrast with that of his predecessor. His biographer and aide, Theodore Sorensen, notes that "from the outset he abandoned the notion of a collective, institutionalized Presidency." Instead:

> He relied . . . on informal meetings and direct contacts—on a personal White House staff, the Budget Bureau and ad hoc task forces to probe and define issues for his decisions—on special Presidential emissaries and constant Presidential phone calls and memoranda—on placing Kennedy men in each strategic spot.[33]

Kennedy therefore rejected the highly bureaucratized Eisenhower structure. He seemed to accept the thrust of the criticism that had been directed at the Eisenhower administration: that the NSC system with its interlocking committees led to countless "coordinated" position papers but little policy.[34] The Eisenhower system reflected an assumption that planning and operations in foreign policy are distinct, hence the Planning and Operations Coordination Board. The rejection of this assumption is clear in the following statement by McGeorge Bundy, Kennedy's Special Assistant for National Security Affairs:

> It seems to us best that the NSC staff, which is essentially a Presidential instrument, should be composed of men who can serve equally well in the process of planning and in the operational followup. Already it has been made plain in a number of cases that the President's interests and purposes can be better served if the officer who keeps in daily touch with operations in a given area is also the officer who acts for the White House staff in related planning activities.[35]

Kennedy sought a more flexible synthesis of these functions, and he wanted control of the processes in his hands in the White House. The result was the complete dismantling of the Eisenhower NSC system: the OCB and Planning Boards were abolished and in the process some thirty to forty committees and subcommittees were eliminated. Kennedy also discontinued the regular and extended meetings of the Cabinet and NSC, and for that matter, stopped regular White House staff meetings.[36] He turned instead to a small foreign policy staff under Bundy that would operate out of the White House. The NSC as a statutorily established and defined body remained, but the decisional and coordinative role assigned to it during the 1950s was now in the hands of the Special Assistant's staff and the *ad hoc* dynamics of the Kennedy White House.[37]

The Kennedy administration's attitude toward and use of the Department of State were ambivalent. Arthur Schlesinger, Jr. reports that Kennedy's personal opinion of the department was split between his "sympathy for the diplomatic enterprise"—his admiration for men like Charles Bohlen, Llewellyn Thompson, and Averell Harriman, and his despair over bureaucratic layering, institutional conservatism, convoluted inbred rhetoric, and other institutional pathologies that infected the department.[38] Kennedy apparently thought the department could be resuscitated, and he attempted to move the department toward a role of leadership in the task of policy coordination. Bundy refers to the leading role of the department in his communication with the Jackson Subcommittee when he noted that there was no question concerning

> the clear authority and responsibility of the Secretary of State, not only in his own Department, and not only in such large-scale related areas as foreign aid and information policy, but also as the agent of coordination in all our major policies toward other nations.[39]

How this was to be achieved is not entirely clear. In a letter to all Chiefs of Mission in May 1961 the President sought to underscore the mission of the department's Chief Officer "to oversee and coordinate all the activities of the United States Government" in the country in question.[40] But a letter to Chiefs of Mission could never be sufficient, and one suspects that Kennedy knew it. For what the Kennedy and subsequent administrations were working against was a deeply embedded organizational culture biased toward caution and even inaction. McCarthy's ghost undoubtedly sat in numerous offices in Foggy Bottom,* and compounding this was Kennedy himself. For Kennedy, the Secretary of State was to take care of the management of the department and operation of ongoing policy. But high politics, diplomacy, and crisis management were, to Kennedy, the business of the President.

By establishing a separate White House staff under Bundy and then using it as an aggressive extension of the President, Kennedy was conforming to the image of the presidency described by Richard Neustadt in 1963: "a President, these days, is virtually compelled to reach for information and to seek control over details of operation deep inside executive departments."[41] In effect, the President became his own Secretary of State and his staff a small surrogate State Department charged with the responsibility of cutting across bureaucratic lines and into the departments and agencies of the foreign affairs establishment—including the Department of State. The very task proposed for State was preempted by the President's own activism and seemingly insatiable demand for action and movement. John Paton Davies, a diplomat victimized by McCarthy, has observed:

---

*A geographical name for the location of the State Department, left over from the days when this part of Washington was a swamp. Foreign Service Officers have frequently said that "Foggy Bottom is not so much a place as a state of mind."

Bold new ideas and quick decisions were asked of men who had learned from long, disillusioning experience that there were few or no new ideas, bold or otherwise, that would solidly produce the dramatic changes then sought, and whose experience for a decade had been that bold ideas and action were personally dangerous and could lead to Congressional investigations and public disgrace . . . purged from the right under Dulles, now purged from the left under Kennedy. . . . How can you expect these men to do a good job?[42]

Kennedy's problem with the department and policy making are summarized in his relationship with his Secretary of State, Dean Rusk. Rusk came to the department with a long background in foreign affairs, including service in the Pentagon and in the Department of State as Assistant Secretary of State for United Nations Affairs and Assistant Secretary for the Far East. Although Kennedy did not know him personally prior to 1961, he nevertheless appeared to be an appropriate choice to run the department, and Kennedy made him Secretary of State. The relationship between the President and Rusk was not what Kennedy had hoped for. Perhaps as a result of his service in the department at the height of the McCarthy attacks and in the bureau that was the target of charges that the department had somehow "lost" China to Mao's communism, Rusk's behavior in many ways epitomized his department. Schlesinger describes him as "a man of broad experience and marked ability . . . a man of exceptional intelligence, lucidity and control, [who] . . . had a tidy and exact mastery of the technical detail of a bewildering range of foreign problems and a talent for concise and dispassionate exposition . . . [and] great ability to summarize divergent views and put his finger on the heart of a question."[43] But also, "he was, more than anything else, a man bred in the large organizations of mid century . . . his organizational instinct was for service, not for mastery."[44] Although hired on the basis of an article in 1960 that advised any new secretary to be responsive to White House direction,[45] Rusk fared poorly in an environment dominated by the President's brother Robert, an aggressive White House staff under Bundy, and the vigorous advocacy of Secretary of Defense Robert McNamara. Rusk, like his department, was shoved aside in the clash of more assertive men and departments.

The McNamara Defense Department

The most assertive of men and departments was the new Secretary of Defense and his department. McNamara's propelling of the Defense Department to the forefront of the Kennedy administration was based on policy and institutional foundations provided by the Eisenhower administration. But the institutional prominence assumed by DOD and McNamara were ultimately tied to the Kennedy administration's dependence on the instrumentalities of force as the basis of its diplomacy.

The combination of McNamara's activist administrative style and the vastly strengthened Office of the Secretary of Defense resulting from the preceding decade of organizational change and upheaval formed the basis of the "McNamara revolution" at DOD. McNamara moved quickly and without congressional consultation to consolidate his personal position as Secretary of Defense. He did so by surrounding himself with a combination of men who were experienced in the administration of the Defense Department and/or possessed awesome and frequently acerbic, even arrogant, analytical brilliance. The upshot was the establishment of vastly augmented programmatic and budgetary control in the hands of McNamara's personal staff, which included as Assistant Secretary of Defense for International Security Affairs (ISA) Paul Nitze, who quickly developed a foreign policy staff and capability that rivaled that of the Department of State.[46]

At the heart of the organization was McNamara himself, a man who described his administrative style in the following manner:

> I think that the role of public manager is very similar to the role of a private manager; in each case he has the option of following one of two major alternative courses of action. He can either act as a judge or a leader. In the former case, he sits and waits until subordinates bring to him problems for solution, or alternatives for choice. In the latter case, he immerses himself in the operations of the business or the governmental activity, examines the problems, the objectives, the alternative courses of actions, chooses among them, and leads the organization to their accomplishment. In the one case, it's a passive

role; in the other case, an active role. . . . I have always believed in and endeavored to follow active leadership role as opposed to the passive judicial role.[47]

The consequence of this combination of administrative style and institutional capability was that the Office of the Secretary of Defense was soon involved at virtually every level of management and military planning. Unified commands and functional activities of the department were rearranged at the further expense of the services. McNamara's pervasive budgeting and programming procedures led to his staff's preempting most traditional military planning.

In less than a year, grumbling could be heard throughout DOD as McNamara's activism thrust him across the lines of interservice bargaining and compromise that had marked the 1950s and that had undermined most reform prior to 1958. Nevertheless, the very characteristics that made McNamara and his staff seem threatening to many of his department ensured his prominence in a White House that admired cold, even ruthless activism that resulted in greater presidential control of the instruments of policy. And by the same token, McNamara's vigor as head of the bureaucracy controlling the chosen instruments of policy in the Kennedy-Johnson years ensured the dominance of the man and his bureaucracy throughout most of those years.

The Johnson Years

The administration of Lyndon Johnson was begun in the shock of John Kennedy's assassination and ended in the tragedy of Vietnam. The former event delayed somewhat the emergence of distinctly Johnsonian policy making innovations, as Johnson was forced to rely heavily on former Kennedy men during his first year to 18 months in office—notably McGeorge Bundy, who remained Johnson's Special Assistant for National Security Affairs until late 1965. The demands of Vietnam, however, meant that changes in policy making institutions and processes when they came were inevitably distorted as the position and needs of the Department of Defense assumed predominance in the policy making establishment.

Standing astride all of these developments, however, was the

President himself, with his desire for personal control of the myriad details of policy and policy making and his demand for absolute loyalty from the officials who worked for him. This meant that the steady accretion and centralization of power in the White House increased dramatically during the Johnson years. It also meant that the relationship between the President and the Secretary of State changed significantly.

The same characteristics of Rusk's personality and administrative style that had so baffled the Kennedy men suited him well in the Johnson administration. Rusk's intense loyalty and dogged determination to be faithful to the objectives set by the President were perfectly matched to a President slogging ever deeper into the mire of Vietnam and beset by growing criticism. And as criticism, raised in many instances by the same Kennedy men, now out of power, who had cut Rusk out of the inner circle during the 1,000 days, became more shrill, Rusk became even firmer. Schlesinger had remarked of Rusk that "he had trained himself all his life to be the ideal chief of staff, the perfect number-two man."[48] And this was precisely what Lyndon Johnson wanted in his Secretary of State.

A symbolic effort was made in 1965 and 1966, before all was sucked into the vortex of Vietnam, to reinforce the position of the Department of State. A series of institutional changes were made that were purportedly designed to reinvigorate the interdepartmental coordination role of the department.[49]

The focal point of this change was to be a new Senior Interdepartmental Group (SIG) comprised of the Deputy Secretary of Defense, the Administrator of AID, the Director of CIA, the Chairman of the Joint Chiefs of Staff, the Director of USIA, and the Special Assistant for National Security Affairs. With the Undersecretary of State at the head of the SIG, the department apparently had "full powers of decision on all matters within their purview, unless a member who does not concur requests the referral of a matter to the decision of the next higher authority."[50] The SIG was to be supported in turn by a number of Interdepartmental Regional Groups (IRG) established for each of the geographic regional bureaus in the Department of State. The Executive Directors of the IRGs were the regional Assistant Secretaries of State, with designated membership drawn from the agencies represented on the SIG. Under this setup it was hoped that the Interdepartmental Regional Groups would be the primary working level.

Finally, the position of the Department of State was to be augmented by the establishment of a planning-programming-budgeting system (PPBS). The concept of PPBS had been taken from the Department of Defense, where Robert McNamara had used it with some success in his strengthening of the Office of the Secretary of Defense during the Kennedy years. The idea was to provide the Department of State with a means of overseeing the budgets of the various agencies involved in foreign affairs. It was reasoned that if budgetary decisions are in fact decisions as to how resources are to be allocated in a particular country or region, then State Department oversight and even intervention in these decisions would provide the department with the most fundamental means for coordinating interdepartmental activity.[51]

The Johnson policy making system was stillborn. Difficulties emerged with respect to several elements of the structure. The SIG, presumably the key point of decision in the event of conflict, was found to be ineffective. The issues that found their way to the SIG level tended to be of such import as to be irresolvable short of White House intervention. Furthermore, the provision for appeal built into the system may have encouraged bucking issues up to the highest levels of decision. In any event, participants in the process have indicated that the SIG was bypassed with great frequency.[52]

Beyond these narrow structural limitations there was the simple fact that the department was being thrust into a role and asked to employ coordination instruments that ran against the grain of the organizational culture discussed above. First, the concept of PPBS was found inapplicable to the Department of State and foreign affairs. It was never apparent to trained diplomats how to quantify "policy" and "interest" or to record the amount of time it took to write one kind of report or another. The attempted innovation failed. Organizational inertia of the department contributed to the failure. But the notion that policy innovation and control could be supervised with the same management techniques that work with Ford Motor Company was probably a defective idea in the first place.

Second, and more generally, the Johnson approach to interdepartmental coordination envisioned the department's taking the initiative in an intensely conflictual milieu of multiagency policy making. But as high-ranking members of the department have noted, this management task was not one that most members of the department were prepared to accept. As Nicholas Katzenbach, the Undersecretary of State for Administration, observed in 1967:

> Especially in the field of foreign affairs—administration has often been regarded as something of a stepchild, rather unfashionable and definitely subordinate, smacking vaguely of filing cabinets, travel allowances, or paper flow. It has also been thought of as separate from and only marginally relevant to the actual making of foreign policy.[53]

The day-to-day essence of foreign policy making for the last 25 years has increasingly become an exercise in interagency coordination. The hammering-out of options for consideration at a higher level or the implementation of policy is no longer the province of a single agency. The field is now crowded with representatives of a number of departments and agencies, some of which, like the Department of Defense, command resources that dwarf those of the Department of State. The demands of policy making and administration in this environment would seem to require, therefore, the marriage of "substance" and "administration," "formulation" and "management"; a certain aggressiveness and involvement in extended bureaucratic conflict; and finally, the ability to cut through and across bureaucratic loyalties. In short, precisely the kind of behavior of which the State Department was incapable without a strong departmental leadership and presidential support. And neither of these were forthcoming because of the overriding and most important element in the hierarchy of foreign policy concerns during the Johnson administration—Vietnam.

The impact of Vietnam on the policy making processes of the Johnson administration cannot be overstated. During late 1966, 1967, and 1968 the prosecution of the war became virtually all-consuming. Consequently, resources were absorbed at an astonishing rate: literally millions of dollars a day and comparable hours of labor and time. Not the least of the latter element was the time and attention of the President and his top policy makers. Clearly, nurturing nascent structural reforms of policy processes was not a high-priority item on the policy agenda. Similarly, the Department of Defense, the CIA, and those elements of the Department of State most deeply involved with the war became the institutional focus of policy and policy making. In this environment SIGs, IRGs, and the evolution of PPBS at State were decidedly less important than other acronyms that pervaded presidential briefing papers—and American households—VC, ARVN, KIA, MIA, and POW. Indeed, John Franklin Campbell argues that SIG and the interdepartmental system established by Johnson was never taken seriously by the President; it was in fact a "kind of window-dressing." Franklin continues:

> One senses that the President expected from the SIG an effort to reduce the heat on him from other parts of the world, while at the same time *not* wanting the new body to complicate matters by proposing significant policy changes. As has been true before and since of well publicized changes in the machinery of foreign policy, the announcement of the SIG was designed to give the public a reassuring impression of change, movement, and novelty while masking an intention that there be no change in policy and no rocking of the presidential boat.[54]

As the policy process evolved in response to an all-consuming war and the style of the Commander-in-Chief, military advice and military agencies dominated all policy processes, and military arguments seemed always in order. Their resource needs were given first consideration. Indeed, the Department of Defense's International Security Agency had by this time developed into a virtual State Department within the Pentagon. DOD's clout in the foreign affairs establishment was augmented by this depth of independent analytical capacity.

The President's personal domination of the policy processes of government proceeded with even greater urgency as he sought to absorb and stay on top of every detail of the war effort. Yet, paradoxically, the dynamic also pulled Johnson toward an ever-smaller group of decision makers—McNamara at Defense, Richard Helms of the CIA, General Earl Wheeler, Chairman of the Joint Chiefs of Staff, Rusk at State, and always W. W. Rostow, his Special Assistant for National Security Affairs. These advisers and the President constituted the so-called Tuesday Luncheon Group. But as the group of top decision makers became smaller, their proceedings more informal, and the focus of the President became myopic, it appears that Johnson's relations and communications with the remainder of the bureaucracy became so tenuous that he lost control. Access to information and political insight that he so vitally needed during Vietnam escaped his grasp.[55]

CONCLUSION

Perhaps the most obvious development of this period was a movement away from the hierarchically structured NSC of the Eisenhower years. The centralization of policy making growing out of the Vietnam War undoubtedly heightens this impression. Nevertheless, both Kennedy and Johnson were Presidents who sought personal control of policy and policy making. Thus both stand closer to Truman's administrative style and use of the NSC system than they do to Eisenhower's.

The 1960s also mark the continued decline of the Department of State as a policy making institution and the continued rise of the Department of Defense, particularly under the aggressive leadership of McNamara. Both Kennedy and Johnson made gestures toward reinvigoration of the department, but in the end a combination of the department's own organizational culture, the resource demands and policy making weight of DOD, and the underlying desire of both Kennedy and Johnson to be their own Secretary of State prevailed. The department reaction was characteristic: another study of what was wrong with the department amidst signs of further deterioration of department morale bordering on open rebellion among some younger FSOs.

A corollary of these developments (or lack of development as the case may be) was the emergence of the Special Assistant for National Security as a key foreign and national security policy maker. Under both Truman and Eisenhower the position was not a major one in the sense that their Special Assistants did not undertake the active roles in both policy making and coordination of departmental and agency positions that both Bundy and Rostow did. Under the latter Special Assistants, the position evolved somewhat informally and was not characterized by extensive institutionalization during the 1960s. Rather, the Special Assistant and his staff inherited and then assumed an expanded role in response to the perceived needs of two Presidents who sought the expansion of presidential power and influence over the foreign and defense policy establishments.

The latter point is the final and perhaps most important development of the 1960s. The collapsing of the functions of the NSC system into the White House staff, the policy making salience of the Special Assistant for National Security Affairs, and the parallel deterioration of State's position are all part of a general and ongoing consolidation of power in the White House. The span and depth of White House control over the Department of Defense and CIA are less clear, but the thrust of developments with respect to the bureaucratic system was apparent by the end of the 1960s. The trends were to culminate during the 1970s.

NOTES

1. Cited by Clinton Rossiter in *The American Presidency*, 2nd ed. (New York: Harcourt Brace Jovanovich, 1960), p. 30.
2. On the "imperial presidency" see Arthur M. Schlesinger, Jr., *The Imperial Presidency* (Boston: Houghton Mifflin, 1973); for a view of the presidency as "imperiled" see Thomas E. Cronin, "An Imperiled Presidency?" *Society* (November-December 1978) and his *State of the Presidency*, 2nd ed. (Boston: Little, Brown, 1980).
3. Cronin, *State of the Presidency*, p. 22.
4. Quoted in John Franklin Campbell, *The Foreign Affairs Fudge Factory* (New York: Basic Books, 1971), pp. 206–207. In 1948 Briggs had requested that, in the interests of efficiency, his embassy staff in Czechoslovakia be reduced by half. The department refused, but Briggs reports delight when some months later, the Czech government declared some sixty–six members of the eighty-person staff personae non gratae—presumably for "espionage activity"—and required them to leave the country. Ibid. p. 208.
5. U.S. Congress, Senate Committee on Government Operations, Staff Report of the Subcommittee on National Security Staffing and Operations, *Administration of National Security: Basic Issues*, 88th Congress, 1st Session 1965, pp. 8–9.
6. Harry S. Truman, *Memoirs: Years of Trial and Hope* (Garden City, N.Y.: Doubleday, 1956), p. 60.
7. Ibid.
8. Paul Y. Hammond, *Organizing for Defense: The American Military Establishment in the Twentieth Century* (Princeton, N.J.: Princeton University Press, 1961), pp. 232–233.

9. Still the best sources on foreign and national security policy making during the 1950s are Sen. Henry Jackson's Subcommittee hearings and reports: U.S. Congress, Senate Committee on Government Operations, Hearings and Reports before the Subcommittee on National Policy Machinery, *Organizing for National Security*, 86th Congress, 2nd Session, 1960. On Eisenhower's administration, see Fred I. Greenstein, *The Hidden-Hand Presidency* (New York: Basic Books, 1982).

10. Ibid., pp. 578–579.

11. Ibid., pp. 582–583 and 601–602 and 608–618 for Anderson's testimony.

12. See Emmet John Hughes, *The Ordeal of Power* (New York: Dell, 1962) and Sherman Adams, *First Hand Report: The Story of the Eisenhower Administration* (New York: Harper & Row, 1961).

13. Adams, op. cit., p. 110.

14. Cited in Hughes, op. cit. p. 243 (emphasis in original); see also p. 218.

15. See James A. Nathan and James K. Oliver. *United States Foreign Policy and World Order*, 2nd Ed. (Boston: Little, Brown, 1981), Chap. 5.

16. See Hammond, op. cit., pp. 288–353.

17. Secretary of State's Public Committee on Personnel, *Toward a Stronger Foreign Service* (Washington D.C.: U.S. Government Printing Office, 1954).

18. See Burton M. Sapin, *The Making of United States Foreign Policy* (New York: Praeger, publishers for the Brookings Institution, 1966), pp. 104–106 and esp. pp. 126–128.

19. Quoted in Eric F. Goldman, *The Crucial Decade—And After: America, 1945–1960* (New York: Vintage Books, 1960), p. 142.

20. For accounts of the McCarthy era see ibid., pp. 212–214, 250–257, and 270–279.

21. David Halberstam, *The Best and the Brightest* (New York: Random House, 1972), p. 119.

22. Cited in Hughes op. cit., p. 81.

23. Ibid., pp. 81–82

24. Ibid., p. 82.

25. Ibid.

26. Ibid., p. 80.

27. Cited in Goldman, op. cit., p. 258.

28. U.S. Congress, Senate Committee on Government Operations, *Administration of National Security: The American Ambassador*, 88th Congress, 1962, p. 53.

29. For a detailed review of the institutional evolution of DOD, see Hammond, op. cit.

30. Ibid., pp. 329–353.

31. Harry H. Ransom, "Department of Defense: Unity or Confederation?" in Mark E. Smith, III, and Claude J. Johns, Jr., eds., *American Defense Policy*, 2nd ed. (Baltimore: John Hopkins University Press, 1968), pp. 366–371.

32. Ibid.

33. Theodore C. Sorensen, *Kennedy* (New York: Bantam Books, 1965), pp. 315–316.

34. This criticism runs throughout the Jackson Subcommittee hearings and reports of 1960.

35. Letter from McGeorge Bundy to Sen. Henry M. Jackson, in U.S. Congress, Senate Committee on Government Operations, Subcommittee on National Policy

Machinery, *Organizing for National Security*, vol. 1, Hearings, 87th Congress, 1st Session, 1961, p. 1338.

36. Sorenson, op. cit., p. 315; and Arthur Schlesinger, Jr., *A Thousand Days: John F. Kennedy in the White House* (Boston: Houghton Mifflin, 1965), pp. 209–210.

37. See Sorensen, op. cit., pp. 319–320.

38. Schlesinger, op. cit., pp. 406–437, esp. 407.

39. Bundy, op. cit., pp. 1337–1338.

40. U.S. Congress, Senate Committee on Government Operations, *The Ambassador and the Problem of Coordination*, A Study submitted to the Subcommittee on National Security Staffing and Operations, 88th Congress, 1st Session, 1963, p. 155.

41. Neustadt, in *Administration of National Security*, p. 77.

42. Quoted in Schlesinger, op. cit., p. 431.

43. Schlesinger, pp. 432–433.

44. Ibid., p. 432–434.

45. Dean Rusk, "The President," *Foreign Affairs.*, 38 (April 1960): 353–369.

46. Ransom, op. cit., pp. 371–373.

47. Quoted in Charles J. Hitch, *Decision-Making for Defense* (Berkeley, Calif.: University of California Press, 1970), p. 27.

48. Schlesinger, op. cit., p. 435.

49. President Lyndon B. Johnson, "White House Announcement of New Procedures for Overseas Interdepartmental Matters, March 4, 1966," *Weekly Compilation of Presidential Documents*, vol. 2 (7 March 1966), p. 506.

50. Department of State Foreign Affairs Manual Circular Number 385, 4 March 1966.

51. The literature of budgeting as policy making and coordination is vast and the literature on the use of budgeting in foreign affairs only slightly less so. With respect to the latter, see U.S. Congress, Senate Committee on Government Operations, *Planning-Programming-Budgeting*, Hearings and Studies prepared for the Subcommittee on National Security and International Operations, 90th Congress, 1st Session, 1968; and Frederick C. Mosher and John E. Harr, *Programming Systems and Foreign Affairs Leadership: An Attempted Innovation* (New York: Oxford University Press, 1970).

52. See Campbell, op. cit., pp. 88–90.

53. Nicholas DeB. Katzenbach, "Administration of Foreign Policy," *Department of State Newsletter* (November 1967), p. 2. And his successor in office, William B. Macomber, Jr., made a similar observation in 1970:

> We are an organization which has traditionally been comfortable with policy-making and with negotiating and promoting policy abroad. We have understood the importance of tact, sensitivity and persuasiveness. But we have tended to be intuitive in nature, weak in planning and unenthusiastic about management . . . it is clear that these change-resistant instincts have caused a great share of our difficulties.

"Management Strategy: A program for the 1970's," *Department of State Newsletter* (January 1970), p. 2.

54. Campbell, op. cit., p. 90.

55. The accounts of Johnson's isolation are many; for accounts of his apparent lack of knowledge of or unwillingness to accept negative information concerning the war see Halberstam, op. cit.; and Townsend Hoopes, *The Limits of Intervention* (New York: David McKay, 1969).

Chapter 3
The National Security Policy Making System in the 1970s and 1980s

In February 1970 Richard Nixon issued a statement concerning his perceptions of the problems of policy making in the 1970s.[1] He observed at the outset that "our fresh purposes demanded new methods of planning and a more rigorous and systematic process of policy-making. . . . Efficient procedure does not insure wisdom in the substance of policy. But . . . adequate procedures are an indispensable component of the act of judgment."[2] The President had some fairly definite ideas concerning the systems for policy making established and utilized by his predecessors. He saw the *ad hoc* approaches of the 1960s as having "the advantages which come with informality—speed, frankness, and so forth."[3] More important, however, he perceived grave inadequacies, for they

> often ran the risk that relevant points of view were not heard, that systematic treatment of issues did not take place at the highest level or that the bureaucracies were not fully informed as to what had been decided and why. . . . They may also suffer from the lack of fixed agenda, methodical preparation, and systematic promulgation or explanation of the decisions.[4]

Likewise, the processes of the 1950s were found inadequate but for different reasons: "The machinery gave too much emphasis to interdepartmental consensus and too little to the presentation of distinct policy alternatives.[5]

THE NIXON ADMINISTRATION

During his first administration, Nixon relied more heavily on a system firmly anchored in the White House under the control of his

Special Assistant for National Security Affairs. At the hub of an interlocking system of review groups, *ad hoc* groups, and formal committees was the NSC or Senior Review Group, chaired by Henry Kissinger. The Senior Review Group included representatives of the Secretary of State, Secretary of Defense, Chairman of the Joint Chiefs of Staff, the Director of the CIA, and other representatives chosen at the discretion of the chairman. The Review Group was responsible for preparing papers for consideration of the NSC and the President. In this capacity it served as a kind of gatekeeper to monitor the flow of paper from the six Interdepartmental Groups (which were reconstituted Interdepartmental Review Groups of the Johnson era) and a handful of *ad hoc* groups responsible for special policy areas, such as the Vietnam Special Studies Group, Verification Panel (Strategic Arms Limitations Talks), "40 Committee" (covert activity), Washington Special Action Group ("crisis management"), and the National Assessments Group (coordination of intelligence estimates). Finally, the Undersecretaries Committee, chaired by the Undersecretary of State, was responsible primarily for the oversight of interdepartmental operational matters.[6]

On the surface this system appeared to be a return to the Eisenhower NSC system. In fact, there was one central difference, and it lay in the pivotal role played by Kissinger. More than any flow of paper or committee arrangements, he and his personal staff were the lynchpins of the Nixon system. Committee representation ran across the major foreign policy departments and agencies, but Kissinger or his representatives chaired the Senior Review Group and the *ad hoc* committees attached to it. The pivotal point of institutional power in the operation was not necessarily the Senior Review Group itself, but rather Kissinger's staff of over 100 and his budget of $2 million (two and a half times the size of Bundy's and three times Rostow's). The magnitude of this operation suggested that Nixon had developed nothing less than a personal foreign ministry within the White House.

Foreign policy "action" was clearly in Kissinger's hands: daily personal contact with the President and the drop in the number of NSC meetings from thirty-seven in 1969 to ten in 1971 are indicative. More important, of course, was the simple fact that on almost every issue of significance—Vietnam, Sino-American relations, strategic arms limitation talks, and European troop reductions—Kissinger was Nixon's primary adviser, negotiator, and contact point with the bureaucracy and in many instances with the press and the public. The only important exception to this pattern was international economic affairs. But even here the policy initiative did not lie with the Department of State, but rather with the Treasury Department and with specialists on the President's staff.

The President's desire for personal control of policy planning, and to a certain extent operations, was furthered by this arrangement. His man held his personal mandate to range widely across the full spectrum of policy issues, pulling together details as well as forcing consideration of issues that the President wanted on his agenda. This almost totally personalized operation was a reflection of the President's own overriding interest and concern for foreign policy. Unlike the 1960s, however, Nixon made not even a gesture toward the Department of State until he moved to colonize it by moving Kissinger to the Secretary's position. Public statements reemphasizing the Secretary of State's position did not obscure the fact that in vast areas of foreign policy planning and operations, the Department of State had been relegated to a staff support role for the President's personal superagency in the White House. Thus, in a sense, Nixon sought to deal with the ongoing "problem at State" by simply ignoring it and building another agency in its place.

In his truncated second term, Nixon retained the arrangement with the inconvenience of having a figurehead at State removed. Kissinger became his Secretary when Secretary William Rogers, increasingly chagrined by scandals and embarrassed by his lack of authority, was rather summarily replaced. The moving of Kissinger to State, however, did not mean that the centralization of presidential authority had stopped. Rather, with Kissinger physically located in Foggy Bottom, there was an opportunity to mobilize the staff resources of the State Department and to aggregate them to the NSC structure. As Nixon noted when he made the announcement of the Kissinger appointment, the advantage of the President's personal adviser's also being the Secretary of State was that there would be "closer coordination between the White House and the Department."[7] In effect, there were now, in the last years of the Nixon/Ford administration, even greater resources placed in the domain of the White House. The prospect that the Department of State itself would see any rejuvenation from Kissinger's stewardship was not bright. For Kissinger's loathing of the foreign affairs bureaucracy preceded his entering the Nixon administration in 1968 and intensified as he fought to gain dominance for the small NSC establishment. He wrote in 1968 that bureaucracy produces policy that merely "emerges from compromise which produces the least common denominator and is implemented by individuals whose reputation is made by administering the status quo."[8] As Kissinger moved to State, there was little promise that those whom he considered but sorry administrators of the "least common denominator" would see much elevation of role in policy formulation or execution. Moreover, the personal style of the new Secretary, deeply suspicious and secretive, did not suggest that he was either willing or able to engage in the reform of the State Department or to involve himself in the reintegration of the State Department's resources in the substance of policy. As Kissinger himself explained, secrecy is a necessary part of policy, and "the only way secrecy can be kept is to exclude from the making of decisions all those charged with carrying [them] out."[9]

As is sometimes the case with institutions and processes, their strengths are at the same time their weaknesses, and this could easily be construed as the case with Nixon's apparatus. The strength of the Nixon/Ford system was clearly Kissinger and the President's dependence upon him; by extension, the weaknesses of the system turned on this fact. At least three specific problems have been identified.[10]

First, Kissinger's NSC staff and Kissinger himself were not able to get on top of international economic problems as they did political and strategic issues. The series of international monetary crises crashed in on the White House between 1970 and 1973 and forced the President into the scrambling reactive posture he so deplored. Kissinger's limited influence on these issues was perhaps a reflection of a conviction on his part that economic issues were in fact secondary to strategic and political questions in the building and maintenance of world order. In fairness, issues of "high politics" such as Vietnam and SALT were certainly commanding most attention when Nixon entered office, and it is understandable that his and Kissinger's attention was focused on specific issues. On the other hand, Kissinger more or less demurred from participation in the policy planning involved in international economics when he proposed in 1971 the establishment of a Council of International Economic Policy. His advice was taken, but the council was not able to establish any semblance of the clout that was built into Kissinger's staff. And policy in the international economics area was not marked by the carefully orchestrated preparation of presidential positions and smooth policy departures.

A second area of concern was the coordination of the activities of the intelligence community. Kissinger is said to have found the intelligence estimates produced by the intelligence community difficult to use in anticipating future crises. They were said to have been overly cautious and generalized in many circumstances, but in other instances these estimates were said to have been too closely tied to the mission and interests of the unit producing the assessments.[11]

The establishment of the National Assessments Group (NAG) within Kissinger's orbit was aimed at producing improved estimates.[12] However, the emergence in 1970 of serious discrepancies and public disagreements between the CIA and DOD over Soviet strategic capability and intent places this complaint in a different light. One cannot help but wonder whether the establishment of the NAG was not a reflection of Nixon and Kissinger's desire to reduce the independence of the intelligence agencies and particularly the CIA. The movement of CIA Director Richard Helms out of the mainstream of intelligence activity in the creation of NAG and the subsequent replacement of him with men more in tune with the White House certainly suggest that concern over the "uneven quality" of multiagency intelligence gathering and the public fanfare attendant to the announcement of NAG masked a White House effort to whip the CIA into line.

Third, some observers have pointed to the emphasis on planning in Nixon's setup as its strength but have noted that this focus allowed day-to-day operations to proceed in traditional modes. Kissinger's reach in all of this was impressive, but his grasp did not seem to extend to such fundamental operational matters as the budgetary operations of key agencies. Perhaps the most significant case in point here was the Department of Defense.

In 1970 a Defense Program Review Committee (DPRC) was established, consisting of the Special Assistant for National Security Affairs as chairman, the Deputy Secretary of Defense, the Chairman of the Joint Chiefs of Staff, the Undersecretary of State, the Director of the Bureau of the Budget, and the Chairman of the Council of Economic Advisors. The DPRC was to become Kissinger's means for infiltrating and then controlling the DOD's budgetary process. To some extent, therefore, the Nixon administration succeeded in imposing a bit more White House control on the DOD. But the Office of Management and Budget found it impossible to penetrate the myriad decision processes that went into making up the final broad program requests of the department. Kissinger found himself similarly deflected during the tenure of Melvin Laird as Secretary of Defense. Unlike Robert McNamara, who saw his role as one of imposing White House priorities on the department, Laird adopted much more the posture of a broker within the department and between the department and the White House. Thus he was opposed to extensive White House intervention and successfully prevented it in the bargaining between service branches and between the branches and the Office of the Secretary of Defense beyond holding the Joint Chiefs and the services to broad policy and budgetary parameters.

In summary, Kissinger and his policy machinery seemed to have filled a presidentially determined need with respect to policy planning. Questions remained, however, especially concerning operational follow-up. To a certain extent, these problems were a reflection of Henry Kissinger's conception of the conduct of foreign policy and the scope of the task itself. On the one hand, there was Kissinger's view that the conduct of policy is similar to the romantic adventures of a Zane Grey novel. As he once confessed to Italian journalist Oriana Fallaci, the conduct of foreign policy is a hard, one-man job:

> I've always acted alone. Americans admire that enormously. Americans admire the cowboy leading the caravan alone astride his horse, the cowboy entering a village or city alone on his horse. Without even a pistol, maybe, because he doesn't go in for shooting. He acts, that's all: aiming at the right spot at the right time. A Wild West tale, if you like. . . . This romantic, surprising character suits me, because being alone has always been part of my style, or of my technique if you prefer. Independence too. Yes, that's very important to me and in me.[13]

In any event, Nixon's obsession for White House control seemed to have required that Kissinger try to be at the head of all caravans simultaneously, whether they were headed for the Middle East, the Paris Peace Conference, the Strategic Arms Limitations Talks, Moscow, or Peking. But in these circumstances I. M. Destler's question became appropriate: whereas in the past there was concern whether the President could exercise control of the policy bureaucracy, the question became, could the Special Assistant?[14]

Nixon chose to make Kissinger his personal extension, and in doing so he drew to a logical conclusion 10 years of development of the White House foreign policy staff. However, this impressive White House establishment seems to have brought the presidency no nearer to creating an integrated and responsive policy establishment outside of the White House "foreign ministry."

The appointment of Kissinger as Secretary of State might have presaged an effort to integrate and make that bureaucracy responsive. However, Kissinger's propensity for personal autonomy unencumbered by bureaucratic constraints—his admiration of "the cowboy . . . entering a village or city alone on his horse [who] acts, that's all"—was not suited to the problems of coordination both created and anticipated by the National Security Act of 1947. Keeping the title of Special Assistant suggested that this and not the institutional role of Secretary of State remained as Kissinger's primary responsibility. "Some day," Kissinger joked, "I will visit the State Department."[15]

But actually, as the Nixon administration lost its authority, both apparatuses, the State Department and the NSC, suffered. In 1972, thirty-seven NSC meetings were held. But in 1973, after Kissinger became secretary and Watergate damage spread, there were only two meetings. After becoming secretary, Kissinger used his numerically shrinking National Security Council staff mainly to circumvent his colleagues at the Department of State. During the Yom Kippur War in 1973, for instance, Kissinger sent messages to the Middle Eastern heads of state, using White House–based CIA communications facilities. The messages were drafted by the NSC staff, and high State Department officials were unaware that they had even been sent.[16] Similarly, Kissinger visited Moscow without telling U.S. Ambassador Jacob Beam that he was in town, and American State Department officials commonly found themselves in the embarrassing position of having to ask Soviet diplomats what the official U.S.

position might be.[17] And after the Greek coup in July 1974, Kissinger invited the new Premier, Constantine Karamanlis, to visit the U-nited States and discuss the Turkish invasion of Cyprus. He did not, however, inform the U.S. embassy in Athens or consult the State Department desk.[18] Kissinger used his position in both the NSC and the State Department to blur responsibility between the two organizations. When, for instance, in November 1974 a diplomatic note had to be hurriedly delivered to Tunisia when Secretary Kissinger was practicing shuttle diplomacy in the Middle East, a Department of State staff aide was asked, "How did you get a letter from the White House so fast?" "Very easy," the official replied. "It arrived as fast as it took me to write it on White House stationery and dispatch it."[19]

Kissinger rarely dealt with anyone but undersecretaries at the State Department and shaped his department staff from some of his best NSC personnel. As a result, at the beginning of the Ford administration Kissinger's power had grown but his formal staff's had withered. And Kissinger's accountability had diminished as he became almost the personal repository of American foreign policy. Kissinger's management of foreign policy ironically conformed to his assessment of the nineteenth-century German Chancellor Bismarck:

> Institutions are designed for an average standard of performance. . . . They are rarely able to accommodate genius or demoniac power. . . . Statesmen who build lastingly transform the personal act of creation into institutions that can be maintained by an average standard of performance. This Bismarck proved incapable of doing. His very success committed Germany to a permanent tour de force. It created conditions that could be dealt with only by extraordinary leaders.[20]

Kissinger could claim, midway through the Ford succession, that "La diplomatie, c'est moi." But he, like Bismarck, had not built a bureaucratic structure to preserve his achievements.

THE CARTER ADMINISTRATION

Predictably, Carter took office vowing to change all of this. Thus, at the onset, he made an effort to distance the new administration from its predecessor and especially from the administrative style that had encompassed the foreign affairs establishment. Part of this effort was an apparent attempt to reduce the visibility of the National Security Council, narrow its functions, and reduce the rivalry between the President's National Security Adviser and the Secretary of State. No longer would the Special Assistant for National Security Affairs be, as he was in Nixon's time, a first among equals in the constellation of foreign policy actors. Instead, the National Security Adviser would work in a "collegial" atmosphere.[21] A smaller staff would be available to the Carter Special Assistant than had been the case during the heyday of the Kissinger system (100 versus 200 individuals).[22] Carter had, after all, campaigned on an array of warnings about the danger of Special Assistants searching for personal aggrandizement and what he termed a "Lone Ranger" style of diplomacy.[23] In the end, however, Carter's decisional and operational procedures and style became as centralized as those of his predecessors but in the process gave the impression of greater confusion.

The Carter "System"

The new Special Assistant for National Security Affairs was a 48-year-old former Columbia University professor, Zbigniew Brzezinski. Comparisons between Kissinger and Brzezinski were almost inevitable. Both were quick, acerbic immigrants with apparently boundless energy and ambition. Both had the ear of the President. And both Kissinger and Brzezinski, in their role as National Security Assistant, faced rivalries with Secretaries of State uncomfortable with bureaucratic brawling. But whereas Secretary of State Rogers seems to have been brought on by Nixon because it was thought Rogers would not be especially strong,[24] Cyrus Vance was chosen by Carter because he was perceived to be an experienced and articulate representative of the "Eastern establishment." Carter had, of course, run for office on a platform that was critical of the traditional foreign and national security establishment. But now that he was in office he felt the need to reassert policy continuity in a post-Vietnam era of conspicuously fragmented consensus.

In general, Brzezinski was to be in charge of "ideas" and to make sure that policy paper flowed regularly and fairly represented every agency position, and that there was policy follow-through. Cyrus Vance was also to have an independent role with coequal access to the President's ear by means of a four- or five-page "Secretary's evening report," summarizing the Secretary of State's impression of the day's events and calling attention to upcoming events and issues requiring presidential action. The President was to return the Secretary's paper by noon the next day with marginal notes. But Brzezinski, by literally being down the hall from the President's office, by managing paper flow, and as the President's jogging and tennis partner, enjoyed almost unfettered access to the President.[25] It was for these reasons, plus Brzezinski's captivating method of describing events, that the Special Assistant became ascendant.[26] "Zbig," Carter was heard to say, "is into my office every 15 minutes."[27] Carter called himself Brzezinski's "eager student" in world affairs.[28]

The methodology for anticipating tensions and maintaining harmony between Brzezinski and his staff and Vance and the State Department was both formal and informal. At the outset great emphasis was placed on the close interpersonal relationship between Brzezinski and Vance. Brzezinski told his friend of 20 years, columnist Victor Zorza, that on election night, he and Vance remained

> together to await the uncertain result, with no one else present—and his account of the occasion conveys the closeness of a relationship that seems likely to withstand the buffeting of political storms. He [Brzezinski] says he is keenly aware of the danger that . . . a bureaucracy as intensely competitive as Washington's . . . could cause trouble among principals, and he will be watching out for it.[29]

There were said to be "ten to fifteen" phone calls a day between Vance and Brzezinski, and Brzezinski was insistent that "it should be the norm and not the exception that the principal members of an administration work well together . . . I am discouraged that people find [this] hard to believe."[30]

There were, however, formal procedures designed to strengthen the coequal roles of the Departments of Defense and State with the NSC. The day he entered office, Carter issued a directive intended to reduce the dominance of the NSC and place more responsibility in the departments and agencies while ensuring that the NSC, with my Assistant for National Security Affairs, continues to integrate and facilitate foreign and defense policy decisions.[31]

By the directive, the number of special NSC staff committees was reduced from seven to two. These two were the Policy Review Committee (PRC) and the Special Coordinating Committee (SCC). The PRC was to develop policies where basic responsibility for the conceptualizing or implementing policy might fall in one agency— say Treasury—but where the policy would touch on other agencies that dealt with foreign relations. It was to be chaired by the Secretary of State, apparently giving him considerable bureaucratic leverage. The Secretary of State, in turn, might designate from the Department of State a representative for chairing "interdepartmental groups" that would be formed and operated under the PRC. The SCC was, essentially, the replacement for the crisis management operations developed by Kissinger.[32] It was to deal with what was to become two of the most critical areas of the Carter administration: arms control issues and intelligence activities. The SCC was chaired by Brzezinski. In addition, there were to be NSC *ad hoc* groups chaired by Brzezinski when "particular policy, including those which transcended departmental boundaries [arose]".[33]

At first glance, it appeared that the NSC's role as an action unit was being replaced by a kind of organizational gatekeeping and "think tank" function. Instead of having seven nearly all embracing committees, all chaired by the special assistant, there were to be only two principal committees, only one of which was chaired by Brzezinski. In fact, however, much of the foreign policy action remained where it had been located for the preceding fifteen years—in the NSC.

The Limits of the Carter National Security Policy System

Two sets of realities eroded the efficiency of this system, plaguing it with incoherence and rivalry, and leading Secretary of State Vance to resign and his successor, Edmund Muskie, to suffer a stinging humiliation at the very outset of his brief tenure. The first is that authority is not easily divisible and that power is almost always hierarchical. The American system of foreign policy making is, by constitutional design and bureaucratic growth, complex. Nonetheless, introducing the second voice of the security adviser necessarily confounds further not only foreign governments, but also, increases confusion within the American bureaucracy as well. Second, incoherence was fostered by the inherent conflict in the policy perspectives of the Vance State Department and the Brzezinski NSC. Whereas the Secretary of State seemed predisposed to the exercise of diplomacy and reconstitution of detente, Brzezinski focused on the necessity of confronting the Soviet Union. In the end Brzezinski's perspective seemed to win out, but between Inaugural Day and the enunciation of the Carter Doctrine in 1980, the tense interaction of these perspectives reinforced the appearance of policy making incoherence and indecision.

The Problems of "Multiple Advocacy." The argument for "multiple advocacy" was explained by the State Department's Special Adviser for Soviet Affairs, Marshall Shulman:

> It would be unfortunate if there were a single orthodoxy so that [the President] did not have to hear a range of possible assessments or speculation. A diversity of views enriches the menu of possible responses.[34]

There is undoubtedly something to be said for such diversity within the context of internal debate over policy. But problems arise when debate is carried out within a policy making framework of considerable informality. Thus when commissioned by the White House to evaluate the NSC system, Philip Odeen concluded:

> The heavy reliance on informal processes . . . may be one reason policy decisions are not systematically translated into action. Follow-up often depends on adequate debriefs by the attendees [at informal policy making meetings], which do not always happen. The agencies have not adjusted to this informal approach and the White House has not developed means to ensure decisions are communicated clearly and promptly to the agencies in cases where the debriefs are inadequate or the perceptions of the results by the principals differ.[35]

The Carter system seemed, if anything, more controlled by the security adviser and NSC staff than even during Kissinger's incumbency. Under the Kissinger NSC, it was calculated that 70 percent of the foreign policy memoranda came from Kissinger's staff and a great deal of the action was held within his staff itself. But one State Department policy planner in the last months of 1980 calculated that out of the thirty important papers reaching Carter's desk in the preceding years, twenty-six had been initiated and supervised by the NSC while only three had come from State and one from the Defense Department. Whereas the full National Security Council—including the Vice President and the Secretaries of State and Defense—met 125 times under Nixon and Ford, full-fledged meetings were held only a dozen times under the Carter system. Cabinet and subcabinet-level meetings were presided over by Brzezinski when there was departmental overlap, and crisis management was largely the domain of the NSC staff. But in spite of the structure there never seemed to be an agenda or set of priorities. For as one NSC staffer said, "rolling his eyes," "we are living the agenda of U.S. foreign policy."[36]

Much of the Carter administration's foreign policy was hammered out in high-level meetings without the President in attendance. The minutes of these meetings were forwarded (by Brzezinski) to Carter and in the margins of the case most convincingly presented, the President would indicate his preferred course. In the Carter administration, therefore, there were few hints of separate courses of action argued tenaciously through the bureaucracy. There was instead merely a top-level free-for-all guided mostly by instinct and wit.

Thus, in the end, multiple advocacy, notwithstanding the existence of formal and informal mechanisms to channel it, exacerbated the uncertainty not only about who made foreign policy decisions but also about who was an authoritative public voice of American policy and the American people to the world community or the parties of negotiations. When political leaders were confronted with the seemingly antithetical pronouncements of Andrew Young, Carter's heretical Ambassador to the United Nations, and Brzezinski, or the incongruous juxtaposition of the Vance and Brzezinski world views in the same presidential address, the result was to confound friend and foe. The use of a special envoy, Robert Strauss, proclaiming his independence of the National Security Council and the State Department, to negotiate the remaining Middle East impasse in the wake of the Camp David summit, was similarly confusing. Especially disconcerting was a threat of the normally imperturbable Secretary of State to resign in the face of Strauss's assertion of independence—and, then, when finally prevailed upon to carry out Department instructions, Strauss, former head of the Democratic Party, was heard to complain that he had been sent off "on a fool's errand."[37]

Carter negotiated; his special envoys negotiated; his Secretary of State negotiated; and his national security adviser negotiated. Brzezinski negotiated with the Chinese, somewhat in excess of agreed upon policy, and then managed its implementation by fait accompli and press conference. Brzezinski insisted on the same television program on which the Secretary of State appeared, that multiple advocacy is what the President needs, whereas Vance, moments later, advised that in foreign policy there must be a single voice. Since there were well-known differences between the two in their approaches to the Soviets,[38] their views on the utility of coercion, and even on the diplomatic method itself, the policy of multiple advocacy was incomprehensible. And a Washington press corps that thrives on interpersonal conflict and bureaucratic struggle could only amplify the cacophony.

Perhaps the best face that could be put on the situation was that advanced by Anthony Lake, the Department of State's Director of Policy Planning:

> [The Carter administration was] managing complexities when they come into conflict—striking a balance among competing objectives . . . our approach is to make constant pragmatic, case-by-case decisions, seeking the most constructive balance among our interests and adjusting our tactics as circumstances change.[39]

Multiple advocacy might have been made to work if the many strands of advocacy could have been confined to the internal policy formulation process. But this would have required far more than centralized policy making procedures. It would have required a

President thoroughly knowledgeable in the ways of bureaucratic politics and a presidential willingness to invest considerable time and effort in the thankless and problematic task of cajoling and convincing the policy making establishment to accept his agenda and priorities, his perspectives. But that establishment assumes that the President has such an agenda and perspective, and Jimmy Carter never succeeded in articulating such a position, much less giving evidence of a willingness to wage bureaucratic political warfare personally. Instead he sought to strike a "balance among competing objectives." In retrospect, it seems clear that even if bureaucratic political skills had been the forte of the President, the construction of a pragmatic balance may have been precluded by the contradictory character of the policy perspectives with which he had to work.

Conflicting Policy Perspectives. The incoherence of the Carter administration's policy processes derived from a divergence of views concerning the substance of policy as well as the nature of the policy making arrangements and the ambitions of those who worked within them. There was, above all, disagreement about the character of the Soviet Union and the centrality of the Soviet-American relationship in the totality of American foreign affairs in the late 1970s.[40]

Moving the Soviets aside to make way for the Chinese, challenging them to "competition in places like Somalia" and changing the idiom of arms control, at least initially, to a public relations exercise, was of course, destructive of the legacy of detente bestowed by Kissinger. But underlying the lurching process whereby this was done was irresolvable tension within the Carter administration between two views of international reality and how to respond to it. On the one hand, there was the view of the Secretary of State who, along with others such as Andrew Young, seemed predisposed to recognizing and working within what was thought to be a new set of international conditions. The Soviet-American confrontation remained important, but from this perspective it was only one of many relationships that would have to be managed through resort to negotiation and diplomacy.

In contrast, Brzezinski represented a perspective that held that the Soviet-American relationship remained most important. Although new forces and relationships were certainly taking their place on the agenda of American foreign policy, they remained peripheral to the Soviet-American confrontation and the conflictual essence of America's international affairs since World War II. Indeed, the new international relations had not supplanted the old as much as they constituted a more complex and dangerous arena within which a much more capable and continually hostile Soviet Union now confronted a more constrained American presence.[41]

Carter tried to straddle both positions, but by late 1978 continuation of that posture had become impossible. If SALT was to have any chance in the Senate, then the demands of conservatives clamoring for defense spending increases and a return to American superiority would have to be acknowledged. But in conceding a massive military buildup during the 1980s, the so-called realist view of international reality was given credibility, and Carter's attempts to adopt a more accommodating or liberal stance vis-a-vis the revolutionary politics of southern Africa and central America was made politically more vulnerable. The fall of the Shah and the Iranian hostage crisis pushed Carter toward the conservatives and a more impressive "Rapid Deployment Force" than any ever imagined during the Kennedy years. With the Afghanistan invasion, Carter finally abandoned any semblance of a departure from the doctrine of militant containment and enunciated a doctrine no less open-ended and, in its details, more belligerent than that advanced by Truman in early 1947. Brzezinski's world view became dominant, and a measure of policy coherence was thereby achieved. But Carter's uncertain approach to and belated acceptance of a more traditional view of international reality, merely confirmed the widespread conclusion that his was an administration marked by hopeless policy making confusion presided over by a Hamlet-like Chief Executive.

Brzezinski Ascendant

Edmund Muskie took over from Cyrus Vance after Vance resigned in April 1980 over the issue of using military force to rescue American hostages in Iran while having promised the Europeans—apparently in good faith—that no such dramatic efforts would be undertaken. Vance learned that the hostage rescue plan was to go forward—a plan in which the Joint Chiefs of Staff feared one third of the hostages and probably thousands of Iranians would be killed—only 24 hours before the ill-fated helicopters took off. He protested, but according to one of Vance's assistants, Carter overruled him, using Brzezinski's logic that the mission was essentially military and not political.[42] There was speculation that Muskie's experience in the Senate would give him a political base from which to combat Brzezinski for primacy in the Carter administration's much criticized foreign policy system. Muskie said,

> My concern about coordinating foreign policy goes far beyond Dr. Brzezinski and the National Security Council staff. . . . We've had no confrontations up to this point. It's conceivable that we might because we're both strong-minded individuals. We both have definite ideas. We both seek access to the President, and it's my job to see that the Secretary of State doesn't take second place.[43]

Early on, however, Muskie, although professing to love his job, complained that in his weekly luncheon with Secretary of Defense Harold Brown and Brzezinski, he had to contend with as many as twenty-five items on an agenda fixed largely at the NSC, leaving him or his staff time for only hasty reaction.[44] There were substantive disputes as well. For example, on the question of whether the United States should establish a military base in Somalia in support of the Rapid Deployment Force, the Department of State's Africa specialists felt that this inevitably would involve the United States in the dispute between the Soviet-backed Ethiopians and Somalia. The status of aggressor in the conflict, from the standpoint of international law, if not equity, belonged to Somalia.[45] On August 22, 1980, however, the issue was decided: the U.S., at a total cost of over $150 million, would purchase basing rights in Somalia.[46]

More significant yet, was Muskie's startling revelation of August 9, 1980 that he knew nothing of Presidential Directive 59, which called for formally shifting strategic policy away from "mutual assured destruction" to incorporate a series of "counterforce" strategic targeting options directed, in part, at Soviet retaliatory capability. Cynics suggested that the decision had been rushed past Muskie not because of his known opposition to the doctrine when he served in the Senate, but because the Republican convention had just adopted a platform that called for just this sort of nuclear strategy. Defenders of the Carter administration said that the timing was coincidence and that both Brown and Brzezinski had been busy with the pressure of events. They had simply not reflected on the diplomatic import of the statement of nuclear doctrine for American NATO allies, a matter of continuing diplomatic delicacy for the Department of State.

The entire State Department, however, apparently had been cut out of the policy from the beginning. According to Leslie Gelb, former director of the department's Bureau of Political-Military Affairs and a long-time observer of bureaucratic politics, Brzezinski took charge of the targeting question in October of 1978 and assigned it to the Pentagon. The State Department was not told of the study for the reason that it was a narrow defense question. In reality, Brzezinski did so "because they assumed they were going to have a real battle with the State Department."[47] Gelb said that only after "several weeks" did news of the study accidently become known to his office, which had the mandate for making "military policy and diplomacy relevant to one another."[48] The Department of State was "invited" to attend one of the planning sessions after arguing for six months in the spring of 1979, that the department should be involved in this kind of political/military pronouncement. "We only got to physically see the [ongoing] study 24 or 48 hours before the first meeting," Gelb recalled. There were to be some three meetings in which State participated. Since there were some objections by State to the evolving study, Brzezinski shelved it but asked Defense to do a new study, this time shutting the State Department out completely on the grounds that it was not really a concern of the State Department or the Arms Control and Disarmament Agency. This was the last time the State Department was to hear about the study until it was about to be announced as policy in August of 1980. Gelb complained the whole issue was "preposterous" and "dangerous":

> It's preposterous because the responsibility for framing nuclear war fighting strategy is the NSC's, not the National Security Council Staff. And the Secretary of State is a member of the National Security Council. . . . I find it dangerous because to think that you can separate defense policy from policy—decisions of nuclear war from foreign policy considerations—shows a dangerously narrow view of war and diplomacy and of life. How are you going to even dream of

ending a nuclear war or dealing with the political problems of nuclear war without the involvement of the Secretary of State and your State Department?[49]

It is noteworthy of the "decline at State" that the Odeen Report, an internal Carter administration assessment of its policy making process, had as one of its major recommendations that

> State should be included in major Executive Office of the President-convened meetings where foreign policy matters are significant. For example, the Secretary of State should participate in Presidential meetings where the NATO commitment to a 3 percent real defense budget increase is a major issue.[50]

That this should have to be said at all indicates the relative weakness of the State Department by the end of the Carter administration.

Carter attempted to begin his administration as an agnostic on the place and character of Soviet-American relations. He subdivided issues in his cabinet, promoted interpersonal cordiality, and tried to ensure the presence of multiple perspectives on foreign policy in the policy process.[51] Without many preconceptions about foreign policy, Carter was, for a while, able to hold conflicting positions simultaneously. His was not the view of the diplomat attempting to mediate longstanding rivalries. It was, rather, the view of the engineer, trying to reach, through experimentation, solutions to dispose of problems. In the end, what "worked" were the old routines of the cold war, managed in much the way they had been handled by his predecessors.

In January of 1980, one Carter administration official at the center of the policy process summed up the outcome, when, for the first time since the early 1970s, there was talk of an armed conflict with the Soviet Union:

> The policy machinery for the first time is working well. There have been no disputes of major substance, no cracks along the Soviet policy fault line as during the first three years of the administration.
>
> There are daily meetings at the top of government. There are assignments for implementation and follow-through. More is being planned and done than appears on the surface.[52]

The bracing effect of a military crisis was captured by the observation that, "Afghanistan was a godsend, . . . It gave point and opportunity for action."[53] And in foreign policy, "action" (or if not action, at least a conflictual approach) and not "diplomacy" has been the management style of U.S. foreign policy for 35 years.

THE REAGAN ADMINISTRATION

If the disarray of the Carter administration confirmed the necessity of a measure of coherence in viewpoint, the early months of the Reagan administration suggested that ideological consistency was not in itself sufficient to ensure orderly and coherent foreign policy making. During his first year in office Ronald Reagan had to convince his Secretary of State not to resign, suppress personal and public feuding between his security adviser and Secretary of State, subsequently ask for the resignation of his security adviser, and undertake a reorganization of his national security policy making setup. It did not seem to matter that the philosophies of those engaged in this bureaucratic warfare were usually distinguished from one another only by nuance. By early 1982, a frustrated Secretary of State Alexander Haig could be overheard angrily declaiming: "This administration is like a rainbarrel. Everyone yells down the barrel and it echoes around, but nothing happens."[54]

The Vicar Defrocked?

It was widely assumed that in an administration whose members and President had little experience in foreign affairs and were generally preoccupied with domestic questions, Secretary of State Haig would quickly dominate foreign policy making. His experience as NATO commander and his service as one of Henry Kissinger's top aides seemed to provide him with a stature sufficient to reverse the decade's long decline of the Secretary of State's position, especially in view of Reagan's intention to downgrade the position of the security adviser.

Haig started very early—indeed, before inauguration day—to consolidate his position by claiming preeminence as the "vicar" of foreign policy making. By and large, Haig had his way in getting hard-line but well-known and generally respected career Foreign Service Officers and others familiar to the Washington foreign policy establishment in place in the upper echelons of the State Department. High-level State Department jobs in Washington were soon filled, while other bureaucracies had positions languishing for months. At the same time, however, Haig's claims to preeminence were clouded by his aggressiveness, which seemed to grate on the nerves of the coterie of California insiders President Reagan brought to the White House.

It was not just Haig's rhetorical bombast that irritated the Californians. From the start, Haig was suspected of coveting the presidency (he had briefly pursued the nomination in 1980) and representing an extension of Henry Kissinger's more moderate detente philosophy. There was speculation that the appointment as Undersecretary of State of William Clark, an old and very close friend of Reagan, but a man with embarrassingly little experience or knowledge of foreign affairs, was designed to constrain Haig at State. Clark, during his confirmation hearings proved unable to identify the leader of South Africa and ignorant of any West European opposition to nuclear proliferation, indeed virtually all of American foreign affairs.[55] He was characterized in Europe as a "nit wit," but it now appears that his task was never to be a major substantive participant in the policy process but rather to serve as a dependable liaison between the State Department, its somewhat alien (to the Reagan intimates) Secretary of State, and the White House. By virtually all accounts, Clark was highly effective in this capacity.[56]

In any event, on inauguration day Haig unsuccessfully lobbied the President to sign a directive formally delegating to him enormous powers in the policy making process. The White House leaked the document to the press, enraging Haig and provoking the first of what was to be many battles over bureaucratic turf. The dispute was settled by assigning much of the authority for crisis management requested by the disgruntled Haig to Vice President Bush. Thus at almost every turn Haig's quest for bureaucratic supremacy was frustrated.

Having been brought up short, early and in public, Haig subsequently managed to further discredit himself by his startling performance before the national television audience watching for word on Reagan's health after a would-be assassin pumped a bullet into the

President's chest in March 1981. Flushed, with hands trembling, Haig proclaimed himself to be "in control." He might have been, but his tight-voiced intensity and inaccurate relating of the constitutionally mandated succession process (putting himself several rungs closer to the presidency than constitutionally warranted) gave impetus to open press speculation about the emotional effects of Haig's triple by-pass heart operation of the previous year. Indeed, that sober mirror of establishment opinion, James Reston of the *New York Times*, felt constrained to query the secretary's emotional state in a year-end interview with Haig.[57]

Haig seemed to suffer an endless stream of both White House managed and self-inflicted humiliations from the spring through the end of the year. Ambassadors were appointed at a maddeningly slow pace with political fidelity to the Reagan brand of conservatism an essential and preeminent test of qualification.[58] By early 1982, a record 50 percent of the ambassadors appointed came from outside the State Department compared to less than 30 percent in the Carter administration. Malcolm Toon, a former ambassador complained, "We have a man in London who owes his place in life to the fact that his parents founded a furniture polish dynasty. His only qualification for the job is that he speaks English." And when John Gavin, the Spanish-speaking actor, was appointed to Mexico—an extremely sensitive post—some Mexicans were heard to complain that if the United States had to send them an actor, why not Wonder Woman?[59]

Haig and Secretary of Defense Caspar Weinberger were frequently at odds on issues that overlapped their respective domains. In some cases such as the development and deployment of neutron bombs in Europe and NATO nuclear strategy, some observers were impressed by what they took to be an almost conscious embarrassment of the Secretary of State.[60] In trade policy, the White House stripped even more of the turf that had been taken from State by the Carter administration and assigned to the Commerce Department and the Office of the Special Trade Representative. A bit later Haig was rather noisily overruled on selling the Airborne Warning and Command aircraft (AWACs) and F–15 fighters to Saudi Arabia. The grain embargo imposed against the Soviet Union by the Carter administration at the time of the Afghanistan invasion was lifted even as the Soviets appeared on the verge of invading Poland. Haig, it was said, believed both moves fraught with danger. Nonetheless he hastened to defend publically what he had been known to be critical of privately—especially the AWACs sale—on the grounds that the standing of the presidency in international affairs would be jeopardized if the decision was reversed by Congress.

Finally, Haig's capacity for injuring himself extended to what could have been allies within the government as well. His natural constituency in the Congress was some of the more senior members of the Senate, especially within the relatively more moderate Senate Republican leadership. However, support he may have had in this sector was undermined by his sins of misstatement and circumlocution—gaffes that were eagerly circulated to the Washington press by White House detractors. For example, Haig sent a letter to Senator Howard Baker, the Republican majority leader, its typed salutation reading "Dear Senator Baker." Haig, seeking a personal touch, struck the formal opening and inked in "Dear Harold."[61]

The Reagan System: A Black Hole?

The Special Assistant for National Security Affairs, Richard Allen, was never able to occupy the openings left as Haig was buffeted by White House rebukes and the Secretary's sometimes erratic behavior. In Reagan's initial conception of his NSC, the security adviser was to be denied direct access to the President. Unlike most of his predecessors, Allen would have to report through a senior White House adviser, in this case White House counselor Edwin Meese, another Californian with little knowledge of foreign and defense policy but an old acquaintance of the President. Moreover, in addition to his diminished institutional standing, Allen had been damaged even before inauguration by a story in the *Wall Street Journal* noting that he seemed to have acted for private business interests while he was on the Kissinger White House staff in the early 1970s. And when, in the midst of increasingly bitter and public feuding between Allen and Haig over the control and direction of policy, it was revealed that Allen had received $1,000 and a gift of wrist watches from Japanese journalists to set up interviews with Nancy Reagan, Allen's credibility was at an end. Even though subsequently cleared of any violation of law, Allen's resignation was requested, and he left the inner circle of the administration in early 1982 amidst unflattering references to his ethical myopia and lack of administrative capacity.

The NSC itself was not well respected. NSC staffers were lesser-known individuals drawn largely from the academic world. They were isolated by presidential directive from speaking to the press in private and were heard to complain that they had been cut off from the traditional flow of information. *Newsweek* reported:

> . . . officials are particularly stung by media reports of their supposed incompetence. "All they're asking is a *chance* to be incompetent," says one sympathetic White House aide. "Right now they're not doing anything." A disgruntled NSC member complains that he and his colleagues are so out of the foreign policy action that "we're an annex of [White House social secretary] Muffie Brandon.[62]

But if the Allen NSC was not supposed to be much of a rival for Haig, and Haig, either as the result of his own blunders or White House attempts to contain his influence within the policy making process, was not in control of policy making, observers and many participants as well were left to wonder as to the nature of the Reagan system.

Initially, a set of informal policy groups had been established in the areas of foreign, defense, and intelligence policy, chaired respectively by the Secretary of State, the Secretary of Defense, and the Director of the Central Intelligence agency, William Casey.[63] Below this level were a series of interdepartmental groups chaired by State Department representatives, in contrast to previous administrations in which such groups were directed by the NSC staff. Formally, the NSC itself was the recipient of the analysis and recommendations generated by the interdepartmental and policy groups and became, in an administration that was to emphasize cabinet government, the central area for decision. Instead, a more informal National Security Planning Group consisting of the Vice President, Secretaries of State and Defense, Director of Central Intelligence, and Reagan's closest personal White House advisers, Meese, James Baker, White House chief of staff, and Michael Deaver, deputy chief of staff, was to serve as the inner circle of policy making. Within this group, as in the domestic policy areas, Meese was to function as the coordinator and director. Allen, the security adviser, was to be a "note taker." In sum, the initial Reagan policy making arrangements were not unlike the informal structures that took shape during the Johnson and to a lesser extent, Carter administrations. Despite the greater ideological homogeneity of the Reagan participants, however, the results of the Reagan system proved to be only marginally less chaotic than those of his immediate predecessor.

Participants and close observers of the process reported that the system's operations were marred by poor preparation, poorly delineated areas of responsibility, and few, if any, systematically prepared and coherent policy statements. In fact, after one year in office the Reagan administration reportedly had failed to produce policy reviews and guidance on most major areas of the world, such crucial bilateral relations as those with the Soviet Union and China, or a clear policy statement concerning U.S. policy in the Middle East. Of the twelve memoranda produced by the system at year's end, most were only a few lines long and were drafted in such a way as, in the words of one official, to leave "most things to the imagination."[64] Lacking minutes or memoranda on the content of discussions, the participants, especially Haig and Weinberger, were frequently and publicly at odds concerning policy. The system, according to most participants interviewed by *New York Times* reporter Leslie Gelb in late 1981, led to a "continuous succession of mixed signals that looked good only if compared with what happened in the Carter Administration."[65] Reagan claimed that there were no differences between the two secretaries, but events made it clear that this was not the case. Thus in early February 1982, Weinberger and Haig clashed over sanctions applied to Poland and over the extent to which American security interests and Israel's coincided. In the latter case, Weinberger and his staff attempted to sell anti-aircraft systems to Jordan when Haig had just finished assuring Israeli Prime Minister Begin that no such sales were likely.[66]

Predictably, Edwin Meese, erstwhile coordinator of the system, saw things differently. "We have," Meese insisted, "a highly centralized but participatory decision-making system for policy implementation with specific responsibility and accountability.[67] But when it was suggested to him that many who participated in the system had taken to characterizing the system as a kind of "black hole" into which issues entered but policy never seemed to emerge, Meese responded:

> Exactly; that's the way we like it. We feel that it is important that the decision-making process be a matter that doesn't get a great deal of public or even internal Government attention other than from those who are directly involved, which are the members of the National Security Council, until the President makes a decision.[68]

If, however, the system was dependent upon presidential activism for its operation and was widely perceived as operating poorly, then it seemed that much of the problem during the first year of the Reagan administration lay with Reagan himself. From the onset, Reagan's interests seemed to run to domestic and economic policy questions. His performance at press conferences was generally given high marks on the latter issues, but his ability to deal with foreign and national security policy questions seemed, by comparison, inept. In fact, in early 1982, when the administration undertook a major reorganization of its foreign policy making arrangements, it was reported that the President had participated in few major foreign and defense policy decisions during his first year in office. Indeed, it appeared that the President seldom sought to involve himself in decisions and that frequently his top aides consciously excluded him from policy questions of significance. Thus, when during 1981 the Department of Defense confirmed a shift in nuclear strategy to one that accepted the likelihood of fighting a nuclear war, the President was not included in the decision making process. "We don't get the President involved in that kind of stuff," said Meese.[69] Similarly in August of 1981, when American naval aircraft had been engaged in a fight with Libyan fighters off the coast of Libya, Meese and the Secretary of Defense had decided that there was no reason to awaken the President, who was asleep at the time. In fact, the press was briefed before the President was informed of the dogfight.

Allen's dismissal as security adviser provided the administration with an opportunity to attend to these problems in early 1982. Allen was replaced by William Clark, and the position of security adviser was to be returned to its position of preeminence in the national security policy making process. There was speculation that Haig's influence would be increased as the result of the changes because he and Clark had reportedly developed a close working relationship during Clark's year at the State Department. On the other hand, it was no less likely that the same institutional tensions that developed between previous strong security advisers and their counterparts at State would reemerge in the Reagan administration. Clark took note of this when he observed that "the conflict of which you speak is inherent in the system. . . . I now must view the area of national security from a Presidential perspective rather than from the State Department perspective."[70]

The observation was prescient, for within months reports of increased tension between the White House and Haig reemerged. In mid-1982, Clark and Haig disagreed on the wisdom of placing an embargo on the sale of technology to the Soviet Union for a natural gas pipeline to Europe. Clark aligned himself with Reagan's desire to deny the Russians American technology and to punish European companies and the European subsidiaries of American firms if they went through with the sales of technology on their own. Haig maintained that the embargo could severely damage American relations with its NATO allies, especially in view of the fact that the President had assured Europeans at the Paris economic summit conference in June of 1982 that he would not press the matter of the pipeline. Nonetheless, Reagan, with Clark's support, reversed himself and Haig, with great emotion, threatened to resign. To Haig's surprise and chagrin, the President abruptly, almost brutally, accepted his resignation and appointed in his place another former Nixon administration cabinet officer, George Shultz.

Shultz's views and style seemed to point to some convergence between State and Defense. His views on arms negotiations at the strategic level and concerning European theater nuclear weapons and force levels seemed somewhat closer to Weinberger's than were Haig's. But Shultz, like Haig, was cautious about attempts to bully the Soviets with embargoes or rhetoric and sensitive to the economic issues that troubled the alliance in a way that seemed to have escaped the Secretary of Defense. Thus some potential sources of difficulty remained embedded in Reagan's policy structure.[71]

In the short run, however, the new Secretary of State's relaxed and low keyed style and his long and close personal relationships with members of Reagan's cabinet could prove more important. Shultz and Weinberger, for example, had both been top officers of the giant international construction firm, the Bechtel Corporation, and the President had reportedly been extremely impressed with Shultz when Shultz had served as a member of transition and international economic policy task forces for the President. This suggested to some observers that the policy making machinery could work with less grinding of gears than during the unhappy tenure of Alexander Haig.

Uncertainties remained, however, as the revised structure took shape. The problem of what exactly was the presidential perspective persisted. In contrast with his first year in office, the President would be briefed on a daily basis by the security adviser. Presumably, he would now be briefed by the Secretaries of State and Defense before press conferences, something that had apparently not taken place during Reagan's first year. And finally, it was reported that Clark intended as one of his primary tasks to insure that the President would become a more active participant in the foreign policy making process itself.[72]

Apart from whether Clark, a man who a year before had admitted that his foreign policy experience consisted of "72 hours in Santiago,"[73] would be able to coordinate the policy process, there remained in place all the problems that demanded precisely such coordination. Notwithstanding a drop in the decibel level of bureaucratic conflict immediately after Haig's dismissal, there remained the longstanding institutional tensions between the State Department, Defense Department, and the Central Intelligence Agency. Moreover, there remained a widely held perception that this was an administration that had not as yet defined its foreign policy objectives and approaches. As always, however, the greatest uncertainty seemed to be in the Oval Office. For as the foreign and national security policy establishment fought for the President's attention, Reagan was confronted in early 1982 with his greatest crisis yet on the domestic front as his economic policies were challenged by the prospect of hundreds of billions of dollars in deficits over the next 3 years, recovery-threatening interest rates, and the highest unemployment levels since the Great Depression.

THE PAST AND FUTURE OF THE NATIONAL SECURITY POLICY MAKING SYSTEM

The present national security policy system came about in response to a world view that emphasized the necessity of American participation and leadership in a global struggle against an implacable communist foe. The need was to create and then orchestrate a broad range of instrumentalities: military strength, intelligence operations, foreign economic and military assistance, propaganda, educational and cultural exchange, and ultimately "counterinsurgency" and other forms of overt and covert means of structuring world order. Down to the Reagan administration, the assumptions about American policy and the policy making structure remained unchanged from those first stated by one of the founders of the NSC and the national security policy system, Ferdinand Eberstadt:

> The great need, therefore, is that we be prepared always and all along the line, not simply to defend ourselves after an attack, but through all available political, military and economic means to forestall any such attack. . . . Much has been said about the need for waging peace, as well as war. We have tried to suggest an organizational structure adapted to both purposes.[74]

The assumptions implicit in this statement have been with us for so long as to make the recitation of them somehow unexceptional. Yet there is an important bias here that should be made explicit—a bias toward action, manipulation, or, to put matters more bluntly—intervention. Policy and policy making became during the postwar period a massive gearing-up for mortal combat with an implacable, zealous foe. The compelling need was for a reorganization of policy processes to strengthen the hand of the President. Thus began the strain toward efficiency traced out in these chapters. There was built into the entire process a steady pull toward rearranging the policy structure to make it more responsive to a modern Presidency involved in struggle and surrounded by great risk unlike that encountered by any of its predecessors. As Professor Neustadt argues:

> Cold War and nuclear weapons make the difference greater. A new dimension of risk has come upon American decision-making. Its effect has been to magnify the President's responsibility, and to intensify his needs for flexibility, for information, for control.[75]

The objective of cold war Presidents, as Eberstadt had put it, was "waging peace," total military effort without a total war.

A consequence of this posture was to push the United States into an interventionist policy that saw America's interests everywhere. The U.S. viewed its national security as synonymous with its conception of international order. A circular dynamic was thereby set in motion: the U.S. had to maintain a presence everywhere, because the ideological confrontation was potentially everywhere; to fail in one place was to endanger the entire structure. Peace was involved in global order, and peace was not divisible. Neither, therefore, was order. Disorder in one place threatened order every place.

The thrust of policy and bureaucratic arrangements that followed a global definition of American interests reflect an approach to the international system that stands in contrast with that of diplomacy. For diplomacy involves something quite different from the dogged commitment to global confrontation described here. Sir Harold Nicholson, former diplomat and authority on diplomatic problems, subscribes to the *Oxford English Dictionary* definition of diplomacy: "Diplomacy is the management of international relations by *negotiation*; the method by which these relations are *adjusted* and *managed* by ambassadors and envoys; the business or art of the diplomatist."[76] The spirit of the diplomatic enterprise is not confrontation but rather accommodation and compromise. During the cold war of the 1950s and 1960s these skills and this approach were not very much in demand in Washington. Not surprisingly, the department responsible for developing and applying these skills, the Department of State, was brushed aside in the scramble for policy control that accompanied the emergence of new bureaucratic actors with skills deemed more appropriate to Presidents who sought a capacity for massive retaliation, "assured destruction," "counterinsurgency," "pacification," and all the accouterments of a diplomacy of violence.

It became commonplace during the 1970s to bemoan the institutional preeminence of the Special Assistant for National Security Affairs and the Defense Department, and the diminished capacity and stature of the Department of State.[77] But the eclipse of State and the rise of crisis-oriented or action-oriented agents of the Executive seem unavoidable. Only if the Secretary of State becomes an exponent of orchestrated force can he also have a hand in diplomacy in an environment of essential hostility. If there is not strong, central White House control, the Secretary of State would probably still be overshadowed by those agencies who are best able to handle a militarized foreign policy servicing far-flung commitments. Secretary of State Muskie during his brief tenure complained as much about the influence of the Defense Department as about the security adviser, and the first year of the Reagan administration was marred by constant bickering and disagreement between the Secretaries of Defense and State.

To argue, then, about the institutional structure of the national security policy system, in some ways misses the point. It might be better to have a Secretary of State who "knew how to fight" on issues of the day.[78] Secretary of State Vance's appearance of ineffectiveness was often attributed to his being too much of a gentleman. But Secretary Haig was certainly no stranger to bureaucratic combat, yet his relationships with others in the Reagan administration at best were mixed. It might be better if there were a national security adviser, who would be, as Henry Kissinger put it in April 1980:

> the orderer of options. He should make sure everybody gets a fair hearing. . . . He should not appear on television. He should not see foreign diplomats. If he does, he is conceived as the alternative to the Secretary of State. . . . When I was the security adviser, I violated every one of these rules except the one that I never went on television.[79]

But the mere existence of a national security adviser who can present any views of his own at all at virtually any time, gives this position the tremendous leverage of what former Kissinger aide Brent Scowcroft has called "propinquity."[80] In this regard, multiple voices are a virtual inevitability. When, however, different songs are being sung in the presence of a conductor who is either unable or unwilling to impose a single score, dissonance and discord become inevitable.

Finally, our review of the development of the system suggests that if a national security adviser did not exist, then some other locus of power would arise, probably in the White House staff, as occurred during the early Reagan administration when the security advisor position was temporarily diminished. Alternatively, given the preeminence of the militarized definition of American commitments, bureaucratic logic would see power devolve to those bureaucratic agents who could command force. In the absence of a strong White House role, bureaucratic influence in foreign policy seems likely to be monopolized by the Defense Department or Central Intelligence Agency. In sum, the reorganization of the role of Secretary of State and the downgrading of the national security assistant could give the Secretary of State a real voice instead of a titular role. But in the context of confrontational politics, that voice is likely to be heard only to the extent that a Secretary of State is steeped in a military idiom. In these circumstances, the diplomat can be either a warrior, or irrelevant.

NOTES

1. See Richard M. Nixon, *U.S. Foreign Policy for the 1970s: A New Strategy for Peace* (Washington, D.C.: U.S. Government Printing Office, 1970), esp. pp. 17–23.
2. Ibid., p. 17.
3. "Letter to Senator Henry M. Jackson concerning the National Security Council from Henry A. Kissinger, Assistant to the President for National Security Affairs, 3 March 1970," in *The National Security Council: Comment by Henry A. Kissinger*, submitted to Subcommittee on National Security and International Operations of the Senate Government Operations Committee, 91st Congress, 2nd Session, 1970, p. 2.
4. Ibid.
5. Ibid.
6. See "Department of State Foreign Affairs Manual Circular, No. 521, February 6, 1969," reprinted in U.S. Congress, Senate Committee on Government Operations, *The National Security Council: New Role and Structure, February 7, 1969*, 91st Congress, 1st Session, 1969, pp. 4–6; John P. Leacacos, "Kissinger's Apparat" and I. M. Destler, "Can One Man Do?" *Foreign Policy* 5 (Winter 1971–1972): 3–27 and 28–40; Don Oberdorfer, "Helms to Oversee U.S. Spy Network," *Washington Post*, 6 November 1971, p. A1.
7. *Time* 3, September 1973, p. 15. A revealing illustration of the relationship between the Department of State and the White House occurred in Kissinger's October 12 Press Conference during the Yom Kippur War.
   Q: "As Presidential National Security Adviser, how do you evaluate the handling of this crisis by the State Department:"
   A: "Well, . . . we are very impressed, in the White House, by the leadership that the State Department has received."
   News Release, Department of State Bureau of Public Affairs, Department of State Office of Media Services Press Conference, Secretary of State Kissinger, 12 October 1973.

8. Henry Kissinger, cited in *Newsweek*, 3 September 1973, p. 28.

9. Henry Kissinger, Report for the Security Studies Project of the University of California, reported in the *Washington Post*, 30 January 1972; or as one State Department official remarked of Kissinger's handling of Soviet-American relations in the October Middle East crisis of 1973: "In a word it is secret diplomacy, secretly arrived at" (*Newsweek*, 5 November 1973, p. 42).

10. For a more extended discussion of these points, see Destler, op. cit.

11. Leacacos, op. cit., pp. 19–22.

12. See Oberdorfer, op. cit.

13. Interview by Oriana Fallaci, *New Republic*, 16 December 1972, p. 21.

14. Destler, op. cit., pp. 39–40.

15. *Washington Post*, 7 April 1974.

16. *New York Times*, 24 December 1973.

17. *New York Times*, 5 March 1974.

18. *Washington Post*, 16 September 1974.

19. *New York Times*, 11 November 1974.

20. "Revolutionary Reflections on Bismarck," *Daedalus* 97, no. 3 (Summer 1968): 889–890.

21. *Washington Post*, 24 January 1977.

22. Dick Kirschten, "Beyond the Vance-Brzezinski Clash Lurks an NSC Under Fire," *National Journal* 12, no. 20 (17 May 1980): 816.

23. "Interview," *National Journal* 8, no. 28 (17 July 1976): p. 100.

24. Henry Kissinger, *White House Years* (Boston: Little Brown, 1979), p. 28.

25. *Time*, 8 August 1977, p. 11.

26. James Wooten, "Here Comes Zbig," *Esquire*, November 1979.

27. *Washington Star*, 27 August 1979.

28. *Washington Post*, 24 January 1977.

29. Victor Zorza, "A Man to Out-Kissinger Kissinger," *Washington Post*, 19 January 1977.

30. *Washington Post*, 20 March 1977.

31. NSC–2, January 20, 1977, released 22 April 1977, text found in *The National Security Adviser: Role and Accountability*, Hearing before the Committee on Foreign Relations, 96th Congress, 2nd Session, 1980, p. 48 (hereafter cited as "NSC Hearings").

32. Executive Order No. 12036, 24 January 1978, Sections 1–302 to 1–304 inclusive.

33. "NSC Hearing," p. 50.

34. U.S. Congress, Hearing before the Subcommittee on Europe and the Middle East of the House Committee on Foreign Affairs, *United States Policy and United States–Soviet Relations, 1979*, Committee Print, October 16, 1979, p. 37. Also, see Leslie Gelb in a speech at the 23rd National Security Seminar, Army War College, 8 June 1977, cited in *Parameters*, no. 3 (July 1977).

35. Philip Odeen, *National Security Policy Integration*, mimeo. President's Reorganization Project: Office of Management and Budget, September 1979, p. 12.

36. Kirschten, op. cit.

37. *Washington Star*, 19 August 1979.

38. Vance worried in private to James Reston that there is a tendency "to poke the stick" at the Soviets. Reston wrote, "He goes even further, and says that he didn't

become Secretary of State in order to revive the vicious conflict of the old U.S.–Soviet 'cold war,' and would 'resign tomorrow' if he thought this was the way things were going." *New York Times*, 11 January 1979.

39. Anthony Lake, "Managing Complexity in U.S. Foreign Policy," speech to the San Francisco World Affairs Council, 14 March 1978.

40. For an extended analysis of this conflict, see James A. Nathan and James K. Oliver, *United States Foreign Policy and World Order*, 2nd ed. (Boston: Little, Brown, 1981), chap. 11.

41. See Brzezinski's exposition of this theme on *Bill Moyer's Journal*, Public Broadcasting System, 16 November 1980.

42. David C. Martin, "Inside the Rescue Mission," *Newsweek*, July 12, 1982: 16–22.

43. *New York Times*, 10 August 1980.

44. Bernard Gwertzman, "It's a Tough Company for On-the-Job Training," *New York Times*—OpEd, 17 August 1980, p. 4.

45. *New York Times*, 14 July 1980.

46. *Washington Star*, 22 August 1980.

47. "All Things Considered," National Public Radio, 13 August 1980, Tape No. 80081304. Also see Thomas Powers, "Choosing a Strategy for World War III," *The Atlantic Monthly* (November 1982), pp. 82–110.

48. Letter to James A. Nathan from Leon Sloss, Director, Bureau of Political/Military Affairs, U.S. Department of State, 26 April 1970.

49. "All Things Considered," op cit.

50. Odeen, op. cit., p. 31.

51. See Carter's Annapolis Speech of 7 June 1978 for a good example of the way virtually every bureaucratic actor was served in what must have been to the Soviets an utterly befuddling address. See Murray Marder, "Behind Carter's Annapolis Speech," *Washington Post*, 11 June 1980.

52. *Washington Post*, 28 January 1980.

53. Ibid.

54. Karen Elliott House, "The State of State," *Wall Street Journal*, 29 January 1982, p. 1.

55. See Hedrick Smith, "Reagan Picks a Mediator," *New York Times*, 5 January 1982, Al.

56. See for example, John M. Goshko, "A Veteran of Order and Precision Unholsters His Troubleshooter," *Washington Post*, 6 January 1982, A3.

57. "A Talk With Haig (I)," *New York Times*, 9 December 1981, p. A31.

58. Tad Szulc "The Vicar Vanquished," *Foreign Policy*, no. 43 (Summer 1981): 173–187.

59. *Newsweek*, April 12, 1982: 38.

60. Morton Kondracke, "The Sinister Force Returns," *New Republic*, 25 November 1981, pp. 10–12.

61. "Briefing," *New York Times*, 20 November 1981, p. 28.

62. *Newsweek*, 16 November 1981, p. 31.

63. This description and analysis is based on two excellent reports by Leslie Gelb, "Foreign Policy System Criticized by Aides," *New York Times*, 19 October 1981,

pp. A1, A8, and "Two Laws Concerning the National Security Adviser," *New York Times*, 7 January 1982, p. A20.

64. Gelb, "Foreign Policy System Criticized," op. cit.
65. Ibid.
66. Gelb, "Is Washington Big Enough For Two State Departments?" *New York Times*, February 21, 1982: 1–4.
67. Quoted in ibid.
68. Ibid.
69. Quoted in James McCartney, "Making of a Foreign Policy," *Philadelphia Inquirer*, 7 February 1982, p. 10-A.
70. Quoted in Gelb, "Two Laws Concerning the National Security Adviser," op cit.
71. See the *Washington Post*, August 29, 1981: C1 and George Will, "Solid Shultz" in ibid.: C7.
72. McCartney, op. cit.
73. Goshko, op. cit.
74. Excerpts from a report of Ferdinand Eberstadt for Secretary of the Navy James Forrestal, 25 September 1945, in Henry M. Jackson, ed., *The National Security Council* (New York: Praeger, 1965), p. 294.
75. Richard E. Neustadt in U.S., Congress, Senate Committee on Government Operations, *Administration of National Security*, 88th Congress, 1st Session, 1965, p. 76.
76. Quoted in Sir Harold Nicholson, *Diplomacy* (New York: Oxford University Press, 1964), pp. 4–5 (emphasis added).
77. Perhaps the best summary analysis is J. M. Destler, "National Security Management: What Presidents Have Wrought," *Political Science Quarterly* (Winter 1980–1981), pp. 573–588.
78. *New York Times*, 26 June 1978, p. 16.
79. Cited in the *National Journal*, 17 May 1980, p. 817.
80. "Communique: State Department vs. NSC," Public Broadcasting System, 9 May 1980.

Chapter 4
The Decline and Rise of Congressional Foreign Policy Power

Congress is the constitutionally mandated partner and combatant with the President for power in the foreign and defense policy making process. During World War II and for decades after it, however, Congress stood acquiescent and supportive of presidential dominance. In part this can be traced to the difficulties posed by the fragmentation of policy making power mandated by the Constitution when that divided and conflict-prone policy machinery confronted the demands of an activist and global foreign policy. Throughout most of the period between the end of the Second World War and the onset of difficulties in Vietnam in the late 1960s, there was a fairly widespread consensus in Congress as well as in successive presidencies that the checks and balances that were the essence of the American constitutional design were simply not adequate to the tasks of world leadership. The perceived threats to American and international security posed by a disorderly and dangerous world demanded greater efficiency than was considered possible or desirable in the late eighteenth century, when the constitutional framework was laid down for a small, weak, and geographically isolated America.

At the same time, it is important to underscore the underlying consensus on policy that developed fitfully during the late 1940s and was firmly in place by the mid-1950s and throughout most of the 1960s. To the extent that Democratic and Republican members of Congress found themselves in basic agreement with Democratic and Republican Presidents throughout the period, it was possible to develop and sustain a system of partisan and executive-legislative relationships that circumvented the difficulties of the constitutional design. Indeed, during the Korean War, when there was no deep policy consensus concerning American objectives and means, intense and bitter partisan debate transformed the policy making process into a major obstacle to the coherent pursuit of any policy. Accordingly, much of Eisenhower's initial effort was directed at reestablishing the bipartisan policy consensus that Truman had developed between 1947 and 1949, when he proposed and Congress accepted the fundamentals of American post–World War II policy: the Truman Doctrine, the Marshall Plan, NATO, and, in general, a policy of active containment of the Soviet Union. Insofar as Eisenhower succeeded in reestablishing this policy consensus he was also able to institutionalize the notion of executive primacy in the policy making process and bequeath that condition to his Democratic successors in the 1960s.

By the late 1960s, however, that policy consensus had begun to disintegrate under the burden of Vietnam. And as the policy consensus gave way, the presidentially dominated executive-legislative relationship began to disintegrate as well. By the early 1970s, with the foreign policy consensus destroyed, Congress was charging through the rubble to create a new executive-legislative relationship in which the controlling concept would not be bipartisanship but codetermination: "an entirely new framework of rules for power sharing among the branches of government."[1] In the meantime, a reaction to the post-Vietnam retrenchment of American activism seemed to be emerging by the end of the decade. With the onset of the 1980 campaign season, both Jimmy Carter and his Republican challenger were asserting a need for a return to the old verities of containment[2]—a call echoed by most in Congress. Moreover, Reagan coupled his call for renewed international activism with an insistence that the presidency itself was in need of renewal as the policy making center of foreign policy. Whether the "new Congress" of the 1970s could maintain its newly asserted position in the 1980s emerges, therefore, as a key question for the new decade.

We assess these and related issues in this chapter and the following chapter. But before doing so, we will establish a context within which we can address the future of the executive-legislative relationship by briefly reviewing its post–World War II development and focusing closely on the reassertion of congressional prerogatives and power in the 1970s. It is essential that at each step of the analysis, we remain mindful of the interaction of policy and policy making processes and institutions, for the one constitutes a reciprocating context for the other, and together they constrain what policy makers can aspire to and achieve.

THE RISE AND DECLINE OF BIPARTISANSHIP

President Truman's view of the presidency and Congress set the tone of virtually every American response to the fast-breaking events of the early cold war period. Foreign policy in his view inevitably and correctly involved consultation with Congress. Thus Truman, conscious of a congressional and a public reluctance for world involvement, carefully prepared the ground for the North Atlantic Treaty in the Senate through his courting of Senator Vandenberg. With respect to the use of military force, however, Truman's "passionately held conviction" was that the President's position was supreme.[3]

Presidential Dominance of Bipartisanship

Truman's view of the presidency and presidential power with respect to the use of force in American foreign policy have been held more or less consistently by each of his successors. They have always genuflected before the broad and somewhat ambiguous constitutional grant of foreign policy power to Congress, but in the area of military force and foreign policy, each postwar American President has sought and exercised broad discretion concerning the commitment and use of force. The importance of this lies in the fact that during Truman's administration, the substance of American *foreign* policy came to be concerned with the commitment and use of American *military* power. Indeed, the two areas were functionally integrated in a concept of "national security." Truman's perception and use of presidential foreign and national security policy power is, therefore, doubly important, for during his presidency the substance and parameters of American foreign policy were established in such a manner that security concerns became paramount. Second, the way in which

Truman responded to these circumstances provided a precedent not only with respect to the substance of policy but also regarding the manner of response. Presidential initiative and reaction, often without prior congressional consultation, became the pattern of Truman policy making.

Subsequent Presidents continued and expanded this practice, and as Congress yielded to it, the American people came to expect, even demand, strong presidential initiative. Presidential government assumed a quasi-constitutional justification. By the mid-1960s members of the executive branch spoke authoritatively of "inherent" and "recognized powers" of the President. These included, according to some of these interpretations, the authority to initiate and sustain military action involving the use of American military personnel no matter whether Congress approved either the initiation or the continuation of such activity. By the early 1970s, however, members of Congress had begun to ask whether the "dog of war" was not permanently off its leash.

Students of executive-legislative relations concerning the commitment and use of American military force frequently point to the Korean War as the pivotal event in the postwar development of overriding presidential war powers.[4] The initiative taken by Truman in this instance was nothing less than a unilateral initiation of American involvement in military conflict. Congressional and popular support for the President was high at the outset of the Korean War in 1950, as it was to be at the outset of the Formosan crisis in 1956, the Cuban missile crisis in 1962, and Vietnam in 1964. However, running through and ignited by the events of 1947, 1948, indeed all the early cold war period, was a sputtering fuse of constitutional crisis, for as Senator Vandenberg noted shortly after the enunciation of the Truman Doctrine:

> The trouble is that these "crises" never reach Congress until they have developed to a point where Congressional discretion is pathetically restricted. When things finally reach a point where a President asks us to "declare war" there usually is nothing left except to "declare war."[5]

Crisis by definition are aberrations in the normal course of events requiring unusual reactions both in terms of the substance of one's response and in the way in which one deals with the situation. The years prior to the outbreak of fighting in Korea had given rise to a pattern of presidential initiative and subsequent congressional reaffirmation of the Chief Executive's policy initiative. In the spring of 1950 the evolution of thinking within the Truman administration carried with it the implication that crisis was to be a permanent part of American policy for the foreseeable future. Finally, insofar as foreign and national security crises required bold and institutionally unfettered presidential action, the executive-legislative imbalance bemoaned by Senator Vandenberg, but rationalized as a necessary though temporary aberration, was now to become a permanent feature of foreign policy making.

The situation presumed to be confronting the country, the President, and the Congress was cogently summarized by Senator Fulbright, 17 years later, after the forces set in motion in the late 1940s culminated in the Tonkin Gulf Resolution and Vietnam:

> The circumstance has been crisis, an entire era of crisis in which urgent decision have been required again and again, decisions of a kind that the Congress is ill-equipped to make with what had been thought to be the requisite speed. The President has the means at his disposal for prompt action: the Congress does not. When the security of the country is endangered, or thought to be endangered, there is a powerful premium on prompt action, and that means executive action.[6]

By the end of the 1950s the idea of an unquestioning congressional acquiescence to presidential initiative was firmly established. In 1959 a new Chairman of the Senate Foreign Relations Committee could be found summarizing the congressional mind:

> So it is the President that must take the lead, and we would help him. We would accede to his requests. If he puts it the other way around, it is going to fail, and I think he makes a mistake in not taking a stronger stand in this field. . . .
>
> I'm talking about political management . . . of the Congress. Our strong Presidents always have, if they are successful in this field, to counteract the parochial interests of our Congress.[7]

The Senator was J. William Fulbright. Fulbright's early conception of the necessary relationship between President and Congress held until the mid-1960s with its high point coming as Fulbright guided the Tonkin Gulf Resolution through the Senate.

The Tonkin Gulf Resolution and After

The scope of presidential activity possible under the Tonkin Gulf Resolution was, of course, enormous. And as the succeeding 4 years were to demonstrate, President Johnson was quite willing to exploit all the ambiguity of the resolution language as the Vietnam War escalated from the retaliatory strike of August 4, 1965, to full-scale conventional conflict involving more than 500,000 American troops. Many in Congress came to associate themselves with the position long held by Senator Fulbright that President Johnson's expansion of the war in this manner was not justified under the original Tonkin Gulf Resolution. The strongest statement of this position is that Congress and the American people were deceived. The Senate, it is contended, understood that the resolution called for a much more limited form of commitment and that the resolution could not and should not be construed as a functional declaration of war.[8]

However, congressional action at this time and in subsequent years cannot be explained solely in terms of executive branch dissembling and deception. As Henry Fairlie has pointed out, there was no lack of information available as to what had been and was going on in Vietnam at the time the Tonkin Gulf Resolution landed in the collective laps of the Senate Foreign Relations and Armed Services Committees. From March 1961 on, the *New York Times, Washington Post, Time, Newsweek,* and other newspapers and journals regularly and for the most part accurately reported on the events in Southeast Asia. In May 1961 the *New Republic* forecast the scenario for the next decade:

> If these Americans are under fire, they will presumably have the freedom to shoot back; and once there are even a few well-publicized casualties, the prestige of the United States will have been for all practical purposes committed irrevocably to the Diem cause. The choices will then be humiliating withdrawal, as the size of the challenge grows, or progressively deeper involvement in a stalemate which may not admit of a "victory" in anything less than a decade—some experts say even longer.[9]

Fairlie notes: "There was always sufficient knowledge within the public realm on which to form a political judgment, and that is all the information which a democracy requires."[10]

Presumably it was also enough for Congress. The fact of the matter is that Congress did make a judgment that at its core was political. There was, of course, a good deal of institutionally based self-deception involved, particularly on the part of Senator Fulbright. In fact, Senator Fulbright accurately foresaw the implications of the resolution. Senator John Sherman Cooper asked Fulbright during the floor debate on the resolution, "Looking ahead, if the President decided that it was necessary to use such force as could lead into war, we will give that authority by this resolution?" The Chairman of the Foreign Relations Committee and Senate sponsor of the measure replied, "That is the way I would interpret it."[11] He was also under the impression, however, "that the President will consult with Congress in case a major change in present policy becomes necessary."[12] Misunderstandings and outright deceit notwithstanding, Senator Fulbright and most other members of the senate were prepared to accept the resolution because in Fulbright's words it was "consistent with our existing mission and our understanding of what we have been doing in South Vietnam for the past 10 years."[13] Furthermore, he asserted: "We are not giving the President any [extra] powers [that he does not have] under the Constitution as Commander-in-Chief. We are in effect approving the use of the powers that he has. That is the way I feel about it.[14]

Thus overshadowing the entire debate on the Tonkin Gulf Resolution was the congressional predisposition toward accepting not only presidential initiative but also the substantive thrust of that policy. Lyndon Johnson maneuvered Congress into accepting the broad statement of presidential authority, but we are dealing here with something far more complex and subtle than one institution of government hoodwinking another. For binding the President and Congress together in 1964 was the mutual conviction and ideological predisposition to combat communist regimes wherever they might appear, even if this involved supporting a corrupt but "pro-American" regime in Saigon or anywhere else for that matter.

Within 2 years, of course, Senator Fulbright and a small number of Senators had concluded that contrary to the rhetoric of almost a quarter century, the meaning of the "national interest" was no longer self-evident; nor did the Executive possess any special wisdom for its definition. Needless to say, Johnson and his successor, Nixon, disagreed. Both Presidents could find agreement with Secretary of State Kissinger's assertion that foreign policy "is not a partisan matter." [15] Indeed, Kissinger reiterated this theme on numerous occasions as Secretary of State. The reason seems clear: if there was continuing partisan debate, he could no longer present himself as the unquestioned personification of American policy—a position essential to the personalized and secret diplomacy that Kissinger preferred.

Kissinger's dislike for partisan debate was, however, but an extension of the operational needs of the cold war presidency. From this perspective the perceived imperatives of American national security require flexibility, responsiveness, and even a measure of ambiguity, precisely the opposite of what is likely to result if policy is subjected to debate and close scrutiny. The logical extension of this principle has been the consistent advocacy and actual centralization of foreign and national security policy operations in the White House. Moreover, Congress itself accepted this view of America's policy and hence what were thought to be the peculiar disabilities of the American political system. Undoubtedly, another advantage to this posture suggested itself to many members of Congress: if the President claimed the initiative in foreign policy, he could also be saddled with the responsibility for disaster if and when it occurred.

In the late 1960s, however, it became apparent that the consequences and costs of a globalist foreign policy could no longer be isolated from the American domestic system. Under these circumstances, a few in Congress, followed in time by increasing numbers of their colleagues, sought to reopen a policy debate quieted for more than 20 years. They found, however, that Adlai Stevenson's fears in the mid-1950s concerning the stultifying effects and costs of bipartisanship had now become institutionalized:

> [Criticism] conjures up pictures of insidious radicals hacking away at the very foundation of the American way of life. It suggests non-conformity and non-conformity suggests disloyalty and disloyalty suggests treason, and before we know where we are, this process has all but identified the critic with the saboteur and turned political criticism into an un-American activity instead of democracy's greatest safeguard. [16]

Especially during the last months of the Johnson administration, the consequences of allowing the atrophy of responsible debate were apparent. The momentous substantive issues involved in Vietnam were submerged in and distorted by personalized vilification on both ends of Pennsylvania Avenue. The patriotism of antiwar members of Congress was publicly impugned by the President, while the sanity of the Chief Executive was questioned by those in opposition to the war. At the same time there was a reiteration of the original rationale for bipartisanship directed at congressional critics, especially when they tried to pass legislation that would limit a President's foreign policy powers. To do so, it was argued, was dangerous because the "dangers" of the contemporary world demanded presidential freedom from legislative restrictions.[17]

But increasingly strident assertions by Nixon and Kissinger to the effect that "the foreign policy of the United States transcends parties and Administrations"[18] were a begging of the most fundamental of questions. For bipartisanship, meaning presidential dominance and initiative, is characterized here as simple institutional dynamics or relationships having no real attachment to the substance and values underlying policy. Indeed, the explicit assumption is that the "national interest" and American foreign policy values are "continuing," somehow self-evident, and agreed upon by all, hence partisan debate is not only unnecessary, it is a threat to those values, given the kind of world in which we live. In fact, however, as was indicated by the sometimes violent Vietnam War debate, the war powers issue, and the final breakthrough on Cambodia and Vietnam legislation, the values and substance of American national security were no longer self-evident to many. Contrary to the Secretary of State's assertion (and wish?), these values proved variable and even discontinuous to many in American society.

To assert, therefore, in the face of majority opposition votes by the Congress, that support of the administration's policies was good bipartisanship but disagreement constituted bad partisanship, demonstrates that bipartisanship had developed as a policy referent the preservation of the status quo. Insofar as administration policy represented a continuation of the quest for an international order reflective of American anticommunist values and that policy was equated with bipartisanship, then bispartisanship had become something more than a simple mode of behavior. For, in fact, bipartisanship was seen as essential to a particular set of policies that may or may not have had anything to do with the necessity of making "quick decisions."

The challenges of the late 1960s were not directed at the need for the President to be able to respond quickly in the event of an emergency. Rather they were directed at the value assumptions of a policy framework that had stood unquestioned for more than 20 years and had lost much of its credibility. The lack of any debate was, of course, the very essence of bipartisanship as the congressional institutional posture deemed essential to the national security. Inevitably, therefore, the challenge to the policies involved a challenge to bipartisanship itself.

THE VIETNAM REVOLUTION

A detailed analysis of the many dimensions of this challenge to the bipartisan orthodoxy follows. For now it is sufficient to note that from spring 1973 until well into 1976, Congress mounted an assault on the prerogatives of a presidency severely weakened by the failure of American policy in Southeast Asia and the Watergate crisis. January 1973 had seen the signing of the Paris Peace Accords confirming the withdrawal of American troops from Vietnam and the repatriation of American prisoners of war. At the same time, however, American support of the Lon Nol regime in Cambodia came under increasing pressure from the Khmer Rouge insurgents, and the Nixon administration resumed massive bombing of Cambodia. The reaction in Congress was no less explosive, for the antiwar coalition that had been building throughout the late 1960s and early 1970s mobilized for a last attack on the policies and prerogatives of the Nixon presidency.

Initial congressional attempts to cut off funding of the Cambodian bombing during February, March, and April 1973 were circumvented by the administration's assertion of its inherent powers to shift funds wtihin the defense budget to pay for the bombing campaign whether Congress approved or not. With American forces out of Vietnam and prisoners of war on the way home, even longtime congressional supporters of American policy balked. In May 1973 the

Senate passed a supplemental appropriations bill for the Defense Department with an amendment, attached by Senator Thomas Eagleton, stipulating that "none of the funds herein appropriated under this act or heretofore appropriated under any other act may be expended to support directly or indirectly combat activities in, over or from the shores of Cambodia or in or over Laos by United States forces."[19] By early June the House of Representatives had agreed to similar language and the measure was sent to a Watergate besieged President Nixon, who promptly vetoed the bill. A veto override failed, but the Eagleton amendment was soon attached to other legislation, such as the State Department appropriations bill and a bill to raise the national debt ceiling, which the President could not veto if the government was to continue to operate. On June 29, 1973, therefore, Nixon accepted the inevitable and acceded to the congressionally mandated end to the Cambodian bombing.

Throughout the remainder of the Nixon administration and the Ford presidency, Congress reduced executive requests for economic and military assistance to the faltering Vietnamese and Cambodian regimes. And as the Saigon and Phnom Penh regimes finally collapsed in the spring of 1975, Congress, notwithstanding administration attempts to lay the blame at its door, refused to extend to Ford initial emergency funds for refugee assistance. In the meantime, Congress had seized the initiative from the President in other areas as well.

Even as the struggle over the Cambodian bombing cutoff was coming to a head, a 4 year effort to reclaim the congressional right to participate in the commitment of American troops to war was reaching its culmination. Beginning in 1969 the Senate passed a resolution asserting that a "national commitment" could come about only through concurrent action of Congress and the President. The resolution failed in the House, but its existence constituted a first shot in the battle to follow. For the next 3 years the House and Senate debated and passed bills concerning the war powers of the President, but no legislation could gain sufficient votes in both houses of Congress. But in 1973 both houses passed such legislation, with the House assuming an even tougher posture than the Senate. Whereas the Senate legislation attempted to define in detail circumstances in which the President could use force without prior consultation, the

House approach emphasized cutting off such commitments through the expedient of the concurrent resolution. Because a concurrent resolution does not require a presidential signature to become law, its use would constitute a legislative or "congressional veto." Prior consultation was called for, a President was required to report to Congress wihin 48 hours after the begining of hostilities, and a President was given a maximum of 60 days to continue hostilities in the absence of congressional authorization.[20] But the heart of the War Powers Resolution, passed in October over a presidential veto, was the congressional veto, which could be initiated at any time by a simple majority vote of both houses of Congress.

As is noted subsequently, the effectiveness of the War Powers Resolution and the congressional veto proved quite ambiguous during the remainder of the 1970s. Nevertheless, the passage of the resolution over Nixon's veto, along with the Cambodian bombing cutoff, was the high point of the "Vietnam Revolution" in Congress. The years 1974 and 1975 saw the Watergate-weakened presidency on the defensive. New restrictions were voted on U.S. military assistance; debate was initiated on increasing the role of Congress in controlling nuclear exports; and in the wake of Watergate-related exposés of abuses of power within the intelligence establishment, House and Senate investigative committees were set up. By the late 1970s House and Senate Intelligence Committees with greater oversight responsibility than Congress had had previously had been established.

Simultaneously, when Turkey invaded Cyprus in July 1974 in response to a Greek-backed coup, thereby upsetting the delicately poised Greek-Turkish balance on Cyprus, strongly pro-Greek members of Congress immediately mobilized to cut off military assistance to Turkey. Notwithstanding Secretary Kissinger's fulminations over "the growing tendency of the Congress to legislate in detail the day-to-day or week-to-week conduct of our foreign affairs,"[21] the anti-Turkish coalition held throughout the remainder of the Ford administration and well into the Carter administration. Later, in 1975 and early 1976, Congress similarly restrained the President's attempts to intervene in the Angolan civil war by voting to cut off aid to U.S.-backed forces in the war. And at the same time that these assertions of congressional power were being played out, Senator

Henry Jackson was mobilizing sufficient forces to compel the administration to adopt a demand for equal numbers of strategic nuclear delivery vehicles in any future strategic arms limitations talks. The Senator had also succeeded in imposing Jewish emigration requirements as preconditions of any trade agreements with the Soviet Union so stringent as to make the agreements unacceptable to the Soviets.

THE "NEW CONGRESS" OF THE 1970s

Clearly the Presidents of the 1970s were confronted with a Congress different from those that had willingly, at times enthusiastically, deferred to presidential leadership in the 1950s and 1960s. Perhaps the most important change in the relationship came from outside, that is, from the collapse of the foreign policy consensus of the earlier period. The institution of Congress, however, had itself changed as scores of new members entered Congress at each election during the 1970s. They brought with them greater skepticism about American involvement abroad and thereby fulfilled the necessary conditions of change in the executive-legislative relationship. But they also brought new expectations and demands concerning Congress, its future role in the executive-legislative policy making process, and their individual roles as members of Congress. The interrelationship of these institutional and personal expectations have not always been compatible, however, and in their incongruity some observers see unresolved problems for the future.[22]

The influx of new members of Congress in the last decade has been remarkable. Since 1972 substantial numbers of Senators and Representatives have retired their seats at each election. In 1972, for example, more than forty members of the House retired; in 1974, a similar number; in 1976, eight in the Senate and forty-seven in the House; and in 1978, ten in the Senate and forty-nine in the House. Moreover, in 1974, some seventy-eight Democratic Representatives were elected from traditionally Republican districts, most, presumably, the beneficiaries of the popular Watergate backlash. Even more significant, however, the overwhelming majority of these "Watergate Democrats" were able to hold their seats during the 1970s. The cumulative effect, therefore, was to produce an institution marked by significant changes in personnel. Thus, after the 1978 election, more than 75 percent of the Democrats in the House had served 6 years or less, and about 50 percent had 4 years or less service. In the Senate, sixty men and women who had served during 1969 had passed from the scene by the time the 1980s opened.

In the midst of this massive personnel turnover, significant institutional reforms were undertaken. In addition to the attempts to redefine the executive-legislative relationship through the War Powers Resolution and the activism displayed in constraining the exercise of presidential power in Cambodia and the other cases noted earlier, Congress turned its attention to its own internal problems. Specifically, many observers of Congress have consistently pointed to serious structural limitations within Congress, such as its fragmentation and its institutional and procedural complexity, all of which have inhibited its capacity for activism as an institution.

In most analyses of congressional structural and institutional limits, the committee and subcommittee system traditionally controlled by a network of autocratic committee chairs has been important. The outcome of this situation has been that the policy making and decisional processes of Congress became fragmented to the point where it is no longer accurate to speak of Congress as making decisions. Congress consists of numerous quasi-autonomous policy making and decisional subsystems, loosely coordinated by the House and Senate leadership. Nowhere is this fragmentation more in evidence and with greater consequence than in the areas of foreign and defense appropriations. Numerous committees and subcommittees consider legislation to authorize and appropriate funds for defense and foreign affairs. But seldom has there been consideration of the relationship between the myriad components of the executive branch appropriations request. The fragmentation and lack of overall perspective complicates immeasurably and probably precludes Congress from acting as a responsible counterweight in the present budgetary process.

Potentially revolutionary reforms in the congressional budgetary process passed Congress in 1974. Under this legislation Congress now has Budget Committees in both the House and the Senate and a Congressional Budget Office (CBO), which has its own director and support personnel with facilities that can produce an independent evaluation of the President's budget requests. Under this new arrangement the Budget Committees are required to prepare and Congress to pass a budget resolution that will recommend guidelines for overall appropriations as well as targets for appropriations in the major functional areas of the federal budget. In addition, these committees must prepare and Congress pass target figures for total federal expenditures and tax and debt targets appropriate to the recommended budget and expenditure levels. To the extent that the system works, Congress for the first time in decades has the potential for viewing the budgetary process as a whole. Thus it has the institutional capacity to compare in a responsible manner the competing claims of the federal bureaucracy.

The establishment of a Congressional Budget Office was also related to another frequently noted deficiency of the Congress; its dependence upon the executive branch for information and analysis of policy options. The CBO was designed to provide Congress with an analysis of executive proposals as well as alternatives to proposals advanced by the Executive. Similarly, Congress moved to increase the responsibilities of the General Accounting Office, (GAO) and the Congressional Research Service (CRS) of the Library of Congress. During the 1970s the GAO sought to shift from an essentially investigative arm of the Congress to one that anticipated public policy issues and provided Congress with more timely analysis. The CRS more than doubled in size during the 1970s and by the decade's end was able to provide 565 professional analysts, with 50 of them assigned to the CRS's Foreign Affairs and National Defense Divisions. Finally, Congress established an Office of Technology Assessment, which also provides expertise on foreign and national security matters.

In summary, Congress more than doubled the institutional support available to it over the course of the 1970s. To be sure, not all of this increase in resources was devoted to foreign affairs. Nonetheless, when added to the tripling of staff available to the House Foreign Affairs Committee and the Senate Foreign Relations Committee during the same period, it is clear that the institutional capacity of Congress as a participant in the foreign policy making process has been augmented in line with the new perception of its role that emerged during the decade.

Even as the new members of Congress were voting to increase the congressional bureaucracy in line with their new conception of the congressional role, they were moving to increase the resources available to them individually. Thus the total of the personal staffs available to each Senator increased from about 1,750 in 1967 to more than 3,200 by 1977. In the House the increases were from just over 4,000 to over 6,900. Here again, much of the new staff assistance was committed to nonpolicy chores such as answering constituent mail. Nevertheless, by the late 1970s, the membership of the House and Senate could count on the services of about 750 and 350 policy-oriented legislative assistants, respectively, or seven and four times the number that had been available in the mid-1960s.[23]

The acquisition of increased personal resources indicates far deeper changes directed at increasing the power of the individual members of Congress. One of the first targets of congressional reform during the 1970s was the leadership of Congress, especially as it was manifested in the committee structure of the House and Senate. As noted previously, the committee system had become dominated by a handful of committee chairs who exercised autocratic control over their fiefs. By the mid-1970s, however, the wave of reform had undermined much of this traditional system, in that it became possible to remove chairs by means of a simple majority vote. Perhaps even more important, power within the committees was decentralized by the establishment of numerous subcommittees, which assured that most members of the Senate majority could, during their first term, chair their own subcommittee.

Paralleling these developments have been changes contributing to a diminution of control on the part of the traditional party leadership. In the Senate, the changes can be traced to the style of the Senate Majority Leader when that post was held by Mike Mansfield throughout the 1960s and early 1970s. Mansfield fostered a low-key and low-profile concept of the leadership, which encouraged individual members of the Senate to develop and pursue their own interests. These decentralizing and democratizing developments had their counterparts in the House, in changes in voting rules of the full

House, such as electronically recorded voting, and by the late 1970s experimentation with televising House proceedings, which tended to increase the visibility of the individual member. Now

> detailed voting records go into the hometown newspapers and, in the words of one member, "everyone scurries to vote on everything." Having lost anonymity, they vote with their eye on the constituency, not on the leaders. The result is that the leadership has far less control over the outcome.[24]

Indeed, to the extent that the leadership is linked to a discredited congressional past, its capacity to exert any authority is diminished. Moreover, in the case of the many new Democratic members of Congress, especially those in the House, who came to office in the wake of Watergate, attention to one's constituency has become very important especially when such a member represents a usually Republican district. Conforming too consistently to the leadership's position could, in such circumstances, lead to political extinction.

The loss of control of congressional leadership became increasingly apparent in the middle and late 1970s. Floor amendments to legislation proposed in committee are indications of dissatisfaction with the normal workings of Congress. One study of amendments to legislation coming out of committee noted that in the 91st Congress, only 39 amendments were offered on 30 bills that came out of the House Foreign Affairs Committee. In contrast, during the 94th Congress 112 amendments were offered to 42 bills and resolutions of the same committee. Whereas earlier more than two-thirds of the amendments were offered by members of the committee, during the 94th Congress almost 75 percent were offered by nonmembers of the committee.[25]

The Panama Canal Treaties ratification process during 1977 and 1978 offered an even more dramatic example of the lack of control of the rank-and-file membership of Congress on a key foreign policy issue. It is remarkable that a junior Senator, Dennis DeConcini of Arizona, could nearly destroy agreements that had taken 13 years to negotiate, by attaching a reservation to the treaties that provided for the use of American force in the event the canal was closed. Yet the Carter administration found itself involved in lengthy and frustrating negotiations with the freshman Senator. Moreover, DeConcini was not the only Senator who felt free to try to renegotiate the treaties. Between early September 1977, when the treaties were signed, and January 1978, more than forty United States Senators visited Panama for talks with the Panamanian leadership. As Frank and Weisband have noted:

> Even Senators who privately supported the treaties as written, felt the need to be seen "improving" (i.e., strengthening) them before casting an affirmative vote. Given the thirteen years of exquisitely detailed haggling over the wording and balance of the agreements, this was bound to cause difficulties. [26]

It has been suggested that if the Carter administration had developed a closer relationship with the leadership of the Senate, some of the problems with the Panama Canal Treaties ratification fight might have been avoided. In fact, much of the damage done by the DeConcini reservation was rectified in the second of the two treaties in a "neutralizing" amendment, which stated an American commitment to nonintervention in Panama's internal affairs, was negotiated with the Senate leadership. [27] Undoubtedly, improvement of the executive-legislative liaison could do much to ease the interaction of the two ends of Pennsylvania Avenue. But given the structural and personnel changes that have emerged from the tumult of the 1970s, it is unlikely that the calm of bipartisanship can ever be restored. On the other hand, it is not certain that the "new Congress" of the 1970s can, as many admirers of presidential power have feared, [28] dominate the executive-legislative relationship. Congress as an institution has certainly been strengthened, but the parallel strengthening of the power of individual members of Congress may prove to be the more important development. Thus the long-lamented structural fragmentation of Congress has been accentuated, thereby making leadership more difficult.

Finally, the early 1980s saw the onset of yet another institutional change: the advent of a period of split party control of the House and Senate resulting from the 1980 elections. Ronald Reagan brought to power with him sufficient Republicans in Congress to give the Republicans control of the Senate for the first time since 1952 as well as reducing the Democratic margin in the House. During 1981, the new President used Republican control of the Senate and a coalition of Republicans and conservative Democrats in the House to write virtually all of his domestic program into law. On foreign and defense policy he succeeded in increasing the defense budget beyond that proposed by the Carter administration and narrowly winning approval of a controversial sale of AWACS surveillence aircraft to Saudi Arabia. Indeed, by the end of 1981 it was plausible to project that Reagan and the new Republicans in the Senate might just succeed in ushering in a new period of presidential domination of the Congress.

In sum, the early months of the new decade only injected new uncertainties into the executive-legislative relationship. Perhaps a better sense of the prospects for the changes sketched in this chapter can be gained by examining more closely and systematically the various elements of congressional power and the executive-legislative relationship.

NOTES

1. Thomas M. Frank and Edward Weisband, *Foreign Policy by Congress* (New York: Oxford University Press, 1979), p. 61.
2. Notwithstanding the fact that the doctrine's father, George Kennan, regarded such rhetoric with dismay.
3. Dean Acheson, *Present at the Creation: My Years at the State Department* (New York: Norton, 1969), p. 415.
4. See, for example, Merlo J. Pusey, *The Way We Go to War* (Boston: Houghton Mifflin, 1969), pp. 79–95.
5. Papers of Senator Vandenberg, p. 342, cited in Walter LaFeber, *America, Russia and the Cold War, 1945–1971,* 2nd ed. (New York: Wiley, 1972), p. 60.
6. Statement of Sen. J. William Fulbright before U.S. Senate Subcommittee on Separation of Powers of the Judiciary Committee, *Separation of Powers,* 90th Congress, 1st Session, 1967, p. 42.
7. J. William Fulbright, "Meet the Press," 7 June 1959, quoted in James Robinson, *Congress and Foreign Policy-Making,* rev. ed. (Homewood, Ill.: Dorsey Press, 1967), pp. 185–186.
8. At least two Senators—Morse and Gruening—were skeptical. See Morse's highly censored colloquy with Secretary of Defense McNamara in U.S. Senate, Joint Hearings before the Senate Committees on Foreign Relations and Armed Services, *Southeast Asia Resolution,* 88th Congress, 2nd Session, 1964, released 24 November 1966, pp. 13–15 and 32–33.
9. Quoted in Henry Fairlie, "We Knew What We Were Doing When We Went into Vietnam," *Washington Monthly* 5, no. 3 (May 1973): 14.

10. Ibid., p. 7.
11. *Congressional Record* 110, pt. 14, 88th Congress, 2nd Session, 6 August 1964, p. 18409.
12. Ibid., p. 18410.
13. Ibid., p. 18407
14. Ibid., p. 18409
15. "Secretary-Designate Kissinger Meets the Press at San Clemente," *Department of State Newsletter,* August/September 1973, p. 7.
16. Adlai Stevenson, "Party of the Second Part," *Harpers,* February 1956, p. 32.
17. See, for example, McGeorge Bundy's testimony before U.S. House, Committee on Foreign Affairs, *Congress, the President, and the War Powers,* 91st Congress, 2nd Session, passim.
18. Text of Henry Kissinger's opening statement before the Senate Foreign Relations Committee, 7 September 1973, in *Department of State Newsletter,* August/September 1973, p. 4.
19. U.S. Senate, Committee on Appropriations, *Report,* Second Supplemental Appropriations Bill, 1973, H.R. 7447, and Additional Views, No. 93–160, 18 May 1973.
20. A President was also allowed an additional 30 days to evacuate American troops if congressional authorization to continue the engagement was not forthcoming.
21. *New York Times,* 25 January 1975, p. 1
22. Richard Haass, "Congressional Power: Implications for American Security Policy," *Adelphi Papers,* no. 153 (London: International Institute for Strategic Studies, 1979), esp. pp. 31–32.
23. For a review of the increases in staff assistance in Congress, see Frank and Weisband, op. cit., pp. 227–245, esp. pp. 228–233.
24. Ibid., pp. 215–216.
25. Ibid., p. 213
26. Ibid., p. 275.
27. Ibid., pp. 281–286.
28. See, for example, Thomas E. Cronin, *The State of the Presidency,* 2nd ed. (Boston: Little, Brown, 1980), passim.

Chapter 5

A New Executive-Legislative Relationship?

The reassertion of legislative position and power is evident in the three traditional areas of congressional power: advice and consent to international agreements and executive appointments, war powers, and the control of the authorization and appropriation of funds—the "power of the purse." These constitutionally delegated powers encompass two roles for Congress. First, Congress has constitutional responsibilities for the *establishment and oversight of programs* designed to further the national interest. Second, the constitutional power to "advise and consent", especially to advise the President, on international agreements, commitments of military forces, and the shape of administration itself, implies a *policy direction role*.[1] Much of the effort during the 1970s to establish as viable executive-legislative codetermination of foreign policy has been directed at the second of these roles ensuring congressional participation in the establishment of fundamental foreign and national security policy direction as well as the programs designed to carry out policy. Success in each of these areas, however, has been rather uneven. Before undertaking an assessment of the prospects for institutionalizing a new executive-legislative relationship, therefore, a review of each of these areas of constitutionally defined power and its implied congressional role is in order.

THE TRADITIONAL POWERS OF ADVICE AND CONSENT

The Constitution provides in Article II, Section 2, that the President "shall have power by and with the advice and consent of the Senate,

to make treaties provided two-thirds of the Senators present concur."
But the Constitution does not make it clear whether the Senate is to
take part in the negotiation of a treaty or merely to deliberate on a
treaty's merits after the executive has concluded the bargaining.
Since Washington's painful experience at the hands of the Senate in
1789, when he was treated as an inferior party and asked to leave the
Senate chamber while his diplomacy was being discussed, the Executive has maintained its distance from the Congress during the
negotiation of treaties. Washington was heard to exclaim after storm-
ing from the Senate that "he would be damned if he ever went in
there again,"[2] and no president did until Gerald Ford volunteered his
testimony before the House Judiciary Committee on the pardon of
Richard Nixon.

Only Wilson's failure to ram American participation in the League
of Nations through the Senate tempered presidential disdain of
senatorial participation in the negotiation of treaties. The fear that
great issues settled at the conference table might come unstuck if the
Senate refused to accept the result seems, until the 1970s at least,
somewhat misplaced. Although the Senate can modify a treaty with
amendments or reservations, as in the case of the Panama Canal
Treaties, Senators have rarely availed themselves of the opportunity.
The Senate has historically seldom rejected or refused to act on
treaties. Rather, it has been cooperative, and the vast majority of
negotiated instruments have passed without difficulty.[3]

Presidents moreover, have developed and employed the "executive agreement" to circumvent Senate involvement in international
agreements almost altogether. Arthur Schlesinger, Jr. notes in his
study of the rise of the "imperial presidency," that "the executive
agreement is one of the mysteries of the constitutional order." He
continues:

> Gradually, in a way that neither historians nor legal scholars have
> made altogether clear, the executive agreement began to emerge in
> the early republic. The executive found this form of compact a practical
> convenience in making once-and-for-all international arrangements,
> at first of minor consequence. The Senate accepted the device if only to
> spare itself the tedium of having to give formal consideration to a
> multitude of technical transactions.[4]

But what began as a convenience to facilitate the pro forma aspects of international intercourse became, by the twentieth century, a potent device in the hands of Presidents such as Theodore Roosevelt and Franklin Roosevelt who sought means to further their conceptions of an energetic presidency. By the turn of the century, these direct agreements between a President and a foreign government constituted a majority of government-to-government agreements. And between 1940 and 1970, about 95 percent of the formal understandings the United States undertook were in the form of executive agreements. Indeed, during this period, when the imperial presidency reached its greatest heights, some 5,653 or 83 percent of all the executive agreements of American diplomatic history up to that time were made. In contrast, 310 or about 28 percent of all America's treaties were concluded during a time when America's global involvement has been more intense than at any time in its history.

Some constitutional authorities have challenged the constitutional standing of the executive agreement. Raoul Berger, perhaps the most forceful proponent of diminishing the executive privilege and prerogative, emphasizes the complete absence of any reference to such agreements in the Constitution and what is, in his view, the extremely specious reasoning of the Supreme Court in the 1936 case of *U.S.* v. *Curtiss-Wright*, which confirmed the constitutionality of the executive agreement as an inherent power of the presidency.[5] Nonetheless, executive agreements have assumed the same force and validity as treaties. They bind succeeding administrations to their provisions. They become part of the international law binding the United States and hence, under the Constitution, of equal force with domestic law. Although an executive agreement has been described by the Supreme Court as lacking the "dignity" of a treaty, the executive agreement is identical in its effect to a treaty.[6]

There have been attempts by Congress to abridge the ability of the Executive to make such agreements. The earliest was the Bricker Amendment of 1954. Senator Bricker's amendment was presented out of fear that the American commitment to the United Nations could lead to agreements with leftist regimes but Bricker's bill lost to the internationalist Congress of the mid–1950s. The second effort was that of Senator Case, who proposed a bill like the Bricker amendment to have these executive agreements—according to

Senator Case there were at least 4,000 secret executive agreements in effect in the early 1970s—reported to Congress. [7] The law passed in 1972, does not, however, require that the President send the text of executive agreements to Congress, but only to the House and Senate Committees on Foreign Relations "under an appropriate injunction of secrecy to be removed only [by] . . . the President."[8]

Nonetheless, the habit of negotiating agreements and neglecting to inform Congress continued in spite of debate, disclosure and legislation. In September 1975, Congress requested information from the Executive that might be pertinent to the Sinai Peace accord wherein 200 American technicians would be sent to an area between opposing Israeli and Egyptian troops. The State Department was forced by a series of leaks to the press to acknowledge that understandings in the form of assurances regarding "the long standing U.S. commitment to the survival of Israel" had been given to the Israelis.[9] Nevertheless, it was insisted by the State Department that these were not international agreements but merely "expressions of intent," which "leave our options open," and thus should not be made public or formally presented to the Senate for approval.[10] A year later it was revealed that more than thirty "agreements" between the American and South Korean intelligence establishments had not been reported to either Congress or the State Department.[11]

A strong argument has been made that it was the intent of the framers of the Constitution that virtually no international business could be conducted by the President alone. Inasmuch as treaties were to be regarded as the law of the land, their consequences were simply too important for them to be entered into without senatorial "advice," that is, consultation before the fact and not merely "consent."[12] Clearly, however, the process of entering into and ratifying international agreements has taken on a different function and character in the late twentieth century.

In some respects, the treaty has become an instrument whereby Presidents have tried to build legitimacy for their action by implicating Congress in the undertaking. If an agreement is controversial or if the Executive feels it would later need to extract domestic legislation or funding from Congress in order to execute the document, then the formal machinery of a treaty is sometimes sought. Thus the Nuclear Test Ban Treaty was signed in 1963 with the Soviet Union only after a massive enlistment of congressional support. Similarly, the Nixon administration submitted the "Interim Agreement" on strategic offensive weapons (SALT I) to the Senate for review and approval along with the ABM Treaty. The latter required advice and consent, of course, but the Interim Agreement did not. Nevertheless, the administration sought to anticipate any objections to so fundamental a policy departure by allowing hearings and a vote on the agreement accompanied by a round of "in-depth" briefings and full-scale lobbying directed at those "hawks" who might disagree with the agreement. At the same time the administration anticipated the argument of those who might demand cuts in the defense budget because of the agreement by allowing Secretary of Defense Laird to threaten ostentatiously that he would not support the treaty unless full defense appropriations were forthcoming.[13]

A similar attempt by the Carter administration to build support for the SALT II agreement with the Soviet Union proved less successful. Carter, anticipating strong opposition to the treaty from Senate Republicans and conservative Democrats under the leadership of Senator Henry Jackson, sought to preserve the option of presenting the agreement much as the Nixon administration had done. By 1978 it was apparent, however, that such a ploy would be resented even by supporters of the agreement.[14] In the meantime, the Carter administration had allowed a number of Senators and Representatives to serve as observers to the negotiations process. With the exception of driving home to the Russians the importance of the verification dimensions of the agreement to ratification, these members of Congress could not be said to have actually participated in the substantive negotiations themselves. Nonetheless, the Carter administration hoped that their presence would ease what everyone in the administration had come to realize would be a brutal test of the President's leadership.

As the negotiations dragged on through the late 1970s, however, it became apparent that no amount of briefing of Senate committees, no number of congressional observers in Geneva, or, ultimately, no defense spending concessions to Senate hawks could guarantee passage of the treaty. Indeed, the treaty, like so much else in the new Congress, had become a lightning rod for congressional activism, individualism, and opposition to Carter foreign policy itself. As Strobe Talbot notes:

> SALT was such a copious grab bag of political and military problems that there was something for almost every senator and representative who wanted to play a part. Sam Nunn [Democratic Senator from Georgia] carved out Eurostrategic affairs in general and cruise missile definition in specific as his specialties. John Glenn [Democrat of Ohio] did much the same thing with verification by national technical means and the problem of telemetry encryption. Depressed trajectory was the hobby-horse of two young, liberal Democratic representatives . . .[15]

Later, when the treaty was before the Senate Foreign Relations Committee, Senator Stone of Florida sought to link the treaty to the Soviet presence in Cuba, Senators Howard Baker and Jesse Helms both emphasized the advantages in missile throwweight given to the Soviets by the agreements, and Senator Richard Lugar chose to dwell on the question of whether the treaty might not undermine the will of the American people to resist Soviet expansionism.

In the final analysis, of course, the treaty was never voted on, as the Soviet invasion of Afghanistan in December 1979 led the Carter administration to withdraw the agreement. It seems unlikely that the treaty would have been treated any less roughly than the Panama Canal accords before it. But in both cases it was apparent that the ratification process had become something other than a debate on the substantive merits of a particular agreement. Rather, they had become symbols of an administration's foreign policy as a whole and tests of strength between the administration and Congress, which could claim (with justification) that it had not been consulted but merely "informed" and then required to "consent." On the other side, of course, was the presidency, which claimed (with justification) that the ratification process was being turned into a rancorous confrontation in which the substance of laboriously negotiated agreement was lost sight of to the detriment of the national interest even if the treaties in question were ultimately ratified. In any event, it is fair to ask whether the powers of advice and consent in such a context can ever be an effective means by which Congress can exercise and the President can accept a measure of congressional participation in the setting of the nation's foreign policy course.

A second major constitutionally mandated power of advice and consent has to do with presidential appointments. Here again, however, the efficacy of the constitutional grant is questionable. In the early period of U.S. history, the Senate power of confirmation was a serious exercise, with the establishment of diplomatic relations sometimes affected by it. But as executive agreements circumvent treaties, the use of personal representatives of the President circumvents the power to supervise appointments. In this century, Wilson's friend, Colonel House, was vastly more influential with the President than his Secretaries of State Bryan and Lansing. Similarly, Cordell Hull, the Secretary of State in much of Franklin Roosevelt's presidency, was largely relegated to diplomatic trivia, while Roosevelt's friend Harry Hopkins became a presidential envoy to Churchill and Stalin. Hopkins never passed through a congressional chamber, and his salary was paid out of "contingency funds" that did not have to be accounted for.[16]

Today, many major foreign policy officers such as National Security Advisers Henry Kissinger or Zbigniew Brzezinski, are rarely seen inside the Senate chamber. White House staff are not subject to Senate confirmation, although it was the clear intent of the framers of the Constitution that all presidential envoys be confirmed. The personalized private envoy who speaks for the President is subject to no such process. The questions, "Who voted for Kissinger or Brzezinski, who confirmed them, and to whom are they responsible?" are answerable only by the names of Richard Nixon and Jimmy Carter and not in any sense by the American people or constitutional representatives.

The appointment process mandated by the Constitution is, then, vitiated by the use of executive agents. Moreover, Congress has not always treated diplomatic appointments in a serious fashion. Congressional committees have spent enormous energies on the scrutiny of Foreign Service Officers—the "rank and file" diplomats of the Department of State—while high- and low-ranking intelligence or military personnel go unexamined. Even more disturbing, the Department of State has upon occasion become a playing field for members of Congress interested in unearthing trivial peculiarities in the security or intellectual background of 22-year-old recruits.[17] Then, too, congressional pique has been ineptly applied to Ambassadors who are almost universally considered competent, such as Charles Bohlen in 1953,[18] William H. Sullivan, named in 1973 for the Philippines; J. McMurtrie Godley, nominated Assistant Secretary of State for East Asian affairs; and Charles Whitehouse, appointed Ambassador to Laos. Nominated in the summer of 1973, the latter were all held up by the Senate because they faithfully carried out their instructions in Southeast Asia. Godley was finally defeated because of the "overzealous" fashion with which he adhered to three different administrations' policies in Asia. Apparently, these men were punished because of their association with policies whose favor had long gone from the Senate.

More often than not, however, the most fatuous of ambassadorial candidates gets easy certification from the Senate. Men and women who have made large contributions to a President's campaign treasury but have no conception of the personalities or problems of the countries or regions to which they are appointed are routinely approved by the Senate with a sigh of resignation from dissenters such as Senator Fulbright, who once philosophized:

> It is ridiculous to send [men and women] with so little preparation to an area where . . . these people are a sensitive and strange people, and I think it will do us no good. However, I am not going to raise Cain. I know it is an old and evil custom that afflicts us.[19]

Moreover, political costs are even more inflationary than the rest of the economy. Whereas in 1956 a $22,000 contribution brought one an ambassadorship to Sri Lanka, the Nixon appointee to Luxembourg, Ambassador Ruth Farkas, reportedly paid more than $300,000 to the 1972 Nixon campaign, and the Ambassadors to the Netherlands, Switzerland, Austria, and France paid over $100,000 to the GOP in the years of the Nixon presidency.[20] But in the spring of 1974, after a year of Watergate disclosures concerning big campaign contributions and a year after some members of the Senate Foreign Relations Committee vowed to "end the sale of Ambassadorships," there remained ample evidence of the perfunctory fashion in which nominees are screened.

On April 10, 1974, during confirmation hearings of industrialist Leonard K. Firestone as Ambassador to Belgium, then Chairman of the Senate Foreign Relations Committee John Sparkman praised Firestone's $114,600 contribution to the 1972 Nixon campaign as a "show of public spirit." In addition to Firestone's "personal" gifts— divided into thirty-three separate "gifts" to each Nixon reelection group to evade campaign finance laws applicable at the time of the 1972 election—Firestone's children, brothers, and wife gave more than $140,000 between 1970 and 1974. Senator Sparkman gently inquired of the prospective Ambassador, "Certainly no contribution you made had any connection whatsoever with your appointment?" Firestone replied, "No." Sparkman then concluded: "We need a lot of public-spirited people who will help those people who are worthy and deserving of help and you have done it." The gifts of Firestone and his family were, after all, he explained, "nicely large but not overwhelming."[21]

It is conceivable that the institution of campaign finance laws for presidential elections that limit the amount of money that can be contributed and provide for public financing of presidential races could eliminate much of this "old and evil custom." There were, for example, fewer examples of the kind of blatant ambassadorial payoffs in the Carter administration following the 1976 election, the first election administered under the new finance law. But there were, nonetheless, egregious throwbacks to the earlier period.

> Ambassador X, a product of the American Midwest, looked quizzically at his staff members in the U.S. embassy somewhere in Southeast Asia.
>
> "Did you say there are two separate Koreas?" he asked. "How come?"
>
> Staff members also swallowed hard when the ambassador said, "You mean there has been a war between India and Pakistan?"
>
> Another stopper shortly after his arrival was, "What's Islam?"

The Ambassador, Richard Kneip, the American envoy to Singapore and former governor of South Dakota and chair of the Midwestern Governors Conference, had also never heard of: Gandhi, Nehru, Sukarno, German Chancellor Helmut Schmidt, Chiang Kai-shek, Deng Xiao-ping, or French President Valery Giscard D'Estaing.[22]

Moreover, as noted above, Reagan's appointee as Undersecretary of State, William Clark, was no better informed than Kneip. Furthermore, under Reagan the number of political supporters appointed to ambassadorial posts soared to its highest levels since the Second World War.

On the other hand, some of Carter's appointees to crucial national security posts received very close scrutiny from Congress. Indeed, Theodore Sorensen, former presidential assistant to President Kennedy and Carter's designee to head the Central Intelligence Agency, was withdrawn from consideration in the face of Senate opposition to his appointment. Ostensibly, the source of this opposition stemmed from revelations of Sorensen's use of classified materials in the preparation of his memoir of the Kennedy years. At the same time, however, many of Sorensen's congressional opponents were skeptical of his dovish views during the Vietnam War and therefore feared that Sorensen would not be a proponent of a tougher position towards the Soviet Union. Similarly, the nomination of Paul Warnke, a strong proponent of SALT and other arms control measures, as head of the Arms Control and Disarmament Agency and chief SALT negotiatior was greeted with dismay and opposition by his foes and by those skeptical of the SALT process. Warnke was eventually approved, but the attendant fight was a harbinger of the Carter administration's subsequent difficulties with SALT itself.[23]

Summary

In some respects, of course, the Congressional opposition to some of Carter's designees as well as to the Panama Canal and SALT II treaties were quite consistent with the constitutional design. The treaties were after all major elements of the Carter administration's policy. However, the lack of substantive consultation between Congress and the Executive has meant that the process of advice and consent is truncated. Executive initiative remains in place, and under such circumstances the Congress's only recourse is to use the consent function as an opportunity to force its way into the process with unforeseen consequences, as an often laboriously crafted agree-

ment must confront a politically volatile mix of honest policy disagreement and resentment at having been excluded from a serious
partnership in setting the direction of policy.

Advice and consent to treaties and appointments have not, therefore, proved effective means for sustained and systematic congressional participation in foreign and defense policy formulation. The
use of the executive agreement has led to the almost total circumven-
tion of congressional involvement in the agreement process. But
even if such agreements were subject to some sort of congressional
review, the question would still remain as to the utility of such review
as a participatory mechanism for Congress. Participation would remain essentially after the fact and would be of necessity episodic and
fragmented rather than ongoing.

Similarly, with the review of appointments, even if this included
personal or special assistants to the President, participation in policy
making would remain indirect. Furthermore, congressional capacities in the appointment process are badly polluted by the pro forma
handling of incompetence and the demonstration of excessive investigative zeal pursued for cheap political ammunition as much as in the
interest of diplomatic quality. It has been further tainted in the past
by the exigencies of great sums of money needed for campaigns by
members of Congress themselves. Frequently, ambassadorships
have been awarded as compensation for large contributions to presidential campaigns. Representatives and Senators have dared not
protest too loudly in this because their campaigns also require great
sums, and these donations are not given entirely altruistically.

There is merit nonetheless in the notion that if executive officials
knew that congressional review of them personally as well as *any*
agreements they negotiate remained a possibility, a more meaningful
concern for congressional opinion might be forthcoming. There are,
of course, negative consequences of such review in that it opens the
possibility of capricious and disruptive congressional interference
with often delicate diplomatic activity. The drafters of the Constitution were willing to take this chance, for to do otherwise left the
Executive unaccountable—a situation that has arisen with the e-
mergence of the executive agreement and personal or special assistants.

THE POWER OF THE PURSE

If no other power except the power to raise taxes and appropriate funds had been given to Congress, the intentions of the framers of the Constitution would be clear. For it is in the budgetary process that a nation makes fundamental choices. The decision to appropriate or not appropriate funds in pursuit of some objective is a critical decision point in any political system; at that juncture resources and rhetoric are married. Without that union no programs can exist, services cannot be provided, and policies have no substantive reality. Those institutions that stand astride the budgetary process have access to and monitor the most important policy making process in modern government.

This power of the purse, as envisioned by the founders, should reside in the legislature. The framers had bitter experience with arbitrary and high taxation. Representatives, they felt, would be more controllable and thus more rational than a potentially arbitrary executive. However, the push during the twentieth century for concentrated efficient executive power has undermined this intent. The Budget and Accounting Act of 1921 provided for the establishment of a federal budget prepared by the President. Much of the initiative in the budgetary process thus passed to the President, and with the emergence of strong Presidents such as Roosevelt and Truman, a large and complex bureaucracy and bureaucratic process built up around the executive budgetary process. But the actual process of raising, authorizing, and appropriating funds remained with Congress.

However, the President succeeded during the course of the cold war in circumventing what congressional control remained in the budgetary process. Several practices have evolved in the presidency's thrust for greater discretion and control. First, Presidents have arrogated to themselves the authority *not* to spend money appropriated by Congress. This process of impoundment has come under periodic attack from Congress but has until recently persisted. The second set of practices has proved even more useful—spending money not authorized by Congress or, perhaps more precisely, spending money authorized by Congress in such a manner that almost total discretion is left to the Executive concerning its expenditure.[24] Clearly, if the President can spend money that is not authorized *and* not spend money that is authorized, Congress is but an ornament on the presidential juggernaut.

Impoundment

The practice of refusing to spend funds for programs and projects that Congress has authorized has been an increasing practise of the Executive. In selective areas of defense equipment procurement, the Executive has chosen an occasional course of frugality that was in opposition to legal authorizations. Contrary to assertions of a legal prerogative of impoundment,[25] however, the authority to do so is not among the presidential powers specified in the Constitution.[26] By the mid–1970s Congress had established procedures designed to thwart impoundment actions by a President. Impoundment itself was declared unconstitutional in 1975, but Presidents, under the terms of the Impoundment Control Act, could make "recision proposals" to Congress. Congress could reject such proposals by a majority vote in either the House or the Senate. In addition, procedures were established to prevent unilateral withholding of funds by a President. Some observers have pointed out, however, that a President still possesses considerable initiative under these procedures to swamp the Congress with proposed recisions and deferrals and thereby accomplish a kind of impoundment through exhaustion of the Congressional process.[27]

Executive Budgetary Discretion

Perhaps more important to the loss of congressional control of the budgetary process during the height of the cold war period was the exploitation of discretionary powers extended to the President by the Congress. The early practice of Congress in appropriating funds was to be fairly specific about what funds were to be spent for what purposes, although there were instances of "discretionary funds" before the onset of the cold war and the demands for executive latitude.[28] But more recently, Congress has made available to Presidents enormous sums of money to be used by the President on a discretionary basis. Contingency and emergency funds have been established under the Foreign Assistance Act or Department of Defense Appropriations Acts. In both 1961 and 1962, for example, President Kennedy had available over a quarter of a billion dollars to be used "when he determines such use to be important to the national interest," and under the Defense Department's appropriations President Johnson had over $1.5 billion that he could employ in Southeast Asia during 1965–1966. In the latter case the funds were employed for military purposes, and in the former Kennedy used his contingency funds to support Peace Corps operations during that organization's first year.

The allocation of funds in this manner proceeds from an ostensibly pragmatic and realistic premise, that neither Congress nor the President can foresee all conceivable circumstances that might arise in a given fiscal year. Consequently, the President should have available funds to meet unusual situations as they arise. In fact, however, Presidents have employed funds for activities that are only marginally related to emergencies. The sums available to the President had little apparent accountability and became, therefore, a kind of private presidential treasury independent of Congress.

According to Senator Frank Church, "the most bizarre" case of the Executive using obscure "discretionary" legislation for national security occurred when the Senate was told in 1972, by then Defense Secretary Melvin Laird, "that . . . [a] Civil War statute could be used to insure the expenditure of funds in Indochina for use by U.S. forces despite congressional prohibition."[29] The act had been originally passed so that cavalry on the Western frontier could maintain themselves while Congress was not in session. But it was used by the Defense Department for Southeast Asia from 1966 to 1972. More prosaic perhaps but certainly no less important are the many other means employed by the Executive during the 1960s and early 1970s—means made available by Congress when presidential discretion was deemed essential to the prosecution of the cold war. And means that, although now constrained somewhat as the result of the upheaval in Congress in the 1970s, are still available in many instances, to a resourceful President.

Transfer authority, reprogramming, control of excess stocks, and the accumulation of so-called pipeline funds are all examples of discretionary techniques available to a President and the President's officers in the foreign, defense, and intelligence establishments. Transfer authority allows a department or agency head to shift specific amounts (specified by Congress) of funds from one category to another within an agency. Reprogramming allows for the rearrangement of funds on specified categories of items within a departmental budget. Excess stocks involve discretionary disposal, either through sale or transfer to another agency, of new or little-used equipment that might be on hand. And finally, pipeline funds are funds that are authorized in one year but not expended and are then carried over to the following year.

All of these techniques were employed with great virtuosity by a succession of Presidents during the Vietnam War period. Almost $100 million in transfer authority was used by President Nixon to fund his secret operations in Cambodia.[30] More than $600 million was reprogrammed by the Navy to accelerate the production of the F–14 fighter, notwithstanding earlier congressional skepticism concerning rapid development of the aircraft.[31] The transfer of excess stocks has been a common means for providing the CIA with resources to conduct covert operations or to continue supplying a government with aid in the face of congressional reductions of military assistance.[32] And finally, pipeline funds have traditionally provided an enormous reservoir for the Executive. Thus in 1973 the Defense Department had $43 billion in unspent authority, more than 60 percent of the $71 billion defense budget for that year. When asked what might happen if funds were cut off for the bombing of Cambodia or were not available from current funding sources, then Secretary of Defense Elliot Richardson indicated that carryover funds would allow the Executive to persevere in the use of air power in Asia.[33]

In other instances the executive foreign and defense establishment manipulated programs ostensibly designed to provide economic and humanitarian assistance. The Food for Peace Program, for example, generates significant funds in the form of currencies of the countries receiving U.S. food assistance. Throughout the early and mid–1970s these funds were frequently employed as military assistance in Southeast Asia. Thus more than $450 million was channeled into Vietnam and Cambodia during fiscal year 1974—over half the aid dispensed under the program worldwide—even as simultaneously famine was striking major areas in Africa and South Asia.[34] Similarly, economic assistance funds were frequently directed toward military assistance with taxes levied on goods imported under economic assistance programs being redirected into the purchase of military equipment.[35] But 1974 saw what is perhaps the ultimate Defense Department budgetary ploy. During the spring of 1974 congressional debate over a $500 million supplemental appropriation for military aid to South Vietnam was brewing. It was apparent that the bill might be in trouble. The Pentagon tried to save the day for the Thieu regime when it announced that it had discovered an "accounting error" and had "found" $266 million "left over" from military appropriations voted for fiscal year 1972–1973. A former Pentagon official and one of the compilers authors of the *Pentagon Papers*, Leslie Gelb, reported in the *New York Times* that none of his sources "provided identical accounts" of where the money came from in the budget. Some said that it was a line item for ammunition; a congressional source simply said that it had no explanation; the money simply appeared. Since the rules of the Senate are such that the spending of carryover funds is not brought to the floor, the Pentagon had planned to increase its aid to Saigon without even having the matter taken to a congressional vote.[36] The Senate for its part very nearly acquiesced. Only after a barrage of angry editorials and perhaps because a Watergate-weakened President deemed another legislative battle less important than remaining in office did the Senate muster a five-vote majority in favor of sending the miraculous $266 million back to wherever it came from.[37] But miraculously, the Pentagon, when pressed, could still raise substance from dust. The place where the $266 million was housed still yielded monies. For in mid-March 1975 Congress appeared unwilling to appropriate any funds for the falling Cambodian government of Lon Nol; and while American and French diplomats burned documents and prepared to evacuate Phnom Penh, it was announced that 22 million epiphenomenal dollars had suddenly "become available." The Pentagon had "overanticipated" the effects of inflation in the budget line reflecting ammunition for Cambodia. Minority Leader Senator Hugh Scott was elated; "good," he said, "tell them they can go back and look for more . . . [miscalculations]; then we'd have a way to deal with this."[38]

And, indeed, almost as the Senator spoke it was revealed that the way was being prepared for similar eventualities in Vietnam. In March 1975 the Saigon regime conceded control of almost half the country to the communists and retreated into the ultimate strategic hamlet–Saigon. In the meantime it was revealed that even as the Ford administration was requesting $300 million in supplemental funds, $178 million of the $750 million fiscal year 1975 appropriation had not been obligated. Moreover, less than 25 percent of the goods purchased with the remaining funds had been delivered. In short, the administration sought almost $500 million in pipeline funds–funds that would surely "appear" in later emergencies.[39]

The largest programs over which Congress had apparently lost control by the end of the 1960s and 1970s, however, were in the area of foreign military assistance. Throughout the early 1970s, as the Nixon administration depended increasingly on military assistance and especially commercial sales as the means for establishing surrogates for an American presence in the Third World, the military assistance program mushroomed. By 1975 the United States was reportedly selling almost $10.4 billion in arms and dispensing another $3.7 billion under grant aid programs. The existence of pipeline funds, excess stocks transfers, and Export-Import Bank subsidies for arms purchases made it difficult if not impossible to pin down exactly how much money was available to a President under these programs. Indeed, by the time the Carter administration entered office, declaring that it intended to reduce significantly the magnitude of American military sales, it was estimated that even with 40 percent reduction in sales in fiscal year 1977, there would remain a $32 billion backlog of orders to be filled during the Carter years.[40]

THE REASSERTION OF PROGRAMMATIC CONTROL

As congressional support for the war in Southeast Asia and presidential fortunes declined and simultaneously the evidence of congressional impotence and loss of programmatic control mounted, the legislature finally roused itself. Initially, as we have seen, Congress resorted to the most straightforward expedient of all: it simply passed the Eagleton amendment, which cut off all funds for the war. Thus with one decisive act the Congress sought to cut through decades of executive discretionary practices and preclude further presidential subterfuges to keep American support flowing. It was nonetheless apparent that structural reforms were necessary to strengthen congressional participation in programmatic decisions. The reformed congressional budgetary process was directed in part at strengthening this role.

The New Budget Process

Initial assessments of the functioning of the new Budget Committees in foreign policy areas suggest, however, that whatever expectations might have been, the process does not seem likely to provide Congress with a sharp new instrument of program control and participation.[41] What seems to have happened is that the Budget Committees, being staffed primarily by fiscal experts, have tended to align themselves with the Appropriations Committees in the House and Senate largely at the expense of the more substantively oriented Foreign Affairs and Foreign Relations Committees. "The effect of this," Frank and Weisband conclude,

> is to lock the foreign relations committees into a sort of legislative padded cell, protected on either side by two fiscal watchdog committees. Nothing is better suited to produce irresponsibility and irrelevance on the part of the very unit which has been designated by Congress to manifest its seriousness and competence in the foreign relations field.[42]

It is clear, therefore, that the new budgetary process remains embedded in the much broader and deeper context of Congress's oversight role to be evaluated later in this chapter.

The Legislative Veto

Another controversial mechanism that Congress brought to bear on the Executive with increasing frequency in the middle and late 1970s was the congressional or legislative veto. In addition to the War Powers Acts (to be examined later), perhaps the most pointed use of the legislative veto has been associated with the attempt of Congress to reassert its role in the military assistance and arms sales programs. The sheer size and salience of these programs in American foreign policy, especially the military sales program, combined with the fact that congressional procedures in the mid–1970s were simply inadequate, gave rise to an amendment to the Foreign Assistance Act of 1974 designed to change the latter situation.[43] The 1974 provision required that any proposed sale of more than $25 million would have to be submitted to Congress for review and that the sale could be precluded by a concurrent resolution of the Congress within 20 days after its submission. Subsequently, this provision was incorporated into the Arms Export Control Act of 1976, which expanded the waiting period to 30 days and included a review of any transfer of major defense equipment in excess of $7 million. Amendments were added that required the President to report to Congress quarterly on prospective and anticipated sales and transfers.

There have been a number of instances in which Congress has challenged proposed arms transfers. In no case were legislative vetoes actually voted, but the mere introduction of concurrent resolutions has proved sufficient to force Presidents to negotiate with Congress and in some cases actually to change the conditions and terms of the sale.[44] In the area of arms sales and transfers, therefore, the existence of the legislative veto seems to have increased congressional leverage. It has been observed, however, that at least prior to the recent amendments to the Arms Export Control Act, Congress tended to be pulled into the process after negotiations had been completed. Conceivably, interference by Congress after an agreement had been worked out with a prospective buyer could damage relations with the country in question. This seems to have been the case for example, in the agreements with Jordan in 1975 and Saudi Arabia in 1976 where congressionally imposed conditions on the use and deployment of equipment to be sold were regarded as demeaning and infringements on Jordanian and Saudi sovereignty. Furthermore, insofar as the mechanism for intervention employed by Congress must be used on a case-by-case basis, there is a danger that congressional review will be carried out in a spasmodic way with little sense of the relationship between a particular sale and the overall arms transfer program. The newly required quarterly reports on projected sales could reduce this prospect.

On balance, however, there is reason for concern as to the long-term operation of these procedures. Clearly, the threat of legislative veto allows significant congressional participation in the arms sales process. However, it is important to underscore the fact that heretofore, almost all major challenges to proposed sales have involved but one region. To be sure, the Middle East has been and continues to be the object of most U.S. sales and is a region crucial to American security interests. But one must wonder about congressional concern for the totality of the program and its implications for the future. Can Congress broaden and sustain its programmatic oversight at a time when the thrust of American policy seems once again to be in the direction of global activism and intervention, especially in the Third World?

Oversight: The Case of the CIA

Proponents of a stronger and more systematic oversight role for Congress could find little more than uncertain prospects by the end of the decade. Even with perhaps the most widely publicized case of purportedly greater congressional activism in the 1970s—the investigation of the intelligence establishment—the future of congressional oversight remained very unclear as the 1980s began. The pattern of congressional activity was not unlike that examined earlier: congressional passivity during the cold war years, increasing activism during the Vietnam rebellion, followed by indecisiveness in the face of conservative pressures for a more activist foreign policy as the 1970s drew to a close.

From the very outset of the cold war period, congressional oversight of the intelligence establishment, especially of the Central Intelligence Agency, was severely circumscribed. In part, Congress gave away its right to oversight, and in part it let the right go by default during this early period. As Harry Howe Ransom has noted:

> In the CIA Act of 1949 Congress went even further, exempting the CIA from existing statutes requiring publication or disclosure of the organization, function, names, official titles, salaries or numbers of

personnel employed by the agency." The Director of the Budget was proscribed from making the usual reports to Congress. The standard procedures regarding the expenditure of public funds were waived, and the Director's personal voucher alone became sufficient for expenditures for purposes of a "confidential, extraordinary or emergency nature."[45]

Moreover, during the early 1970s, the Senate Armed Services Subcommittee charged with oversight responsibility and chaired by Senator Stennis, did not meet in 1971, met only twice in 1970, and met only once in 1972; no staff were present, and no records were kept.[46] The members of the Senate Foreign Relations Committee were invited to attend, but according to Senator Fulbright, meetings were infrequent, bound by a rule of 10 minute question time per Senator, and the Director tended to tell "them what they wanted to know." "It seems to me," Fulbright complained to one former insider of the CIA, "that the men on the Committee are more interested in shielding CIA from its critics than in anything else."[47] In all there were four committees charged with looking at the CIA. But the attitude of those charged with these oversight responsibilities, at least until the disclosure in early 1975 that the CIA had amassed secret dossiers on at least 10,000 Americans, was less than vigilant. Thus Senator Stennis could be found arguing in debate on November 23, 1971: "You have to make up your mind that you are going to have an intelligence agency and protect it as such and shut your eyes and take what is coming."[48] Ignorance, it seems, was the essense of reponsible oversight during much of the 1950s, 1960s, and 1970s.[49]

Congressional permissiveness was once again on display at the confirmation hearing for Director William Colby in the summer of 1973. Senators were told that "although disclosure of the total figure of the intelligence community budget would not present a security problem . . . it [might] stimulate requests for additional details." Colby concluded, therefore, that he could not "recommend the publication of the total or any subdivision thereof."[50] In spite of the refusal of the new Director to tell Congress how much the agency or other government intelligence activities were costing the taxpayers, he was overwhelmingly confirmed. In June 1974 Senator Proxmire proposed an amendment to the DOD procurement bill that would have required disclosure of the total amount of money spent on intelligence activities by the U.S. government. The measure was defeated by a vote of 55 to 33, with eight of the nine members of the oversight committee voting against it.[51] In fact, more than 288 different measures have been introduced since 1948 to make the CIA more responsive. Few passed prior to the late 1970s.

In 1977 the Senate Select Committee on Intelligence asked that a one-line figure on the CIA's gross budget be published. Earlier, the Supreme Court had refused to hear a taxpayer's 1974 challenge concerning the public right to know of the appropriation of public money. The challenge was brought under Article I of the Constitution, which states in part: "no money shall be drawn from the Treasury, but in consequence of Appropriations made by law; and a regular statement and accounting of receipts and expenditures shall be published from time to time." But most in Congress agreed with Senator William Hathaway who argued, "Once we've opened the door and given them a little peek, the demands will grow. . . . And quite frankly, gentlemen, I don't know if we'll ever be able to slam the door shut."[52]

The consistency and margin of these votes throughout the quarter century after World War II suggests that congressional inaction in this area was caused by something more fundamental than structural inadequacies. Rather, Congress acted throughout this period to support, even strengthen, an institutional relationship that ensured congressional ineffectiveness. Unless one is prepared to argue that Congress was populated by incredibly obtuse men and women, one is forced to conclude that this behavior represented consistent support not only for the instrument of policy represented by the Central Intelligence Agency, but also the policy it served. Indeed, once the congressional consensus behind America's global role began to crack under the blows of Vietnam, economic distress, and evidence uncovered by the press that the CIA had been employed by the presidency against domestic dissent, Congress moved to investigate not only the CIA but other elements of the previously sacrosanct and secret intelligence agencies, the Federal Bureau of Investigation, and what many observers regard as the largest and most mysterious component of the intelligence system, the National Security Agency.

In an attempt to anticipate congressional action, President Ford appointed a commission under the direction of Vice President Rockefeller to study and make recommendations for the reform of the intelligence establishment. The commission's report was issued in June 1975, and the President made recommendations to Congress and issued an executive order of his own in January 1976 designed to increase presidential control of the intelligence establishment and correct many of the abuses revealed during the preceding months. Critics charged, however, that the administration's response provided for too many exceptions to the President's prohibitions and might actually lead to an expansion of intelligence agency surveillance of domestic political activity.

In the meantime, investigative committees had been set up in Congress.[53] The House committee soon become immobilized by internal conflict when it was revealed that its proposed chair Lucien Nedzi had received secret briefings on previous illegal activities carried out by the Central Intelligence Agency while the Representative served as chair of the House Armed Services Special Subcommittee. Subsequently, the House Committee's work was disrupted by allegations of lax internal security and the leaking of the committee's report to the press. In the Senate, however, Senator Church's Select Committee began work in early 1975, and by the fall of that year it had documented a series of illegal and questionable activities of the various intelligence agencies, especially the CIA and the National Security Agency. Foreign operations made public by the committee included documentation of the CIA's planned assassination attempts directed at Fidel Castro and Patrice Lumumba, covert operations against Rafael Trujillo of the Dominican Republic and Ngo Dinh Diem of South Vietnam, and CIA involvement in the attempt to block the assumption of power by Salvador Allende in Chile. Domestically, it was revealed that the CIA had directly disobeyed a presidential order to destroy certain deadly poisons and had engaged in a 20 year mail surveillance program that involved photographing the exterior of 2.7 million pieces of mail sent to the United States from the Soviet Union and opening 215,820 such letters between 1953 and 1973. In addition, it was revealed that between 1967 and 1973, the National Security Agency had monitored international telephone and cable traffic of American citizens. Though ostensibly directed at international drug traffic, terrorists, and would-be presidential assassins, antiwar activists were also targeted. Moreover, a House Government Operations Subcommittee on Government Information and Individual Rights revealed in November of 1975 that for 30 years virtually all international telegrams originating in or forwarded through the United States had been routinely turned over to the government by the three largest international telegraph companies.

Other areas of operations that were deleted from the final Senate report for protection of intelligence sources and methods included such areas as budgetary oversight, relations between intelligence agencies and American academic institutions and religious groups, and the use of the Department of State's diplomatic corps as a cover for espionage operations abroad. Subsequent revelations made it clear that the intelligence establishment had extensive contractual research arrangements throughout American colleges and universities, including research on mind control drugs, that sometimes included experimentation on unsuspecting subjects. In addition, journalists and representatives of religious institutions were revealed to have served as CIA informants.

The Senate committee's recommendations covered more than eighty proposals, including new statutory authority or "charter reform" designed to clarify the purposes of various elements of the intelligence establishment and the lines of responsibility and authority; a tightening of executive branch administrative and review mechanisms as well as recommendations concerning the quality of the intelligence product; tighter restrictions on intelligence activities, especially covert operations, and outright prohibition of such operations as political assassinations, subversion of democratic governments, support of governments systematically violating human rights, and prohibition of the use of academics, journalists, or religious leaders for covert operations; and an expansion of congressional oversight arrangements. Concerning oversight arrangements, the committee recommended that there be established a permanent Select Committee on Intelligence that would have responsibility for: (1) receiving prior notification of all covert operations, (2) authorizing the national intelligence budget annually, and (3) preparing the new charter for the intelligence establishment.

By mid–1976, the Select Committee was in place, and review of the intelligence budget and covert operations was under way. Although implementation of these aspects of the oversight function proceeded relatively smoothly, the problem of charter reform was much more difficult. Indeed, as congressional opinion began to drift toward a generally harder line on foreign and national security issues in the late 1970s, the charter reform process began attracting the criticism of those who were now advocating a more activist American posture with an attendant unleashing of the intelligence establishment. As the reform efforts of the mid–1970s began to lose steam, the reform process came to a virtual halt. Not until May 1980 did a new CIA charter proposal emerge from the Senate Intelligence Committee, and that proposal was a drastically scaled down 4–page version of a comprehensive 132-page proposal that had been developed in the committee over the preceding 3 years.[54]

Apart from reducing the number of committees to which the CIA had to report regarding covert operations, perhaps the most important changes passed by the Senate were what some critics regarded as an expansion of the presidential opportunity to avoid reporting covert operations to the Congress. Senator Proxmire, the only Senator to vote against the proposal (the final vote was 89–1), argued that language in the preamble to the bill requiring the intelligence establishment to report to Congress only "to the extent consistent with due regard for the protection from unauthorized disclosure of classified information and information relating to intelligence sources and methods" could be seized upon as a means to avoid virtually all reporting requirements. Most, however, including those highly critical of the intelligence establishment's operations and the failure of congressional oversight throughout the cold war, regarded the Senate compromise as acceptable if for no other reason than that it did not overtly reverse the earlier reforms, while at the same time maintaining the opportunity for more comprehensive charter reform at a later date.

The likelihood and ultimate shape of such reform remain very much in doubt with the onset of the 1980s, however. The operation of the Senate Intelligence Committee has generally received very favorable marks, but the fate of charter reform thus far suggests that oversight of the intelligence establishment could once again disappear within a small circle of coopted overseers. The contraction of the number of committees receiving prior notification of covert operations is arguably acceptable to proponents of active oversight, if the House and Senate Intelligence Committees are truly committed to oversight and accountability on the part of the intelligence establishment. On the other hand, the House has proved far less aggressive thus far; and in the face of rising congressional ambivalence concerning tight control of the intelligence establishment, the House Foreign Affairs Committee voted in July 1980 to allow the President to ignore reporting requirements "to meet extraordinary circumstances affecting the vital interests of the United States or to avoid unreasonable risk to the safety of the personnel or methods employed." The chair of the House Committee, Clement Zablocki was prepared to phrase the issue before Congress in language reminiscent of the 1950s: "Do we want an efficient intelligence agency or do we want to be informed?"[55]

Oversight and Programmatic Control: Defense Budgeting

No less consequential and budgetarily even more significant congressional oversight responsibilities lie in the authorization and appropriation of funds for the defense budget. Here, of course, Congress must dispense and oversee the administration of tens of billions of dollars to pay for the personnel, operations, maintenance, and procurement of weaponry and equipment, and research and development on new weapons for the armed services. Perhaps no greater opportunity for congressional programmatic control and influence exists than in the processes whereby American foreign and national security policy are made.

Given the importance of these processes and decisions, it should not be surprising that they have become the focus of some of the most intense political activity in the American political system on the part of governmental and nongovernmental actors[56] with interests in the outcome of the process and the course of congressional oversight. No group has been more active and expended more resources on this activity than the executive branch itself. During the cold war the Pentagon developed and has maintained a massive bureaucracy, which by its own admission has spent more than $30 million a year and by some private estimates as much as $190 million to advance the Department of Defense's positions.[57] Such activity was perhaps most evident in the 1960s, but the Vietnam backlash against foreign policy activism and defense spending did little to change the most common lobbying techniques during the 1970s.[58]

That the executive-legislative relationship can become ultimately corrupting needs no extensive elaboration. Most important from a policy making standpoint is the simple fact that not only can Congress become dependent upon the Executive for information, individual members of Congress can become dependent on military spending for the economic well-being of their districts and states. Concern for base operations and placement is instructive. In the first place, the presence and level of operations of a military base in a congressional district can have important consequences for the local economy. The base payroll constitutes an infusion of millions of dollars a year into the local economy, which results in turn in the development of local support service industries that rely almost totally upon the spending of base personnel and their dependents. Even slight shifts in operations mandated by a zealous congressional committee can mean local economic dislocations of some magnitude. There is little incentive to be concerned for the policy premises from which such bases spring, especially if concern might suggest no real need for maintaining the bases. In 1967 Secretary of Defense Robert McNamara began a program of closing bases in several states. This action caused the immediate surfacing of political sensitivities. Within hours of the announcement, the Office of the Secretary of Defense was besieged by irate and fearful members of Congress demanding a reversal of the decision. Similarly, in 1973 Secretary of Defense Elliot Richardson ordered 274 base closings or reductions eliminating 21,072 jobs, and received the same treatment as McNamara. Ironically, some of the most vocal members of Congress in this latter case were the most vigorous attackers of Nixon's foreign policy and levels of defense spending. Indeed, one cannot help but surmise that the location of the bases to be closed and the policy position of some members of Congress were entirely unrelated. In any event, this case illustrates the political leverage provided a President by the economic and political dependency of many in Congress.

As with bases and base operations, Congress's potential role in the development and procurement of new weapons systems can be undermined by its interrelated political and economic dependence. Thus states such as Washington, California, Texas, and Georgia find 10 to 40 percent of their labor forces involved in the production of weapons systems and related technologies. Under these circumstances Senators and Representatives from these states find it difficult not to avert their attention from evidence and analysis that cast doubts on threats to the national security and imply reduction in production and procurement of weapons. Here again there is subtle pressure to concur in the worst-case analysis of the executive branch defense and weapons analyst.

On the other hand, members of the Armed Services or Appropriations committees find themselves caught between somewhat conflicting sets of expectations. On one side there is the pull of the constituency and electoral needs, which imply a compliant and uncritical posture and behavior if military appropriations benefit their districts. But there is also the tug of another set of congressional norms, which, in the case of the appropriations committees, demands a posture of toughness and scrutiny of department and agency requests.

The way out of this dilemma has been to bore in on the details of State and Defense operations while at the same time avoiding broader policy questions. Thus Representatives and Senators could be found throughout the 1950s and 1960s spending inordinate amounts of time questioning Defense, State, and AID personnel about the minutiae of base operations, personnel problems, the number of automobiles in the motor pool in London, the liquor bill for the Paris Embassy, or how much it cost to ship the NATO Commander's poodle from Washington to Brussels. But the corollary of this behavior was a lack of interest in the policy premises underlying the actions of the Department of State or, more important, the Department of Defense. During the late 1950s, for example, Professor Lewis Dexter sought to determine the role of the House Armed Services Committee in policy matters and received this candid reply from a member of the committee:

> What the hell is the point of that? What would you do with it? I don't see that any public service could be performed by it. You can't find anything particular to say. In fact, how do we [members] know what should be considered? We mostly reflect what the military people recommend; military policy is made by the Department of Defense.
> Our committee is a real estate committee.
> How do we check the military recommendations? I don't know. We just ask a lot of questions—questions that are not resolved. It's most difficult to make inquiries. Take bases. Well, we want to know why

such-and-such a size. But we don't mostly know how to evaluate the answers; we aren't equipped to do so. So 95 percent of the legislation is what DOD recommends.[59]

Analysis of congressional budgetary behavior during the late 1960s and much of the 1970s—the period of most intense reaction to Vietnam and the arrival of the "new Congress"—provides a mixed but somewhat more flattering picture. Conclusions concerning whether Congress has, in spite of DOD lobbying and control of information, exercised a measure of programmatic control over the defense budget depend on the analyst's methodology and level of analysis. The latter seems especially important, for those students of congressional budgetary behavior who have tended to focus on the changes made by Congress in the total or aggregate defense budget find, at most, marginal congressional changes and therefore conclude that congressional programmatic impact is itself marginal or, at best, undertaken for economic or fiscal reasons, such as a desire to cut waste or otherwise save money.[60] On the other hand, most analysts who have attempted to examine congressional actions on specific elements and programs within the defense budget have concluded that Congress does in fact make nontrivial adjustments (i.e., greater than 5 percent changes) in DOD requests, especially in the areas of procurement and research and development.[61] Still others who have examined specific programs would agree that Congress has indeed been more active in its programmatic oversight during the last decade but suggest that in many instances the effect has been merely to delay rather than redirect or eliminate programs that the Defense Department wants.[62] One of the present authors, in a study of congressional actions on U.S. Navy shipbuilding requests in the 1970s, found considerable congressional budgetary activism. However, most of the reductions involved low capability ships or the stretching-out of procurement programs for expensive and higher capability ships. Indeed, Congress encouraged the Navy to buy vessels of higher capability than the President requested.[63]

As with the previous overview of congressional oversight of the intelligence establishment, therefore, caution is in order concerning projections for the 1980s. There is evidence that Congress is no longer supinely acquiescent to DOD budget requests, as perhaps it was in the late 1950s and early 1960s. Studies of the voting behavior of freshman members of the House and Senate during the 1970s generally parallel the conclusions of the programmatic analyses of congressional budgetary behavior: the Congress has been more skeptical and thus more observant in its oversight function during the Vietnam revolution.[64] However, by the late 1970s there were indications that the effects of the revolution might be shortlived.[65] As detente declined and the political rhetoric and public opinion of the late 1970s and early 1980s came to echo that of the 1950s, congressional budgetary behavior moved in tandem with events. The Carter administration, which had promised reductions in defense spending, was confronted with a Congress that insisted on a fifth nuclear-powered aircraft carrier despite the President's objections, and wished to increase defense spending more rapidly than the White House. And when the Reagan administration swept into office with its proposals for reasserting American superiority over the Soviet Union, the Congress enthusiastically endorsed the new President's expanded defense budgets. Only when, in 1982, projected budget deficits exceeded $150 billion, did echoes of early 1970s style defense budget cutting reemerge, and even then with greatest reluctance.

In the strictest sense, of course, this recent congressional behavior can be regarded as a manifestation of a more activist Congress. A more hawkish or interventionist Congress need not be viewed as weaker or a weakening partner in the executive-legislative relationship. On the other hand, postwar experience suggests that promotion of such a posture carries with it dangers for Congress.

Congressional votes on Greek-Turkish aid in 1947, Point Four, NATO, the Mutual Defense Assistance Program, and the Formosa, Middle East, Cuban, and Tonkin Gulf resolutions represented the points at which the cold war Presidents went before the Congress to seek approval for the expansion of American global presence. In some instances, of course, there was more than a little duplicity exercised by the Executive, but by and large, especially at the outset of the cold war, Congress was aware of the implications of what it was doing when it provided the President with what he wanted. In sum, the executive-legislative relationship of the last 25 years developed and was sustained because the members of Congress accepted the policy and ideological assumptions of that relationship. Having accepted that set of premises, there was little left to do but become spectators to the implementation of the policy, occasionally intervening on the programmatic margins, but by and large acquiescing in and trying to benefit politically from what was taking place. They may have become corrupted and enfeebled by the resulting one-side relationship, but it was ultimately a corruption and enfeeblement rooted in the conviction that what America had set out to do in the world was right and the instrumentalities America had chosen—including an imperial presidency and congressional membership in the military-industrial complex—were proper.

There is insufficient evidence to predict that this institutional history will repeat itself. The Congress that has entered the 1980s is certainly a more vigorous institution than the institution that emerged from World War II and the cold war. But if the attempt to fashion new instruments of programmatic control has had some success, the major effort invested in the reassertion of a policy direction role—the War Powers Act—has been, at best, problematical. And in this development there is cause for concern for those who envisioned a new executive-legislative relationship emerging from the upheaval of the late 1960s and early 1970s.

THE WAR POWERS ACT AND THE SEARCH FOR A POLICY ROLE

The passage of the War Powers Act over a presidential veto on November 7, 1973, was hailed by many as a historic breakthrough for Congress. Senator Javits declared, "Never in the history of this country has an effort been made to restrain the war powers in the hands of the President. . . . [This bill] will make history in this country such as has never been made before."[66] In contrast, there were a few skeptics who, like Senator Barry Goldwater, complained that under the language of the act, "the President is no longer prohibited from initiating original actions. He needs only to report during the first 60 days. . . . This language puts into law language that is not contained in the Constitution."[67] Senator Eagleton, one of the originators of the War Powers resolution, also felt that the final product was simply a license to make war. Despondent, he explained his ultimate opposition:

> If this becomes law we have given a predated declaration of war to the President . . . courtesy of the U.S. Congress. . . . [This] is not what the Constitution . . . envisaged when we were given the authority to declare war. We were to decide *ab initio*, at the outset, and not *post facto*. . . . This is an historic tragedy. It gives the President and all of his successors *in futuro* a predated 60 day unilateral war-making authority.[68]

Goldwater and Eagleton's interpretation of the War Powers bill was, not surprisingly, accepted by several spokesmen of the Executive. On November 30, 1973, for instance, Secretary of Defense Schlesinger explained that the new War Powers legislation might actually enable President Nixon to order new bombing in Indochina—bombing specifically prohibited by the Aguust 15, 1973, cutoff mandated in the Church-Case provision of the State Department Authorization bill.[69] It was obvious, however, that Congress intended something quite different. Though it mandated reporting procedures and the explicit threat of legislative veto, Congress hoped to compel executive consultation and thus codetermination of policy requiring the commitment of American military personnel. Subsequent instances involving the commitment of American military personnel, however, have justified neither the despair of Senator Eagleton nor the exultant optimism of those like Senator Javits who thought that the passage of the War Powers Act heralded the onset of a new congressional role in the setting of foreign policy direction. Rather, the act's effect remains essentially untested, though events since its passage warrant a skeptical view of its utility as a means for ensuring executive-congressional codetermination of policy.

In four instances where American military personnel were committed by the President—the transport of refugees from Da Nang, Vietnam, in April 1975; the evacuation of American nationals from Cambodia and Vietnam in April 1975; and the evacuation of Americans and others from Lebanon in 1976—presidential reports were filed with Congress but in a perfunctory manner.[70] In a fifth case, involving the transport by American aircraft of European and African troops into Shaba Province, Zaire, in 1978, President Carter refused to file a report, contending that the fact that the aircraft landed to the rear of combat operations exempted the airlift from the War Powers Act's reporting requirements. This position was challenged by a handful of members of the House, but after hearings the matter was dropped, with administration representatives adamantly refusing to file a report and denying that their participation in the hearings constituted fulfillment of any obligations under the act.[71] But perhaps no incident better elucidates the limits of the act in practice than the executive-legislative interaction attendant to the capture of the American freighter *Mayaguez* by Cambodia in May 1975 and the lack of interaction in the Iranian hostage rescue debacle in April 1980.

The act enjoins the President to consult "in every possible instance . . . before introducing U.S. armed forces into hostilities or into situations where imminent involvement is clearly indicated by the circumstances." But in mid-May 1975, President Ford did not "consult Congress." Rather, Ford informed a select congressional group well after he had decided to send American warplanes to fire on Cambodian gunboats presumed to be involved in the *Mayaguez* incident. The decision to invade Koh Tang Island was made around 4 P.M. on Wednesday, May 14, 1975. The order to commit troops went from the White House to the Defense Department at 4:45. The assault forces began operations at 5:14. Yet the 17 specially chosen members of Congress were not informed until 6:40 P.M.[72]

Hardly had the 24 hour ultimatum the White House said it had issued expired, when on Wednesday, May 14, at 7:07 P.M. the Cambodian radio began to repeatedly broadcast a rather pathetic capitulation that included an indication that Cambodia was releasing the *Mayaguez* crew.[73] Neverthless, the ground attack on Tang Island was begun. By 8:30 Wednesday night American Marines had arrived at the *Mayaguez*, moored on Tang Island, only to find the crew gone. While fighting raged on Tang Island, at 10:45 P.M. Wednesday night, the American destroyer *Wilson* reported a small boat approaching flying a white flag. Eight minutes later "at least 30 Caucasians" were spotted. They were presumed to be the crew of the *Mayaguez*. Just the same, 20 minutes after the crew of the *Mayaguez*, aboard a fishing boat flying a flag of truce, had been seen by the *Wilson*, and 4 hours after the Marine assault on Tang Island had begun to rescue this same *Mayaguez* crew, U.S. warplanes struck the Cambodian mainland to "protect the marines" on Tang Island from the "Cambodian Air Force" [sic].* If the U.S. military feared the Cambodian Air Force, one might wonder why the strikes were not launched at the time of the invasion of Tang Island. And why, too, were U.S. air strikes directed at the mainland launched after the Cambodian radio broadcast had been received and after the U.S. merchant crew had been sighted? Moreover, the *Mayaguez* crew departed to search for the *Wilson* 3 hours before the attack on the mainland began. It is improbable that this small vessel, sailing more than 5 hours, carrying U.S. merchant men waving sheets, shirts, and underwear, heading toward a U.S. destroyer engaged in belligerency off Tang Island 25 miles away, would not be noticed by the watch on the bridge of the destroyer *Wilson*. Indeed, at least one published report indicates that the *Mayaguez* crew was spotted by a U.S. plane "within sight" of Tang Island.[74]

It was apparent that the United States wanted to completely unfurl its display of firepower so that American arms could be seen to awe what former Chairman of the Joint Chiefs of Staff Admiral Moorer termed in the *Washington Post* the previous week "the little revolutionaries" of Asia and elsewhere. Three weeks before the *Mayaguez* incident began, President Ford grumbled at a White House strategy session that the American setback in Indochina was causing him to look "indecisive." "I know what the mail is saying," he complained. "I have to show some strength," he concluded, "in order to help us . . . with our credibility abroad."[75] A few hours before the incident Secretary Kissinger told a St. Louis audience, "Given our central role, a loss in our credibility invites chaos."[76] And the day after the incident, "high ranking sources" told *New York Times* reporter Philip Shabecoff "privately" "that the seizure of the vessel might provide the test of American determination in Southeast Asia . . . the United States has been seeking since the collapse of allied governments in South Vietnam and Cambodia."[77]

The rescue of the *Mayaguez* was an exercise to show that America was still a global cop, and even though its patrol might be a bit

*The Cambodian Air Force was an assortment of captured and probably inoperable U.S. aircraft.

circumscribed, a mighty stick could still be brandished. The administration had attempted for weeks to shift American policy failures to the 94th Congress. Congress had been called "niggardly," "isolationist," and worse. Now the Ford administration could claim that if only given a free hand, American arms could, after all, secure American interests. Congress had thus been placed in the political position of having to demonstrate that the successful use of military action to secure the release of the *Mayaguez* was unnecessary. Congress was forced into the impossible *post hoc* proof that success might have been achieved by patient and quiet undertakings. Even so, Congress failed to demand real consultations as the War Powers Act requires. Moreover, those prohibitions (and the four other specific legislative acts that forbid military "activities in or over or off Cambodia, or North Vietnam or South Vietnam," financed from "past, present or future appropriations") were virtually ignored.[78]

Harvard legal historian Raoul Berger wrote heatedly 2 weeks after the chorus of congressional yahoos began to subside:

> The Senate Foreign Relations Committee hastened to set its seal on the President's "exercise of his constitutional powers" in sinking Cambodian patrol boats in order to regain the captured merchant vessel *Mayaguez*. . . . Suppose that the patrol boats that the United States sunk, instead of belonging to pygmy Cambodia, had been those of the Soviet Union. Is it for the President alone to make the fateful judgment that may plunge us into war? Such situations call for the "collective judgment" of President and Congress, as the War Powers Resolution of 1973 requires. . . .
>
> That requirement is not satisfied by merely "informing" selected members of Congress of the forthcoming hostilities, but by genuine "consultation" *before* a decision is made. . . .
>
> It is a reproach to Congress that having just shaken us loose from a disastrous war, sustained in no small part by Congressional acquiescence—it is once more ready to approve a Presidential exercise of its own power. Thereby it gives its sanction to yet another dismal "precedent" that future Presidents will not be slow to invoke against Congress.[79]

But the next President did not deign to seek precedent when American forces were committed in Zaire, nor later in Iran in the abortive rescue attempt of April 1980. In both instances the commitments were simply defined as falling outside the scope of the War Powers Act. The commitment to Zaire was said to involve an airlift to a noncombat area. In the Iranian case, the Carter administration asserted that because the mission was a rescue attempt, it was humanitarian and thus beyond the scope of a War Powers Act. It is important to note, however, that this rescue attempt involved the insertion under cover provided by an awesome naval task force in the Indian Ocean of more than a hundred heavily armed men aboard more than ten military aircraft hundreds of miles inside the territory of a presumably hostile foreign power. Moreover, there were implications far beyond Iran, for an elaborate counterintelligence effort involving Egypt and Israel was undertaken for the purpose of obscuring the mission not only from the Iranians but also from the Soviet Union, lest the latter intervene militarily and thereby initiate a dangerous escalation in a volatile region containing enormous superpower military capability. The mere statement of the fear suggests that there was potentially far more involved than a humanitarian rescue. Once again, however, the war powers question was pushed aside. Given the character of the mission, a plausible rationalization of nonconsultation could be constructed without resorting to the semantic gymnastics engaged in by the Carter administration. But the same characteristics of the mission make for a no less plausible case that at least an ex post facto presidential report was in order after the mission was aborted. Finally, in the early months of the Reagan administration, it was reported that most of the 120 or so U.S. military personnel in El Salvador drew an extra $65 a month "hostile fire" pay, though the Pentagon deemed that their jobs were not hazardous enough to warrant reporting to Congress under the War Powers Act. Similarly, reports circulated that U.S. troops went on patrols and flew armed helicopters in support of counter-insurgent missions in Honduras. But Congress—despite public hostility to an involvement in the area—did not raise the issue.[80]

Thus a succession of administrations that have come to office applauding the reassertion of congressional activism in foreign policy have nonetheless consistently denied the applicability and even constitutionality of the major institutional innovation in the executive-legislative relationship to come out of the congressional upheaval of the 1970s.[81] No less important, however, has been congressional reticence in the face of this posture on the part of both Republican and Democratic Presidents. To be sure, the pace of events and public response to presidential initiative in the *Mayaguez* and Iranian incidents made it practically and politically difficult, if not impossible, for Congress to bring the sanction of the legislative veto to bear in either case. But insofar as this has been true thus far, it merely confirms the skepticism of those who felt from the outset that the War Powers Act would prove a poor means for reestablishing the consultative role anticipated for Congress in the constitutional design for the American foreign policy making process.

CONGRESS ON THE THRESHOLD OF THE 1980s

This review of recent changes in Congress supports the conclusion that reformers in Congress have been most successful in reasserting and perhaps even in expanding Congress's capacity for programmatic participation and oversight but have been much less successful regarding participation in setting foreign and national security policy assumptions and objectives. The issue of the last decade has indeed been largely one of "codetermination", but there has been at best only partial resolution of that issue. Moreover, partial success could prove especially unfulfilling, for if majorities in Congress are limited to oversight of programs but cannot gain access to the process of developing the assumptions and the objectives of programs, then the congressional role must remain essentially that of the reactive outsider. The political vulnerabilities of such a position are considerable, for executive control of information and initiative allows the presidency and its agents to force executive-legislative debate into a framework of "the President's policy vs. No-policy."[82] Programmatic control and participation are essentially the capacity to block, deflect, obstruct, or marginally modify programs. Without systematically developed policy alternatives, congressional majorities can at most redirect programs away from aims to which they object. But without some sense of new direction, deadlock of the sort that developed around the cutoff of aid to Turkey may result, or, worse yet, direction will be supplied by whichever special interests can command congressional attention.

Furthermore, one wonders how long the programmatic oversight role can be sustained. Checking, balancing, modifying,—the activities associated with institutionalized skepticism—are crucial. But how satisfying or creative can they be if individuals or the institutional consensus demands the more positive or active role of policy conceptualizer? And with Congress being frustrated in the desire for policy codetermination, one must wonder how long even programmatic oversight and activism will be conducted responsibly. Perhaps it can be sustained in the midst of a politically salient executive-legislative confrontation such as Vietnam, but what happens when public attention shifts or oversight becomes drawn out, tedious, or politically unrewarding, such as with the CIA charter reform?

But if the programmatic role is constrained, perhaps the ultimate constraint on further reform is to be found in the emerging policy response to the events of the late 1970s and early 1980s. Even as the course of American policy and its fate in the late 1960s and early 1970s provided the impetus and opportunity for reform of the executive-legislative relationship, the thrust of events after 1976 may be deflecting, even distorting, those reforms and closing off opportunities for further change.

It will be recalled that the reformers had been, for the most part, men and women who desired both a new executive-legislative relationship and a foreign policy requiring a less globalist and interventionist implementation. Vietnam and the Watergate-truncated Nixon presidency served both of these ends. But by 1978 the harbingers of new Soviet-American tension emerged, and by 1979 "Cold War II" appeared on the horizon—a condition made manifest with the 1980 election—and with it a shift in congressional policy sentiment became apparent. The paradoxical result has been that at the moment Congress began to reassert and even expand its institutional capacity and prerogatives, the substantive thrust of congressional activism became less and less distinguishable from the kind of globalism against which the reformers of the early and mid–1970s had rebelled.

Thus even as institutional changes were crystalizing, it was possible that American policy was returning to a posture that had, in the years after World War II, carried with it the seeming necessity for an imperial presidency and an acquiescent Congress. The resurgent demand for greater and more forceful American activism seems to require that more resources be committed to the development and maintenance of military instrumentalities, hence, higher defense budgets. But will the executive-legislative corollary be less congressional oversight? Detente has all but vanished, and with it the future of strategic arms limitations becomes more uncertain. Will congressional initiative in this area also diminish? Raw materials, energy, and other resource conflicts with the Third World seem likely to escalate. Does this imply a corollary decline in congressional foreign aid and human rights concerns? The return of some approximation of cold war carries with it the need, in the view of many, for an unleashing of the intelligence establishment and its covert operations. Does this imply the end of charter reform? And finally, the exigencies of increased globalism have been used to justify executive initiative in the cases of the *Mayaguez*, Zaire, and Iran. Does this imply that the War Powers Act is destined to become a historical curiosity or worse, an *a priori* justification for presidential unilateralism, as feared by Senator Eagleton?

Thus the undoubted strengthening of Congress institutionally that came out of the early 1970s does not necessarily represent the institutionalizing of a congressional renascence in the executive-legislative relationship. For if Congress once again accepts as necessary a foreign policy directed at maintaining an international order inspired, constructed, and supervised by America as the crux of American and international security, then the position of Congress could once again become subordinate to a presidency of imperial dimensions. For an extensive system of international commitments carries with it certain institutional imperatives: efficiency, centralization of control, and the flexibility of a large, indeed, an almost infinitely expandable, reservoir of presidential power. "World order" and "implied" powers have gone hand in hand as Presidents pursued the cold war and simultaneously revolutionized the constitutionally prescribed executive-legislative relationship. Thus, if Congress seeks a redefinition of its role *within* a policy based primarily on American military power, the role of Congress will probably remain peripheral. An effort to circumscribe presidential war powers and foreign policy making initiative, while simultaneously accepting the objectives and values of a world superpower along with its attendant national security and foreign policy bureaucracy, will be most likely frustrated.

NOTES

1. This distinction has been developed in U.S. Senate, Committee on Foreign Relations, Committee Print prepared by the Foreign Affairs and National Defense Division of the Congressional Research Service (prepared by Harry L. Wrenn), *Congress, Information and Foreign Affairs*, 95th Congress, 2nd Session, 1978, p. 90.

2. John M. Berry, "Foreign Policy Making and the Congress," *Editoral Research Reprints* 1, no. 15 (April 19, 1967). Reprinted in House Document No. 298, 90th Congress, 2nd Session (Washington, D.C.: Legislative Reference Service), p. 181.

3. See Joseph E. Kallenbach, *The American Chief Executive: The Presidency and Governorship* (New York: Harper & Row, 1966), p. 506.

4. Arthur M. Schlesinger, Jr., *The Imperial President* (Boston: Houghton & Mifflin, 1973), pp. 85–86. For the data in this paragraph see Schlesinger and Louis Fisher, *President and Congress: Power and Policy* (New York: Free Press, 1973), p. 45.

5. See Berger's testimony in U.S. House, Hearings before the Subcommittee on International Security and Scientific Affairs, Committee on International Relations, *Congressional Review of International Agreements*, 94th Congress, 2nd Session, 1976, pp. 69–70. See also *United States v. Curtiss-Wright Export Corp.*, 299 U.S. 304 (1936).

6. *B. Altman Co. v. United States*, 224 U.S. 601 (1912).

7. S. 4556, 91st Congress, 2nd Session, 2 December 1970.

8. Public Law 92–403; see also Adam Carlyle Breckenridge, *The Executive Privilege: Presidential Control Over Information* (Lincoln: University of Nebraska Presss, 1974).

9. "U.S. Documents Accompanying the Sinai Accord," *The New York Times*, 17 September 1975.

10. *Washington Post*, 28 September 1975.

11. U.S., General Accounting Office, Reports of the Comptroller General of the United States, *U.S. Agreements with the Republic of Korea*, 20 February 1976.

12. For a presentation of this argument see Berger, op. cit., pp. 69–70. In Berger's view, only the "housekeeping" aspects of foreign affairs, e.g., receiving the credentials of Ambassadors, were to be left to the President to carry out without consultation.

13. *New York Times*, 6 June 1972.

14. Strobe Talbot, *Endgame: The Inside Story of SALT II* (New York: Harper & Row, 1979), pp. 215–216. This survey of executive-legislative relations regarding SALT II is drawn largely from Talbot's account.

15. Ibid., p. 207.

16. See H. Wriston, "The Special Envoy," *Foreign Affairs*, 38, no. 2 (January 1960): 219–257.

17. See U.S. Senate, Committee on Foreign Relations, *Background Information on the Foreign Relations Committee*, 90th Congress, 2nd Session, 1968, pp. 27–32; and ibid., 92nd Congress, 1st Session, 1971.

18. Charles E. Bohlen, *Witness to History, 1929–1969* (New York: Norton, 1973), pp. 309–336.

19. Cecil V. Crabb, Jr., *American Foreign Policy in the Nuclear Age*, 2nd ed. (New York: Harper & Row, 1960), p. 60.

20. *New York Times*, 17 March 1974.

21. *Washington Post*, 30 April 1974.

22. We would like to thank Professor Reid Reading for providing us with this case from the *Pittsburgh Press*, 29 January 1980. p. 1. In addition it should be noted that subsequent liberalization of contributions to "political action committees" and the campaign operations of private groups and committees not officially affiliated with an official presidential campaign operation could reopen this door. See *Buckley v. Valeo*, 424 U.S. 1 (1976).

23. In fact, some observers viewed the opposition block as a rough indicator of how many votes Carter would need for SALT ratification, although the text of the treaty remained to be completed.

24. See Timothy H. Ingram, "Billions in the Basement," *Washington Monthly 3*, no. 11 (January 1972).

25. *Washington Post*, 6 February 1973.

26. The prevalent view, except at the White House, was expressed by Justice William H. Rehnquist in 1969, when he was Assistant Attorney General. He wrote: "With respect to the suggestion that the President has a constitutional power to decline to spend appropriated funds, we must conclude that the existence of such broad power is supported neither by reason nor precedent," in ibid.

27. There was some evidence that the Ford administration attempted this. See Louis Fisher, *Presidential Spending Power* (Princeton, N.J.: Princeton University Press, 1975), p. 200. For an account of impoundment legislation, see *Congress and the Nation, vol. 4, 1973–1976* (Washington, D.C.: Congressional Quarterly, 1977), pp. 60–61.

28. Louis Fisher, "Dark Corners in the Budget," *Nation*, 19 January 1974, p. 75.

29. U.S. Senate, Hearings before the Special Committee on the Termination of the National Emergency of the United States, *National Emergency*, Part 2, 93rd Congress, 1st Session, 24 July 1973, p. 529.

30. Fisher, "Dark Corners in the Budget," P. 77; and Ingram, op. cit., p. 38.

31. U.S. House, Committee on Appropriations, *Department of Defense Appropri-*

ations Bill, 1970, House Report 91–698, 91st Congress, 1st Session, 3 December 1969; and U.S. House, Committee on Armed Services, *Authorizing Appropriations, Fiscal Year 1971,* House Report 91–1022, 91st Congress, 2nd Session, 24 April 1970.

32. L. Fletcher Prouty, "The Secret Team and the Games They Play," *Washington Monthly* 1, no. 11 (May 1970): 11–19; and Ingram, op. cit., p. 38.

33. Ingram, op. cit., p. 42; and *The New York Times,* 8 May 1973.

34. Aid 1974 program presentation to Congress: *Indo-China Reconstruction Assistance,* p. 9, cited by the National Action/Research on the Military Industrial Complex Documenting the Post War War (NARMIC), American Friends Service committee, January 1974, pp. 170–174; Center for Defense Information, *The Defense Monitor* 3, no. 5 (May 1974): 1–3; and *The New York Times,* 2 February 1975.

The exact character of these expenditures was sometimes hard to decipher. But one example of the use of these funds derived from "humanitarian" food sales emerged when members of Congress inquired where the Department of the Navy got $400,000 worth of Vietnamese piasters to grant a contract to an American construction firm with headquarters in San Antonio to build the notorious "tiger cages" (cells 4 feet high, 6 feet long, and 4 feet wide in which four or five prisoners were kept stooped and crammed on a remote island off the coast of Vietnam); the Navy and AID replied that it was "assistance in kind," generated by the Food for Peace program. See U.S House, Committee on Foreign Affairs, *Mutual Development and Cooperation Act of 1973,* 93rd Congress, 1st Session, 1973, p. 203; and NARMIC, p. 172.

35. NARMIC, p. 173, letter from John Mosler, USAID Mission, Saigon, to GVN Director General for Budget, 23 February, 1973.

36. *New York Times,* 17 April 1974.

37. "Senate Blocks Pentagon Request for More Vietgnam Aid," *Congressional Quarterly Weekly Report* 32, no. 19 (11 May 1974): 1234–1235.

38. *Philadelphia Bulletin,* 18 March 1975.

39. Leslie Gelb, "Indochina Deja Vu," Week in Review, *New York Times,* 23 March 1975.

40. See Philip J. Farley, Stephen S. Kaplan, and William Lewis, *Arms Across the Sea* (Washington, D.C.: The Brookings Institution, 1978), pp. 8 ff.; Congressional Research Service, *Implications of President Carter's Conventional Arms Transfer Policy* (Washington, D.C.: Foreign Affairs and National Defense Division, CRS, Library of Congress, 1977); and U.S. Senate, Committee on Foreign Relations, Committee Print, *Arms Transfer Policy,* 95th Congress, 1st Session, 1977.

41. This assessment is drawn from Thomas Frank and Edward Weisband, *Foreign Policy by Congress* (New York: Oxford University Press, 1979), pp. 253–257.

42. Ibid., p. 256.

43. This analysis is indebted to ibid., pp. 92–110, and Richard F. Grimmet, "The Legislative Veto and U.S. Arms Sales," in U.S. House Committee on Rules, A report prepared by the Congressional Research Service for the Subcommittee on

Rules of the House, *Studies on the Legislative Veto*, 96th Congress, 2nd Session, February 1980, pp. 248–320.

44. See Grimmet, pp. 252–268.
45. Harry Howe Ransom, *Can Democracy Survive the Cold War?* (Garden City, N.Y.: Doubleday, 1964), p. 178.
46. *Congressional Record* 120 (4 June 1974), 93rd Congress, 2nd Session, 1974, p. S9606.
47. Victor Marchetti and John D. Marx, *The CIA and the Cult of Intelligence* (New York: Knopf, 1974), p. 345.
48. David Rosenbaum, "Intelligence Oversight Is Done with a Blindfold," *New York Times,* 29 December 1974.
49. Ibid.; and Fisher, *Presidential Spending Power*, p. 218.
50. *Washington Post*, 2 August 1973.
51. *Congressional Record*, 4 June 1974, pp. S9601–9613.
52. U.S., Congress, Hearings before the Select Committee on Intelligence on *The Disclosure of Funds for Intelligence Activities*, 95th Congress, 2nd Session, 24–25 January 1978 and Rosenbaum, op. cit.
53. See *Congress and the Nation, vol. 4, 1973–1976*, pp. 182–197; and the useful collection of documents covering the congressional investigation in all of its phases, T. G. Fain, ed., *The Intelligence Community: History, Organization, and Issues* (New York: Bowker, 1977).
54. On the development of the Senate proposal, see John Felton, "Intelligence Charter Disputes Emerge Again on Key Issues," *Congressional Quarterly Weekly Report* 38, no. 8 (23 February 1980): pp. 537–538; Richard Whittle, "Senate Committee Votes Changes in Intelligence Reporting Requirements," *Congressional Quarterly Weekly Report* 38 no. 22 (31 May 1980): 1520–1521; and Whittle, "Senate Passes Compromise Intelligence Oversight Bill," *Congressional Quarterly Weekly Report* 38, no, 23 (7 June 1980): 1588–1589.
55. Quoted in *New York Times*, 1 August 1980, p. A7.
56. The activities of the nongovernmental actors are discussed in Chapter 7.
57. See transcript of *CBS Reports: The Selling of the Pentagon*, broadcast 23 February 1971 and reprinted in the *Congressional Record*, 26 February 1971, p. S2110; Adam Yarmolinsky, *The Military Establishment: Its Impact on American Society* (New York: Harper & Row, 1971); and J. William Fulbright, *The Pentagon Propaganda Machine* (New York: Vintage Books, 1971), passim.
58. Yarmolinsky, op. cit.
59. Quoted in Lewis A. Dexter, "Congressmen and the Making of Military Policy," in Davis Bobrow, ed., *Components of Defense Policy* (Chicago: Rand McNally, 1965), pp. 99–100.
60. See the classic analysis by Richard Fenno, *The Power of the Purse: Appropriations Politics in Congress* (Boston: Little, Brown, 1966); and Otto A. Davis, A. H. Dempster, and Aaron Wildavsky, "A Theory of the Budgetary Process," *American Political Science Review* 60, no. 3 (September 1966): 529–547.
61. Perhaps the most important analysis of this sort was that undertaken by Arnold Kanter, "Congress and the Defense Budget: 1960–1970," *American Political*

Science Review 66, no. 1 (March 1972): 129–143. Studies extending and generally confirming Kanter's analysis include: Edward J. Laurance, "The Changing Role of Congress in Defense Policy-Making," *Journal of Conflict Resolution* 20, no. 2 (June 1976): 213–253; and Robert L. Bledsoe and Roger B. Handberg, "Changing Times—Congress and Defense," *Armed Forces and Society* 6, no. 3 (Spring 1980): 415–430.

62. See Lawrence J. Korb, "The Bicentennial Defense Budget," *Armed Forces and Society* 2, no. 1 (November 1975): 128–139; and Korb, "Congressional Impact on Defense Spending, 1962–1973: The Programmatic and Fiscal Hypotheses," *Naval War College Review* 28, no. 3 (November–December 1973): 49–61.

63. James K. Oliver, "Congress and the Future of American Seapower: An Analysis of United States Navy Budget Requests in the 1970s," paper presented at the 1976 annual meeting of the American Political Science Association in Chicago, September 1976.

64. James R. Dennis, "Roll-Call Votes and National Security: Focusing in on the Freshmen," *Orbis* 22 no. 3 (Fall 1978).

65. A fear that this would be so was voiced by Rep. Les Aspin at the height of the Vietnam revolution: Les Aspin, "The Defense Budget and Foreign Policy: The Role of Congress," in Franklin Long and George Rathjens, eds., *Defense Policy and Arms Control* (New York: Norton, 1976), pp. 155–174.

66. Thomas F. Eagleton, *War and Presidential Power: A Chronicle of Congressional Surrender* (New York: Liveright, 1974), p. 11.

67. Ibid., p. 207. The final language of the War Powers Act authorized 90 days for troops to be committed by the Executive without congressional action.

68. Ibid., pp. 218–219.

69. Ibid., pp. 220–221.

70. See Allan S. Nanes, "Legislative Vetoes: The War Powers Resolution," in *Studies on the Legislative Veto*, pp. 579–687.

71. See U.S. House, Committee on International Relations, Hearings before the Subcommittee on International Security and Scientific Affairs, *Congressional Oversight of War Powers Compliance: Zaire Airlift*, 95th Congress, 2nd Session, 10 August 1978.

72. Roy Rowan, *The Four Days of Mayaguez* (New York: Norton, 1975), pp. 179–180. As a House report on the incident (No. 93–87) made clear, consultation is not "synonymous with merely being informed." Rather, "consultation in this provision means that a decision is pending on a problem and the Members of Congress are being asked by the President for their advice . . . and . . . their approval of action contemplated. For consultation to be meaningful, the President must himself participate, and all information relevant to the situation must be made available." See U.S. House, Committee on International Relations, Hearings before the Subcommittee on International Security and Scientific Affairs, *War Powers: A Test of Compliance*, 94th Congress, 1st Session, 7 May and 4 June 1975, pp. 46–47, 71, and 105–112.

73. The Cambodians are, the communiqué said, "a small, poor, and needy people just emerging from . . . war. . . . The Cambodian nation . . . [has] no intention of

provoking anybody nor do we have the wherewithal to provoke anybody." Text of communiqué. *The New York Times,* 16 May 1975.

74. Rowan, op. cit., p. 210.
75. Jack Anderson, "Washington Merry-Go-Round," *Washington Post,* 26 May 1975.
76. *Washington Post,* 13 May 1975.
77. *New York Times,* 14 May 1975.
78. See *Congressional Quarterly Weekly Report* 31, no. 52 (December 29, 1973): 3435; and HR 9055–PL 93/50, H.J. Res. 636–PL 93–52, HR 7645–PL 92/126, HR 9286–PL 93/155, and S 1443–PL 93/189; and "Text of Resolution on Warpowers," in *The New York Times,* 8 November 1973.
79. Raoul Berger, "The Mayaguez Incident and the Constitution," *New York Times,* 23 May 1975. See also Anthony Lewis, "A Chorus of Yahoos," *New York Times,* 26 May 1975.
80. Don Oberdorfer, "Most U.S. Troops In Salvador Get Hostile Fire Pay," *Washington Post,* 30 July 1982; On Honduras, see *New York Times,* 20 April 1982:3.
81. See Jimmy Carter, "Legislative Vetoes: Message to Congress," *Weekly Compilation of Presidential Documents* 14, no. 25 (26 June 1978): 1146–1149. For an overview of the question of the constitutionality of the legislative veto, see U.S. Senate, Committee on Government Operations, Subcommittee on Oversight Procedures, *Congressional Oversight: Methods and Techniques,* 94th Congress, 2nd Session, July 1976, pp. 18–19. For an elaboration of the argument that the legislative veto is unconstitutional, see the testimony of Monroe Leigh, Legal Adviser, Department of State in U.S. House, Committee on International Relations, hearings before the Subcommittee on International Security and Scientific Affairs, *Congressional Review of International Agreements,* 94th Congress, 2nd Session, 1976, pp. 177–180. Indeed, in late 1982 the courts declared certain aspects of the legislative veto unconstitutional.
82. See the discussion of this problem in *Congress, Information and Foreign Affairs,* pp. 90–97.

Chapter 6

Public Opinion and Foreign Policy

The several generations of individuals involved in the conduct or study of U.S. foreign affairs since World War II have not been sanguine about public opinion. The public has seemed too steeped in lethargy and parochial self-interests to offer responsible contributions to the decision making process. The public could not be ignored, given the democratic framework of American politics. But no less important were the rejection of the Versailles Treaty at the end of World War I, the isolationism of the period between the two great wars, the post–World War II reaction to the division of Europe, the "loss" of China, the rampage of Senator Joseph McCarthy, and the demonstrations of the Vietnam years, for all were iridescent and painful memories for officials and observers. Thus it seems to many that the public cannot be discounted; yet, at the same time, the people cannot be counted an asset in the pursuit of any long-term diplomatic design.

One diplomat-turned-historian, Louis Halle, has attributed many of the ills of this century to the broadening of public participation in politics. The inference of this criticism is that the public acts as an unwelcome kibitzer at a most dangerous game. Halle suggests, therefore, that the price paid for the "shift of political power from a cosmopolitan elite to a nationalistic and often xenophobic" mass has been the "decline in standards of interest and conduct."[1] The public has been condemned for paying insufficient heed to foreign affairs or, when concerned, for having the analytic capability of a large reptile. As George Kennan despaired:

> I sometimes wonder whether . . . a democracy is . . . similar to one of those prehistoric monsters with a body as long as this room and the brain the size of a pin: he lies there in his comfortable primeval mud

and pays little attention to his environment: he is slow to wrath—in fact you practically have to whack his tail off to make him aware that his interests are being disturbed; but, once he grasps this, he lays about him with such blind determination that he not only destroys his adversary but largely wrecks his native habitat.[2]

American leaders have frequently thought the public little fit to face the hard realities of the international system. They see the public at its best when it can be mobilized to support policy rather than be instrumental in policy formulation. Scholar George Liska put the case plainly. The "game" of foreign policy

is the most fascinating of sports: the masses provide an audience to applaud success and boo failure, and the imperial elites contend with their counterpart in other countries and their internal counterelites, who use dissent as a circuitous avenue to direction.[3]

In this view, the day-to-day operations of diplomacy are best left to the professional managers of foreign policy.* Indeed, "crisis managers" proliferated in the cold war. Where diplomacy had previously been marked by negotiation, it was, in this period, marked by crisis and confrontation. The management of force was the coin of the realm of foreign policy. The public could not know the delicate signals and maneuvers of such operations. These were skills that were acquired through lengthy apprenticeship. The penchant for and mastery of the craft of foreign policy was, in the words of a former State Department official Roger Hilsman, "like blue cheese, . . . an acquired taste."[4]

This traditional skepticism of political elites concerning the foreign affairs capacities of both the American people and American system is shared by contemporary leadership. In an extensive survey undertaken in the wake of the Vietnam war, political scientists Ole Holsti and James Rosenau found widespread pessimism on several points. Institutionally, a majority of their more than 1,000 respondents agreed that the inevitability of executive-legislative conflict "negates" the likelihood of an effective foreign policy. In general, those surveyed felt that the political system was "poorly suited to conduct limited war" and that the American people "are lacking in

*Portions of the next 8 pages are adapted from James Nathan, "The Roots of the Imperial Presidency," *Presidential Studies Quarterly*, January, 1975, by permission of the publisher.

two important requisites for a sound foreign policy—patience and an understanding of the role of power in world politics." Or as Hans Morgenthau once concluded:

> The kind of thinking required for the successful conduct of foreign policy must at times be diametrically opposed to the kind of consideration by which the masses and their representatives are likely to be moved.[5]

In their skepticism of public wisdom in foreign affairs, social scientists are companions to observers and practitioners of foreign policy. "Public ignorance," wrote Thomas Halper, "persists like a winter cold."[6] An early excavation of the public's intellectual resources in foreign affairs was conducted by political scientist James Robinson, who found that "the vast majority of citizens hold pictures of the world that are at best sketchy, blurred and without detail or at worst, so impoverished as to beggar the imagination."[7] Public knowledge about foreign affairs in the early 1970s, despite augmented exposure offered by television, has not been increasing. One longitudinal study concluded: "Interests in, and knowledge about foreign affairs have seemingly made little inroad into the psychological field of . . . the bulk of the population."[8]

Further, it has been argued by social scientists as well as policy makers throughout the post–World War II period, that the public is volatile, swinging back and forth, not so much setting the boundaries of discourse and decisions as churlishly clubbing the unsuccessful or those who could be portrayed as unpatriotic. The classic study by Gabriel Almond in the 1950s asserted that "Americans tend to exhaust their emotional and intellectual energies in private pursuits. . . . On questions . . . such as foreign policy, they tend to react in formless and plastic moods which undergo frequent alteration."[9] Only within the last decade have analysts seen any necessity to reappraise and qualify Almond's portrait.[10]

Insofar as this uncharitable view of the American public holds, the argument for an attempt by responsible leaders to be wary of candor is strong. The view encourages an attempt to see to it that information is structured so at least the damage can be minimized. Since a negotiation might be compromised if the public were incapable of real understanding of some of the ambiguities of an agreement, perhaps a secret accord would be best. This is, after all, one of the fillips to the decline of formal treaties submitted to Senate debate and a partial explanation of the concurrent rise of executive agreements. Even if the public mood were thought sluggishly stable, as some recent evidence suggests,[11] there is still an argument that the public cannot make judgments: "In the quicksilver world of international politics," Thomas Halper argued, "the public is concerned about situations which have ceased to exist. . . . Information, once accurate, becomes obsolete, and consequently, erroneous . . . the results . . . may be even more deleterious than . . . no information at all."[12]

Since the margin of error in foreign affairs is often so small and the consequences of error potentially catastrophic, temptations abound to restrict public access to information—even if it could be comprehended and even if it did not jeopardize secrets. As a 1960s version of one classic civics book explained: "The reason is clear. In a time of international tensions and crisis, democracies *must act*. . . . The methods we use may flout ideals of responsibility and popular control, but they seem to be a part of the price we must pay for living in a disorderly world of sovereign nations."[13] Or as a Kennedy press aide put it at the height of the Cuban missile crisis, the government had a "right, indeed the duty, to lie."[14]

Clearly such views of the capacities and inclinations of the American people have serious implications for American foreign policy and the democracy whose interests that foreign policy is to protect and advance. Though by no means a direct or "pure" democracy in which all the people participate directly in all the decisions that affect their lives, a premise of a twentieth-century democratic system such as the United States purports to have is that people are capable of understanding their interests and of forming reasonable judgments concerning the wisdom of policies associated with those interests. In addition, those officials directly engaged in the formulation and conduct of foreign policy are to represent the interests of and be accountable to the citizenry. If, however, one assumes that the people are incapable of knowing and of making informed judgments concerning their interests and prone to irrational and unpredictable behavior regarding international affairs, then strict adherence to democratic norms of accountability by public officials may no longer be prudent.

Assessment of this dilemma requires attention to several ques-

tions and problems. Are the American people benighted and belli-
cose when it comes to grasping the nature of international affairs?
Apart from the knowledgeability of the public, what is the character
of the relationship between those who formulate and conduct foreign
policy and the public they represent? Thus two distinct though
obviously related issues must be explored: (1) the constraints imposed by the public on policy makers and (2) the approach toward the
public adopted by public officials, especially the President, who has
been the focus of foreign policy making since the Second World War.
In this relationship lies the crux of the practical and philosophical
questions under review in this and the following chapters.

THE AMERICAN PUBLIC AND THE WORLD

The evidence concerning public knowledgeability is not always con-
clusive. One is never sure whether the glass of water that one is
examining is half full or half empty. Judgments are frequently rooted
in the judge's prejudices concerning the issues on which the public is
being tested. Responses by the public have varied with the wording
of a question or the placement of a question relative to other questions in an interview schedule. Thus respondents have favored increases in defense spending when asked about the issue in isolation
from other programs, but when placed in the context of competing
programs such as education, sentiment for cutting defense
emerges.[15] Finally, in any analysis of public opinion on foreign
policy, it is useful to distinguish between the knowledge of specific
events and issues possessed by the public and their more general
attitudes toward American involvement in world politics. This distinction is especially important in understanding the relationship
between the public and policy elites.

The Knowledgeability of the Public:
Who Knows What?

Judgments concerning the knowledgeability of the public are complicated by the agreement among public opinion analysts that it is not
very useful to view the public as a monolith. It is common to distin-

guish between "mass publics," "attentive publics," and "opinion leaders." Unfortunately, there is disagreement among analysts as to what portion of the public falls into which of these categories and as to how to define the boundaries of the categories.

One recent analysis[16] suggests that perhaps 30 percent of the American public should be grouped as the "mass public." These people have very low levels of knowledge about anything but the most obvious and dramatic foreign developments. Their opinions are poorly formed and very inconsistent. A larger group, perhaps 45 percent, constitutes the "attentive public" and is made up of people with some general knowledge of international affairs. However, the knowledge of this group is not deep; their attitudes are not always consistent; and the intensity of their views is frequently weak. Finally, the "opinion leaders" are those with high levels of knowledge, consistent views, and attitudes that are held with considerable intensity. This group makes up about 25 percent of the population, and perhaps 1 to 2 percent of them are the most active in public affairs within their communities or on the national level.[17]

If we keep these distinctions in mind, some of the often contradictory findings on public knowledge of foreign affairs may become somewhat clearer. In 1964, for example, a cross-section of American people were asked, "Do you happen to know if there is a communist government in China now?" Twenty-eight percent confessed they did not know.[18] But whether this is cause for despair is not certain. After all, about 70 percent gave the correct answer. Similar ambiguities attend other efforts to assert a persistent inability of Americans to make reasoned judgments based on minimal information. In an American Institute of Public Opinion (AIPO) poll in May 1950 that asked, "Will you tell me offhand what the Marshall Plan is?", 63 percent of respondents answered "reasonably correctly." Yet only 5 percent could give meaningful answers to a related question about the term "Point 4."[19] Similarly, items presented in an important study by Free and Cantril to demonstrate public ignorance about foreign affairs show that an "astounding" 28 percent of the public could not identify the acronym "NATO" in 1964.[20] Yet the researchers might have noted that, on the other hand, an equally "astounding" 72 percent of the population could. It would seem, then, that drastic conclusions based on any single item would be hasty.

Nonetheless, failure to recognize often obscure information or perform esoteric operations is sometimes used as proof of public incapacity. At this point we would ask if our readers can spell the name of the late Swedish Secretary General of the United Nations? If our readers cannot correctly spell D-A-G   H-A-M-M-A-R-S-K-J-O-L-D, they should not despair, for they are in the company of 99 percent of the adult population who were asked to perform the same task in a 1953 effort to demonstrate the public's ignorance about foreign affairs. Still, in the 1960s, nearly 60 percent of the public could correctly identify Mao Zedong as the leader of Communist China; only 2 of 557 respondents in a Detroit study said that Russia had not developed and tested its own atomic weapons; and in 1960, 96 percent of the public had heard of the U-2 incident.[21]

By the late 1960s, after a decade of intense national preoccupation with foreign affairs, research emerged that people's knowledge was not all that insignificant. More important, individuals seemed to possess fairly firm and complex belief systems, which they could, with some acuity, match against parties, politicians, or a single issue.[22] Yet at the end of his professional life, V. O. Key, one of the founders of the study of voting and political behavior, after studying the data, nevertheless despaired with his colleagues that it was now a "perverse and unorthodox argument" to hold "that voters are not fools. . . . In the large[,] the electorate behaves about as rationally and responsibly as we should expect given the clarity of the alternatives presented to it and the character of the information available."[23]

Findings concerning the knowledgeability and attitudes of the young are no less perplexing. One systematic study of youth attitudes and information about national and international politics in the late 1960s and early 1970s detected no significant differences from their predecessors in the range, richness, or intensity of their views.[24] At the same time, nobody has doubted in recent years that among young people—those under 30—political consciousness has slipped from its peak in the Vietnam era. Explanations include the pervasiveness of television, the breakdown of families, poor school instruction, and a composite malaise consisting of marijuana, narcissism, and permissiveness. Moreover, recent tests of college students' grasp of world politics conducted by the Council on Learning and the Educational Testing Service concluded that perhaps 90 percent of college students have an "inadequate" grasp of world affairs. Fewer than a third of the 3,000 students who took the test understood recent global population trends and patterns of world energy consumption or could answer satisfactorily questions concerned with global politics, security, nutrition and health, and world cultures and religions. On the other hand, questions have been raised about the validity of the test itself, in that many of the areas tested are devoid of consensus among experts.[25]

In the final analysis, one is unsure of the meaningfulness of any assessments of youthful activity and attitudes when, in terms of voting and political participation, most political activity occurs after the age of 30. The same problem exists more broadly, for electoral participation seems to be increasingly confined to those in the upper reaches of the attentive public and the quarter of the population that consists of the opinion leaders. That 40 percent or more of the population is thereby excluded from the most basic form of participation is no comfort for the democrat. But if the 50 percent or more of the population that does participate possesses more than minimal levels of knowledge and consistency of belief systems, then the picture cannot be regarded as entirely bleak.

For adults, with some years of care about families, incomes, and taxes, public events seem increasingly well heeded. For this reason, the network evening news has expanded from 15 minutes in the 1950s to at least 30 minutes, and 1 hour broadcasts by the mid-1980s seem likely. One could justifiably be concerned about the quality of much local news coverage—the fires, murders, and "happy talk." But at the time of the Afghanistan crisis in late 1979, when Carter was proclaiming his doctrine for the Persian Gulf, network news was achieving its highest weekly ratings since ratings have been kept. CBS alone estimated that an average of 13.3 million homes witnessed the nightly narratives of events in Southwest Asia and the Middle East. Hence when the occasion is significant, it is hard to argue that the public averts its gaze.

A Belligerent Beast?

But even if the public is granted some capacity for attention, analysis, and retention of information, are they overreactive and churlish?

Perhaps if belligerence were an indelible feature of the American psyche, news and information would have to be managed, lest the consequences be an orgy of rage ending in catastrophe. But it is not evident that the public's volatility of opinion is dramatically greater than the mood changes of opinion leaders such as Presidents, pundits, and politicians. By and large, during the course of the cold war, the public reacted cautiously to some rather pronounced swings between optimism and despair about the future of great power relations on the part of public officials.[26] Poll data collected between 1949 and 1969 by William Caspary and John Mueller show from 60 to 80 percent of the American people consistently voicing support or at least acceptance of the necessity for active American involvement in world affairs.[27] In the wake of Vietnam, such sentiment was replaced by a much more complex internationalism, which we explore later. But when the public mood has changed, it has not been with the suddenness with which Jimmy Carter confessed to ABC interviewer Frank Reynolds on New Year's Day, 1980:

> My opinion of the Russians has changed [more] drastically in the last week than even the previous two and a half years before that. It's only now dawning on the world the magnitude of the action that the Soviets undertook in invading Afghanistan.[28]

Still, if there is any basis for Kennan's fear of a people roused to a beastly wrath when their interests are in jeopardy, then the case for the careful parceling of information in times of crisis or potential crisis can be compelling. But an examination of the data yields uncertainty concerning the classic fears that Americans were too pacifist in peace and too belligerent in war.[29]

It was certainly this official perception and fear that drove much of American foreign policy during Vietnam. Indeed, Dean Rusk once told one of the present authors that it was the proudest achievement of his years in public office that the national security policy making establishment did not "make the eagle scream." Robert McNamara echoed this sentiment when he told an interviewer:

> The greatest contribution Vietnam is making—right or wrong beside the point—is . . . an ability . . . to go to war without the necessity of

arousing public ire. In that sense, Vietnam is almost a necessity of our history, because it is the kind of war we'll most likely be facing for the next fifty years.[30]

Yet when American involvement finally ended with the embarrassing collapse of the American client, the popular reaction was not the upheaval and "divisive and destructive debate" feared by Johnson and every administration from the beginning of American engagement with Vietnam.[31] The recriminations were largely confined to President Ford's trying to shift blame for the final collapse onto Congress. The attention of the American people, on the other hand, was focused on the inflationary effects of presidential mismanagement of the wartime economy by Presidents Johnson and Nixon.

In the postwar period, Americans have usually rejected rash solutions and quick fixes. Even in the darkest days of the Korean War, Americans rejected by a margin of three to one the use of atomic weapons. Similarly, when asked, "Do you think the United States should start an all-out war with Communist China or not?" only 14 percent of those polled wanted war.[32] With 500,000 troops suffering heavy casualties in Vietnam, Americans were asked in 1967 and 1968 to agree or disagree with the statement: "Some people say we should go all out to win a military victory in Vietnam, using atom bombs or other atomic weapons." Sixty-five percent disagreed.[33] Finally, all through the 1979–1981 hostage crisis in Iran, there was never a majority favoring the use of force. Diplomatic solutions were preferred by margins of 20 percent or more. And when an accord was signed with the Iranians for release of the hostages in exchange for remitting frozen Iranian bank accounts, less than 10 percent of the public favored a vengeful military retort. This moderation persisted despite the ill treatment of many of the Americans, despite any obvious necessity of honoring an agreement signed under duress, and despite public antipathy to Iran and a deep sense of humiliation over the crisis.[34]

Rather than bellicosity, the American public throughout much of the cold war might be considered as pliant and generally supportive of international involvement, especially to the appeal of success. As Professor John E. Mueller noted, opposition to the wars of Korea and Vietnam was largely a function of casualties. Americans generally support what works. If escalation means a success that is identifiable, and American losses remain low, the public acquiesces. If withdrawal can be called a success, then this too receives support. Ralph B. Levering has recently summarized the Korean War period thus:

> Most Americans . . . consistently wanted an end to American involvement in war. The majority of Americans in 1951 and 1952 considered entering the war a mistake, wanted to pull American troops out of Korea as fast as possible and supported numerous proposals to achieve a negotiated peace. . . . Proposals for a compromise peace were [also] popular.[35]

Notwithstanding the public urge to oppose communism, which has been a constant in post–World War II public opinion, there also seems to persist an intense desire to experiment with any formula that might bring about peaceful resolution of disputes with the Soviets. This disposition to seek diplomatic settlements is not confined to the starker frictions of Soviet-American relations. It extends to the conflicts that are symbolic of East-West relations as well. In May 1953, when asked about sending help to the French, then besieged in Vietnam by the forces of Ho Chi Minh, who was generally thought by Americans to be an "Asian Stalin," 56 percent were against sending any American troops.[36] On the eve of the Cuban missile crisis, when CIA operations against Castro were at their height and anti-Castro sentiments were a major issue of the upcoming congressional campaign, a clear majority (65 percent) opposed an invasion of Cuba to rid the United States of this nuisance.[37] Similarly, in those arenas that bear directly on the U.S.–Soviet strategic contest, relatively few Americans are anxious for conflict. Thus at the onset of the 1970s, albeit a time of officially proclaimed detente, large majorities favored cooperation with the Soviet Union concerning: limiting antimissile systems, exploring outer space and the oceans, educational and cultural exchange, expanded trade, and even combining U.S. and Soviet efforts to control the spread of nuclear weapons and the outbreak of war in Europe and Asia.[38] And in 1982, a majority of the American people responded positively to the idea of a nuclear weapons freeze between the U.S. and the Soviet Union despite months of effort by the Reagan administration to portray the Soviet Union as untrustworthy regarding strategic arms negotiations and agreements.

At the same time, presidential initiatives or actions in the direction of belligerence can take sizable pluralities and majorities with it—at least in the short run. Presidential popularity and approval ratings rise at moments of crisis. Truman at the onset of Korea, Eisenhower during the Quemoy and Matsu crises and when he sent marines to Lebanon, Kennedy during the Bay of Pigs invasion and the Cuban missile crisis, Johnson and Nixon at various crisis points during the Vietnam period, and Ford during the *Mayaguez* crisis—all benefited from a surge in public support. But popular support receded in every case, and there is evidence that with each succeeding crisis of the cold war and Vietnam periods, the moment of heightened public support has grown shorter.[39]

Finally, if Americans are responsive to presidential initiative, it does not follow that this translates into unbridled belligerence. All the peace moves of the cold war have found public acceptance. Professor Rita Simon of the University of Illinois has called attention to a January 1948 poll that indicated that "78 percent thought the United States ought to halt its production of atomic bombs even before an international control agency was established."[40] Fear of public retribution has stymied previous administrations' overtures to communist powers, but the American people have invariably favored summit meetings with Soviet leaders. The polls do not reflect any significant ebbing of support throughout the cold war for high-level talks with any Russian head of state.[41] During the cold war, 75 percent of the public approved the Korean armistice, and over 65 percent supported both the Limited Test Ban Treaty and the Nuclear Non-Proliferation Treaty.[42] At the peak of the Quemoy and Matsu crises and in the early period of the Vietnam War, there was strong popular sentiment for a compromise solution—either UN arbitration or, in the case of Vietnam, a coalition government.[43] And even when the effects of Arab oil price rises led many officials in early 1975 publicly and seriously to examine the possibility of using force in the Persian Gulf, the American people opposed a military response by a margin of 10 to 1.[44] As Seymour Lipset notes, alongside the American urge to oppose communism, there also reposes an intense public desire to experiment with any formula, no matter how remote, that might bring peace.[45]

COMPLEX INTERNATIONALISM IN THE
1970s AND 1980s

The complex implications of the public's ambivalence toward military solutions to diplomatic difficulties combined with its broad internationalism are apparent in the difficulty the Carter administration faced in trying to respond to events and vocal elite critics of American military power in the late 1970s. Carter, his Secretary of State, State Department appointees, and segments of the public seemed, at the outset, to attempt to abandon part of the cold war repertory, moving away from an emphasis on the use of force. But Carter's administration also included a National Security Adviser, Zbigniew Brzezinski, who confessed, at the end of his tenure, that turning the country again toward preparedness was both his "overriding goal" and his most significant achievement. In addition, there was a clamoring on the right, a vocal, highly organized, and well-funded establishment of the once reigning "national security managers." Their advocacy of military preparedness was in turn echoed by many opinion leaders and members of the attentive public.

On November 11, 1976, a working group of 141 prominent postwar policy figures announced at the National Press Club a "Committee on the Present Danger." In the following years, the committee offered elite decision makers, Congress, and the press a reservoir of papers, pamphlets, and studies advocating a massive conventional and strategic buildup to match the committee's perception of the threat in the early to middle 1980s of an "overwhelming preponderance of power" being constructed by the Soviets worldwide.[46] This remarkable constellation of former public officials aligned themselves with organized labor, ethnicity, and traditional virtues and values, and argued on ideological grounds that the cold war was still the basic characteristic of world politics. This reconstituted cold war internationalism not only feared burgeoning Soviet military prowess but also the tendency of the Carter administration to appeal to an embryonic post-Vietnam public opinion about the necessity of diminishing the role of force in American foreign policy.

At the other end of the spectrum, a smaller and less well endowed organization called "New Directions" was formed to advance a more liberal and cooperative version of internationalism. But these proponents of adapting to and working within the constraints of interdependence were never to achieve the prominence of the Committee on the Present Danger. For by the beginning of the 1980s, the complex internationalism that had emerged from the Vietnam era began to coalesce around a more assertive posture.

Complex Internationalism

The positions represented by the Committee on the Present Danger and New Directions reflect a spectrum of internationalist sentiment evident by the mid-1970s. Whereas earlier in the decade the trauma of Vietnam had moved many Americans, perhaps a majority, to a posture frequently characterized as neo-isolationist, distance from the Vietnam experience reveals a more complex set of attitudes. By the mid-1970s, public opinion analysis began to reveal that the American people had retained their historic internationalist posture, though at lower levels than at its peak prior to Vietnam.[47] The internationalism of the late 1970s, however, was divided between a liberal, cooperative or "nonmilitary" internationalism (perhaps 25 percent of the population) and a more conservative, competitive, or "military" internationalism (perhaps a third of the population).[48] The remainder of the population can be identified as noninternationalist. This remainder is not isolationist as much as it is simply indifferent toward foreign policy questions most of the time. This group does, however, hold attitudes that make it a more likely ally of the conservative internationalists when the noninternationalists' attention is stimulated by world affairs.

The opinions and attitudes of liberal internationalists tend to cluster around support for essentially nonaggressive and cooperative forms of international engagement. Resort to various economic instruments such as economic aid, development assistance, and arms control, and strengthening of various international cooperative organizations such as the United Nations and related agencies tend to be preferred by liberal internationalists. Conservative internationalists are no less supportive of world involvement but tend to emphasize the enduring character of Soviet-American competition, the salience of military instruments, and the imperatives of more aggressive intervention abroad to advance American economic and political interests and leadership. Noninternationalists, when pressed as to their attitudes toward the world, reveal a preoccupation with power and strength akin to that advanced by conservative internationalists. However, unlike conservative internationalists, noninternationalists have little enthusiasm for entanglement with the world: "Noninternationalists want the United States to be strong and independent— not interdependent."[49] Michael Mandelbaum and William Schneider have summarized the three positions:

> Clearly, what conservative internationalists favored was *U.S. world leadership itself*, no matter what the area of endeavor. Liberals were much more selective in their responses and tended to favor world leadership in some areas (avoiding war, achieving scientific progress) but not in others (moral values, military strength). Noninternationalists tended to support U.S. world leadership in areas of "strength" (economic strength, military strength, standard of living) and in the avoidance of war but not in areas of cooperation, aid, and alliance with other countries.[50]

At the time of Jimmy Carter's 1976 campaign, this mix of attitudes was as yet unfocused. Carter succeeded, through vague references to rekindling the moral spirit of American foreign policy, in appealing to ideals common to most Americans. Such a position was sufficiently abstract to appeal to all segments of an internationalist but badly split public. Once in office, however, Carter found his administration splayed across contradictory rhetoric and policies designed, in part, to sustain his appeal to a cleaved internationalist consensus.

The Carter administration's often contradictory rhetoric and policy initiatives were also, however, a reflection of a no less fractured elite view of international reality. Holsti and Rosenau's survey of American elite opinion on foreign affairs was conducted as the Carter administration entered office and revealed an elite opinion structure that corresponded closely to that revealed in analyses of general public opinion in the middle to late 1970s. As Holsti put it in his 1979 presidential address to the International Studies Association, American elites represented a kind of three-headed eagle on foreign policy: one, the cold war internationalists, looking back to the axioms of the cold war for its bearings; the second, the post–cold war internationalists, concerned primarily with the new issues of North-South politics and global political economics as well as a preoccupation with the problems of strategic arms control; and a third, the isolationists, who tended to look inward to the problems of American society, maintaining that American security and influence in the world were ultimately a function of America's ability to tend to its own garden rather than meddling in those of their neighbors to the east or south.[51]

The internationalists agreed on the necessity of sustaining American international involvement in the face of an essentially expansionist Soviet Union. However, about half of the internationalists, the post–cold war internationalists, were ambivalent concerning a continuation of the cold war internationalist's commitment to an active containment of communism, especially if it entailed the use of force and intervention of the sort undertaken during the run-up to the Vietnam War. Internationalists of both types were convinced of the operation of some kind of domino theory in which American difficulties or defeats could be seen as encouraging additional instability. But the post–cold war internationalists were not persuaded that such instability inevitably worked against the interests of the U.S., given their belief that revolutionary activity was not necessarily inspired by or beneficial to communism. Rather, in this post–cold war internationalist view, the major threats to American security grew out of the agenda of new issues that emerged during the 1970s: world political economics, energy, the environment, and law of the sea. Here, rather than the cold war internationalist focus on East-West strategic issues was the post–cold war internationalist locus of activism—an activism in which international organizations would play an important role.

In contrast with this bifurcated internationalism, there are the isolationists who denigrate the bipolar view of the world and the notion that the Soviet Union is bent on expansion and the provocation of nuclear war. The Third World, with its poverty and anti-Western resentment, is seen as inevitably unstable, but essentially beyond the influence of the West as long as the non-West is not prepared to act on its own behalf. From this perspective the United States can export neither democracy nor development. In any event, the isolationists argue, the real threats to American security are domestic and must be tended to if American influence is to be extended.

Of perhaps greatest significance for the future of elite opinion on foreign and national security affairs, it would appear that the differences in perspective that exist are not generational. That is, those who retain an allegiance to the axioms of the cold war era are not necessarily of an older generation than those who express a post–cold war internationalism. In fact, Holsti and Rosenau's research suggests greater differences within generational groupings than between them. Rather than being a function of age, differences on foreign affairs within American elites seem to have more to do with occupation; business and military leaders appear to be more prone to cold war internationalism; those in the media, education, and the clergy and some Foreign Service Officers more likely to adhere to post–cold war internationalism; and labor leaders most likely to be isolationist.[52] Similar findings have resulted from studies of the American population as a whole.[53]

One implication of these findings is that American public opinion—both mass publics and the elite sector–is cleaved by contradictory views of international reality and an appropriate U.S. response to the world. Constructing and, more important, maintaining a consensus behind a course of action—an essential condition in the view of many students of American foreign policy[54]—is likely to remain a demanding task in the 1980s. Yet even as this inference was being drawn concerning public opinion,[55] poll data began to show what appeared to be precisely the opposite: a crystallizing of public opinion around "a much more assertive, or hawkish, posture in world affairs, . . . a widespread determination to rebuild American military capabilities and to reaffirm a readiness to use those capabilities in defense of perceived interests abroad."[56]

A New Internationalism?

Late 1979 seemed to mark the coalescence of new concern about America's defense posture. Confronted with Afghanistan, the hostage seizure in Tehran, and, at times, near hysteria in semiofficial and official policy circles regarding the Soviet threat, much of the public seemed to have concluded that, despite what it may have wished in the wake of the Vietnam war, the cold war had returned. The Gallup organization asked in February 1980, "Ten years from now, do you think the U.S should be playing a more important and powerful role as a world leader, a less important role, or about the same as it plays today?" Fifty-five percent of the 1,111 registered voters responding preferred a more assertive role. A similar response was given by 47 percent of the sample polled by the Chicago Council on Foreign Relations in 1978 and 33 percent in 1974.[57] In mid-1978, 53 percent of respondents in a CBS News/*New York Times* poll replied that the U.S. should toughen its posture toward the Soviets and on defense spending, 60 percent supported an increase in defense spending before the Iranian crisis in the fall of 1979, with support increasing to 76 percent in March of 1980. Ten years earlier a majority of the people could be found who felt that defense spending was too high.[58] In the words of Lloyd Free and William Watts, a "defense-oriented internationalism had come of age."[59]

The mid-1970s, as opinion analysts Free and Watts noted, were a "watershed period."[60] It was a time of reevaluation. Especially after Watergate and Vietnam, there was potential within the body politic and among opinion makers to choose a new direction. The attentive public as well as the elites displayed a qualified acceptance of continued U.S. military intervention. A mid-1970s survey of American corporate executives conducted by Professor Bruce Russett found that a majority believed that the commitment of U.S ground troops in Vietnam was incorrect, bad for the economy, and bad for American social and political institutions. Furthermore, only in the cases of West Germany and Mexico did a majority favor U.S. military intervention in the event of an armed attack by communist forces.[61]

By 1980, however, support for the use of American troops in Europe to defend vital interests had increased from a low of 30 percent in 1973–1975 to an average of 65 percent by the spring of 1980.[62] By 1978, 42 percent of the business community was willing to use troops in the Mideast in case of an oil cutoff, and other opinion leaders were only 5 to 7 points behind on this issue. In contrast, in 1974 the overall percentage of the elite willing to use force in such contingencies stood at only 22 percent.[63] When the Soviets were introduced into the oil/U.S. security equation, an overwhelming percentage of the Harris poll respondents of January and February

1980—some 75 percent—agreed with the "Carter Doctrine"—that force, if necessary, should be used to protect the oil fields. [64]

Free and Watts's longitudinal data concerning the continuum of internationalist/isolationist opinion in America in the 1970s seemed to summarize the situation on the threshold of the 1980s. Free and Watts note that

> to qualify as "completely internationalist" a respondent has to disagree with the notions that the United States should go its own way, mind its own business, and concentrate more on national problems, while agreeing that the United States should cooperate with the United Nations, take into account the views of its allies, come to the defense of Japan and Western Europe. To be classified as 'completely isolationist,' a respondent must give precisely the opposite answer.

Their findings are presented in Table 6.1.

Table 6.1.   Internationalist/Isolationist Trends, 1972–1980

Opinion	1972	1974	1976	1980
Internationalist	56%	41%	44%	61%
Mixed	35%	38%	33%	26%
Isolationist	9%	21%	23%	13%

Source: Lloyd Free and William Watts, "Internationalism Comes of Age . . . Again," Public Opinion, April/May 1980, pp. 48–49, especially Figure 1, p. 49. Used by permission.

Significantly, the internationalist total was by 1980 the highest it had been since the early 1960s.

To conservative internationalists the new mood was welcome. But to George Kennan, who, 30 years before, had decried mass hysteria in America's dealings with the Russians, the "war atmosphere in Washington" at the beginning of 1980 was clearly the responsibility of the policy making establishment. He despaired:

> Never since World War II has there been so far-reaching a militarization of thought and discourse in the capital. An unsuspecting stranger, plunged into its midst, could only conclude that the last hope of peaceful, nonmilitary solutions had been exhausted—that from now on only weapons, however used, could count. We are now in the danger zone. [65]

Nonetheless, even conservative analysts were uncertain as to whether this mood reflected a new consensus upon which a new cold war internationalism could be based. It was noted, for example, that though support for getting tougher with the Soviets, increased defense spending, unleashing the CIA, and defending traditional allies had all increased to encompass majorities of the American people, ambiguities remained. Thus as the Soviet invasion of Afghanistan and the shock of the hostage seizure receded, public support for using force in the region subsided. Within six weeks, fewer than 20 percent of the public were reported willing to use military force in either Afghanistan or Iran. Only in the immediate wake of Carter's advocacy of using force in the Persian Gulf if necessary to protect U.S. interests could bare majorities (52 percent) be found supporting such a move. Here again, within weeks a majority could be found advocating economic and other approaches rather than a resort to force. Simultaneously, domestic issues began to assume more importance than foreign affairs in polls testing issue salience among the American people.[66] Moreover, in the midst of deteriorating relations with the Soviet Union during the early Reagan administration and increasing defense budgets, the American public, in numbers and with an intensity that surprised most observers, seemed to support the idea of a nuclear freeze.

The new internationalism did not, therefore, flow from a wellspring of animus and bellicosity stored in the American collective mind. It emerged, instead, from a congruence of events that seemed to confirm the projections of conservative or cold war internationalist Cassandras of preparedness, and it was encouraged by a Carter administration desperately scrambling after the movement of conservative opinion. The return to military means was a process of public reaction that moved from a yearning for respite, to bewilderment, to frustration, and then to angry determination to reassert American credibility at arms in the face of humiliation in Teheran. Hence the appearance of an American capacity to orchestrate force, no matter how problematic the outcome, seemed the minimum precondition of any foreign policy or, in the presidential debate of 1980, an instrument for explaining domestic priorities. Even if force was not seen as relevant to a great range of problems, especially on the part of liberal internationalists, the renascent centrality of the issue of Soviet power seems to have confirmed a reinvigorated foreign policy program that called for a trillion dollar buildup by the mid-1980s. It was more than simply the portent of Soviet power and the possibility of slipping to a position of parity with Soviet arms prowess that seemed to drive American opinion to a firmer embrace of military instruments. The new assertiveness in the 1980 election campaign fed on itself as candidates Carter and Reagan sought to outdo one another in their assessments of the security challenge before the United States in the 1980s.

Moreover, it proved to be potent electoral politics for Ronald Reagan, because it allowed him to form a coalition of conservative internationalists—long desirous of reasserting American strength, leadership, and involvement—and noninternationalists, attracted to the prospect of the reestablishment of American strength and independence. It remains to be seen whether the coalition can be sustained if the conservative internationalist penchant for intervention becomes policy in the 1980s. It is perhaps significant that the Reagan adminstration found it extremely difficult to rally any broad and deep public support for its backing of an El Salvadoran regime that seems incapable of survival without ever-escalating levels of U.S. support and was caught completely by surprise by the nuclear freeze movement.

Internationalism has indeed reasserted itself in the late 1970s and early 1980s. But it seems premature to conclude as some analysts have that "leadership has much to build on in its efforts to forge a consistent foreign policy, [it] can count on most Americans to view the world beyond our shores with considerable realism and maturity."[67] Americans may indeed view the world with realism and maturity, but it need not follow that "realism and maturity" means support for a return to the 1960s kind of activism, interventionism and strategic confrontation. Indeed, by the end of 1981, three out of four Americans supported George Kennan's proposed 50 percent mutual reduction in nuclear weapons. The plan, reported George Gallup, received solid support in all regions, classes, and in both parties.[68] Thus the Reagan administration's assertion of a mandate from the 1980 election may constitute a too simple judgment on an election in which the President received the explicit support of only about 27 percent of those eligible to vote. The public outlook at the onset of the 1980s, wrote public opinion analysts Daniel Yankelovich and Larry Kagan, may

> make it easy for the Reagan Administration to win support for bold assertive initiatives, but much more difficult to shape a consensus behind policies that involve compromise, subtlety, patience, restrained gestures, prior consultation with allies, and the deft geopolitical maneuvering that is required when one is no longer the world's preeminent locus of military and economic power.[69]

The public mood was in large measure shaped by an officially inspired nostalgia for the time when the United States was such a preeminent power. However, a combination of changed international circumstances, deep cross-currents in public sentiments, and the shift in elite and public opinion might well augur, as Samuel Huntington recently warned, an opening for "dramatic initiatives, dramatic achievements and dramatic disasters."[70]

NOTES

1. Louis Halle, *Dream and Reality: Aspects of American Foreign Policy* (New York: Harper, 1959), p. 155.

2. George Kennan, *American Diplomacy, 1900–1950* (New York: New American World Library, 1959), p. 59.

3. George Liska, *Imperial America: The International Politics of Primacy* (Baltimore: Johns Hopkins University Press, 1967), p. 18.

4. Roger Hilsman, *To Move a Nation* (Garden City, N.Y.: Doubleday, 1967), cited in John McDermitt, "Crisis Manager," *New York Review of Books* 14 September 1967, p. 8.

5. Hans J. Morgenthau, *American Foreign Policy: A Critical Examination* (London: Methuen, 1952), p. 223; and Ole Holsti and James Rosenau, "Vietnam, Consensus, and the Belief Systems of American Leaders," *World Politics* 32 (October 1979): 46–47.

6. Thomas Halper, *Foreign Policy Crises: Appearance and Reality in Decision Making* (Columbus, Ohio: Charles E. Merrill, 1971), pp. 18–19.

7. James P. Robinson, *Public Information About World Affairs* (Ann Arbor, Mich.: Institute for Social Research, 1967), p. 1.

8. "Dark Areas of Ignorance Revisited—Current Knowledge About Asian Affairs," in Dan Nimmo and Charles Bonjean, eds., *Political Attitudes and Public Opinion* (New York: David McKay, 1972), pp. 267–273.

9. Gabriel Almond, *The American People and Foreign Policy* (New York: Praeger, 1954), p. 53.

10. Recent summary analyses include: Barry B. Hughes, *The Domestic Context of American Foreign Policy* (San Francisco: Freeman, 1978), pp. 21–56; Michael Mandelbaum and William Schneider, "The New Internationalisms," in Kenneth A. Oye, Donald Rothchild, and Robert J. Leiber, eds., *Eagle Entangled: U.S. Foreign Policy in a Complex World* (New York: Longman, 1979); and Daniel Yankelovich and Larry Kagan, "Assertive America," *Foreign Affairs* 57, no. 3 (1981).

11. William Caspary, "The Mood Theory: A Study in Public Opinion and Foreign Policy," *American Political Science Review* 64 (June 1970): 536–547.

12. Halper, op. cit., p. 19.

13. James MacGregor Burns and Jack W. Peltason, *Government by the People*, 7th ed. (Englewood Cliffs, N.J.: Prentice-Hall, 1969), p. 500 (emphasis in original).

14. Paul N. McCloskey, Jr., *Truth and Untruth: Political Deceit in America* (New York: Simon and Schuster, 1972), pp. 47, 216–232. Sylvester's comments are in his editorial in the *Saturday Evening Post*, 18 November 1967, p. 10. Actually, "False, fictitious or fraudulent statements of representations" by officials in areas of their jurisdiction is a federal crime punishable by fine and up to 5 years' imprisonment: U.S. Code, Title 18, Section 1000.

15. See the discussion in Mandelbaum and Schneider, op. cit., no. 5, pp. 87–88.

16. Hughes, op. cit., pp. 23–25.

17. For another categorization, see James Rosenau, *Public Opinion and Foreign Policy* (New York: Random House, 1961).

18. A. T. Steele, *The American People and China* (New York: McGraw-Hill, 1966), p. 257.

19. R. J. Simon, *Public Opinion in America, 1936–1970* (Chicago: Rand McNally, 1974), p. 184.

20. Lloyd A. Free and Hadley Cantril, *The Political Beliefs of Americans* (New Brunswick, N.J.: Rutgers University Press, 1968), p. 60.

21. Robinson, op. cit., p. 2.

22. A good summary of this literature can be found in Henry T. Reynolds, *Politics and the Common Man: An Introduction to Political Behavior* (Homewood, Ill.: Dorsey Press, 1974), pp. 182–189.

23. V. O. Key, Jr., *The Responsible Electorate* (Cambridge, Mass.: Harvard University Press, 1966), pp. 7–8.

24. James A. Nathan, *International Socialization*, unpublished doctoral dissertation, John Hopkins University, School of Advanced International Studies, Washington, D.C., 1972.

25. See *The New York Times*, 16 April 1981; the *Washington Post*, 16 April 1981; and the editorial in the *Post*, "Flunking the Global Test."

26. For comparison of leading columnists' opinions and the public mood regarding Soviet-American relations in the 1950s, see James A. Nathan, "Detente, the Public and the Pundits," unpublished paper, Washington Center for Foreign Policy Analysis, Johns Hopkins University, Washington, D.C., 1965.

27. Caspary, op. cit.; and John Mueller, *War, Presidents and Public Opinion* (New York: Wiley, 1973).

28. *New York Times*, 1 January 1980.

29. See Walter Lippmann's classic statement in *The Public Philosophy* (New York: New American Library, 1955), pp. 24–25.

30. Cited by Douglas Kiker, "The Education of Robert McNamara," *Atlantic Monthly* 219, no.3 (March 1967): 53. For a discussion of the role played by the official perception of public opinion, see Leslie H. Gelb, "The Essential Domino: American Politics and Vietnam," *Foreign Affairs* 50, no. 3 (April 1972): 459–475.

31. Lyndon Johnson, *Vantage Point* (New York: Holt, Rinehart and Winston, 1971), p. 15; and Gelb, op. cit.

32. Mueller, op. cit., p. 176.

33. Ibid., p. 181. It should be noted that the data presented by Mueller were to buttress an argument different from the one we are advancing. Mueller's contention is that the public will essentially concur with almost any presidential initiative. To Mueller, the process is in two steps, is lasting, and can be dramatic. First, presidents convince the "attentive elite" by dramatic initiative, and then mass opinion inevitably follows. In general, however, Mueller believes that the Vietnam experience and even wars form less a part of support for an administration than economic variables, matters of style, and a general tendency of the public to lower their evaluation of Presidents as time passes. See pp. 224–241.

34. *New York Times*, 27 January 1981 and 3 February 1981.

35. Ralph B. Levering, *The Public and American Foreign Policy, 1918–1978* (New York: Morrow, 1978), pp. 102–103.

36. Ibid., p. 116.

37. Ibid., p. 117.

38. Hughes, op. cit., p. 36.

39. Jong R. Lee, "Rallying Around the Flag: Foreign Policy Events and Presidential Popularity," *Presidential Studies Quarterly* 7, no. 4 (Fall 1977): 254.

40. Simon, op. cit., p. 162.

41. Ibid., p. 155.

42. Harris Polls, 1 September 1963 and 10 October 1966.

43. Seymour Martin Lipset, "Doves, Hawks and the Polls," *Encounter* 27, no. 4 (October 1966): 40.

44. *Washington Post*, 26 January 1975, reporting a Gallup Poll of 25 January 1975.

45. Lipset, op. cit., p. 40.

46. Committee on the Present Danger, "Common Sense and the Common Danger," and "What Is the Soviet Union Up To?" 4 April 1977; John D. Watson, Jr., interview with Eugene V. Rostow, 31 May 1979; *Washington Star*, 4 April 1977; Committee on the Present Danger, "Is America Becoming Number 2?" 5 October 1978; Alan Tonelson, "Nitze's World," *Foreign Policy*, no. 35 (Summer 1979): 74–90; Robert Zelnick, "Paul Nitze: Nemesis of SALT II," *Washington Post*, 24 June 1979. For a comparison with the 1950 pressure group of the same name also spearheaded by Paul Nitze, see Samuel F. Wells, Jr., "Sounding the Tocsin: NSC 68 and the Soviet Threat," *Working Papers No. 7* (26 September 1979),

International Security Studies Program, The Wilson Center, Smithsonian Institution, Washington, D.C.

47. See Hughes, op. cit., p. 31; and John A. Reilly, ed. *American Public Opinion and Foreign Policy 1975* (Chicago: Chicago Council on Foreign Relations, 1975).
48. The terms "nonmilitary" and "military" are Hughes's, op. cit., p. 30. The liberal, conservative, and noninternationalists distinctions are originally drawn by Mandelbaum and Schneider, op. cit., and are based on Reilly's data.
49. Mandelbaum and Schneider, op. cit., p. 54.
50. Ibid. (emphasis in original).
51. Ole Holsti, "The Three-Headed Eagle: The United States and System Change," *International Studies Quarterly* 23 (September 1979): 339–343. The empirical and conceptual elaboration of Holsti's metaphor are to be found in a series of papers published by Holsti and James Rosenau. The most comprehensive of these and the two upon which the following survey rests are "Vietnam, Consensus, and the Belief Systems of American Leaders," op. cit., and "Cold War Axioms in the Post-Vietnam Era," in *Change in the International System*, ed. Holsti, R. Siverson and A. George (Boulder, Colo.: Westview Press, 1980), pp. 263–301.
52. Holsti and Rosenau, "Does Where You Stand Depend on When You Were Born?" *Public Opinion Quarterly* 44 (Spring 1980): 1–22.
53. See Mandelbaum and Schneider, op. cit. See also Lloyd Free and William Watts, "Internationalism Comes of Age . . . Again," *Public Opinion*, April/May 1980, pp. 46–50.
54. See for example, Alexander L. George, "Domestic Constraints on Regime Change in U.S. Foreign Policy: The Need for Policy Legitimacy," in Holsti, Siverson, and George, op. cit., pp. 233–262.
55. See Holsti and Rosenau, "Cold War Axioms . . .," op. cit., Michael Roskin, "From Pearl Harbor to Vietnam: Shifting Generational Paradigms," *Public Opinion Quarterly* 89 (Fall 1974): 563–588; Bruce Russett and Miroslau Nincic, "American Opinion on the Use of Military Force Abroad," *Public Opinion Quarterly* 91 (Fall 1976): 411–432; and the present authors' *U.S. Foreign Policy and World Order* (Boston: Little, Brown, 1976), pp. 574–580.
56. Russett and Donald R. Deluca, " 'Don't Tread On Me': Public Opinion and Foreign Policy in the Eighties," *Political Science Quarterly* 96 (Fall 1981): 382; and David Gergen, "The Hardening Mood Toward Foreign Policy," *Public Opinion*, February/March 1980, pp. 12–13.
57. *Newsweek*, 3 March 1980, p. 28.
58. See Gergen, op. cit., p. 12; and Russett and Deluca, op. cit., Table 1, p. 383.
59. Free and Watts, "Internationalism Comes of Age . . . Again," op. cit., p. 47.
60. Ibid., p. 49.
61. Bruce Russett and Betty C. Hanson, "How Corporate Executives See America's Role in the World," *Fortune*, May 1974, p. 165; and Bruce Russett, "The American's Retreat from World Power," mimeo, n.d., pp. 7–9.
62. "A Study of American Attitudes Towards Its Allies and the World," prepared for *Der Stern* by Louis Harris and Associates, Inc., April 1980, p. 3.
63. Ibid.

64. Ibid.
65. *New York Times*, 1 February 1980.
66. Gergen, op. cit., p. 13.
67. Free and Watts, op. cit., p. 50.
68. The Gallup Poll, 13 December, 1981, p. 2.
69. Yankelovich and Kagan, op. cit., pp. 696–697.
70. Samuel P. Huntington, "American Foreign Policy: The Changing Political Universe," *Washington Quarterly* 2, no. 4 (Autumn 1979): 41.

Chapter 7

Policy Making and
the People

Our review of the available data and analysis of the character and quality of American public opinion on foreign policy confirms none of the simple stereotypes of the public. It would be a mistake to characterize the public as either beast or savant. Public attitudes and propensities emerge as a complex mix of mood and pragmatism within a broad context of internationalism that is arrayed along a continuum from conservative internationalism that is comfortable with military means and liberal internationalism that eschews military intervention for political and economic involvement. People are not well informed on the full range of foreign issues at any particular time, but there seems little warrant for the contention that they are incapable of dealing with information when it is provided or of ultimately reaching plausible judgments concerning their interests. These judgments on specific issues are often, as Daniel Yankelovich has put it, *"ad hoc"* and may therefore be somewhat "inconsistent and unstable, particularly on issues that the public has not completely thought through."[1] But whether conservative or liberal, there has been and remains general public support for international activism.

Close observers and students of public opinion have been impressed throughout the last decade or more with the opportunity that this situation presents to national leadership. Yankelovich observed: "Such a situation is made to order for leaders who are gifted in their ability to communicate with the public. They (the leaders) realize that they have great latitude for leadership in applying to specific situations a principle that the public supports."[2] But in a democratic society the opportunities available to leaders are accompanied by great responsibilities. Inasmuch as a distinguishing characteristic of a democratic society remains a responsible and accountable relationship between the leaders and the people, those who would lead must also listen. For in a democratic society, the principles to be applied in foreign policy are presumed to emerge from a dialogue. In the American system both the opportunities and the responsibilities for initiating and preserving the quality of this dialogue have tended to fall on the President.

THE PRESIDENCY AND THE POLICY PROCESS

Constitutional complexity, circumstances, and political socialization all contribute to the centrality of the President in the relationship of the public to the policy making process. For most of the cold war period, the institutions responsible for the political socialization of Americans—family, schools, and peer groups—have tended to reinforce the image of the President as the figure best able to lead the American people in a complex and increasingly dangerous world. More recently, as a consequence of Vietnam and Watergate, the previously positive image of the President has suffered.[3] Nonetheless, in a fragmented political structure, the President remains the focus of popular expectations and demands. Hence the President retains significant capacity—perhaps more than any other figure in the American system—to structure the terms of national debate and propose the direction and particulars of policy. But this position also means that a President readily becomes a target of popular frustrations. And in a complex international environment that has been increasingly unresponsive to American initiatives in the 1960s and 1970s, these frustrations have mounted.

The combination of presidential visibility, inevitable frustrations, and the relatively brief time available to a President has worked to constrain and complicate the leadership potential of the presidency. Indeed, throughout the 1960s and 1970s, Presidents and their administrations, in trying to respond to these converging and often contradictory demands and expectations, have often found it difficult to maintain a distinction between leadership and a destructive manipulation of public opinion. This is especially ironic in view of the evidence of a public generally supportive of the international engagement Presidents have espoused. Nonetheless, in a political system in which there are numerous and often aggressive competitors for the public's attention—such as the media, interest groups, and other forms of private power[4]—gaining and holding the attention of the public has become a preoccupation of the President. In some instances this preoccupation has become pernicious, as Presidents, when their policies were failing or under attack, have sought to maintain or regain the initiative in setting the framework of debate. Often as not, this struggle centers on the control of the flow of information to the public.

The President and Information

Concomitant with the expanded demands on the Executive, revolutionary changes have occurred in communications technology and media, and with them a new component of power has emerged. The attributes of power have come to include information and its dissemination and control. Knowledge had a part in forming state power in previous times. But the very existence of state machinery, decision making, and leadership relies increasingly on information and its use.

The President is superbly placed to exploit this technological revolution in knowledge and its dissemination, which can be dated back to the 1940s. The revolution in presidential access to media was well used by Franklin Roosevelt, who averaged more than a press conference a week. The exigencies of war further elaborated executive purview and control of foreign policy information. By the time of the administration of Lyndon Johnson, there were standby crews with "hot" TV cameras positioned in the White House. The 24 hour studio could be exploited on the shortest notice to rally the public. Johnson frequently startled millions as he burst in on regular network programming with almost no introduction. He once went on the air so fast that the presidential props could not be put in place. When the technician asked for another minute to hang the Great Seal, Johnson said, "Son, I'm the leader of the free world, and I'll go on the air when I want to."[5] Although President Nixon subjected himself to press conferences only a fraction of the time of his predecessors, a study of Nixon's use of TV showed that in his first term Nixon used prime time almost three times as frequently as Lyndon Johnson. In contrast, in the first two years of the Reagan presidency, the President averaged slightly less than one press conference every 2 months; a rate even lower than Nixon's. However, Reagan employed a spate of effective radio and television speeches—more than any other first term president by some estimates. Thus Reagan minimized the potential damage to his public image that could result from frequent probing by newspeople of what often emerged during his infrequent press conferences as a limited grasp of information on major issues. His personal popularity, despite low performance ratings for his administration, remained high. People blamed his policies, the Congress, his aides, but not the "great communicator."[6]

The President's informational initiatives can be used in less direct ways to condition the context of debate. Thus public information can be controlled by restrictive classification, planting stories with favored reporters, and using a large public relations apparatus to keep the public informed about what the Executive wants known and ignorant about things the public would not likely support. If it is the judgment of the Executive, as in 1965, that the public needs to be convinced that it is fighting a just war, a White Paper might be released to explain that violence in South Vietnam, for example, is controlled, directed, and carried out by invading North Vietnamese forces. It was a misrepresentation, but only the most careful scholarly and legal exegesis of the record could rebut it. When Johnson ordered the sustained bombing of North Vietnam, it was said that it was in retaliation for the attack on American forces at Pleiku in February 1965. But it is now clear that Pleiku was but a much desired pretext for the initiation of a course of action that had previously been contemplated.[7] Similarly, in early 1981 the Reagan administration produced quantities of "captured documents" as the basis of their claim that Soviet and Cuban support for insurgents in El Salvador required an American response.

Another means of regulating and shaping the flow of information by the Executive is an enormous public relations apparatus. One executive agency, the Defense Department, has the largest public relations operation in the government, designed to purvey DOD's image of the "threat" and an appropriate response to it.[8] Presidents are no less concerned with the active shaping of an image and the selling of policies to the American people. Gerald Rafshoon, whose public relations and advertising firm was responsible for packaging the 1976 Carter presidential campaign, occupied a central role in the Carter administration, including a massive effort to sell the Panama Canal and SALT II treaties to the American people. Similarly, Carter's attempt to exploit the Iranian hostage crisis during his reelection campaign in 1980 led some cynics to suggest that the Ayatollah Khomeini should qualify for federal matching campaign funds or, at a minimum, he and the Islamic revolution should be registered as a political action committee for the Carter campaign, given the President's attempted use of the crisis. Yet, when the Carter administration's rescue mission of late April 1980 was aborted, the White House declared an end to the state of emergency that the hostage issue had given rise to and deemed the crisis "under control." Until just before the election, when it reemerged, the hostage issue virtually stopped being news. As one *New York Times* analyst reported:

> A number of officials and public opinion specialists cite the Iranian situation as an example of how even a weakened President has the power to set the context, and the degree with which public issues are discussed around the country.[9]

The arrival of the Reagan administration promised, if anything, an increase in public relations activity. During 1981, for example, as the administration sought to convince the American people of the threat to American national security posed by anti-American insurgents in El Salvador, the State Department released an archive of captured documents concerning purported arms transfers into El Salvador from Nicaragua and Cuba. Later in the year as administration rhetoric against Libya escalated, news of a secret Libyan "hit squad" detailed to attack American leaders was fed to the press and media. The assassination team did not materialize by year's end and administration officials conceded that they never had firm information concerning its composition or plans. Though the story vanished from the front pages and evening news broadcasts, its very appearance was an important indication of the capacity of administration inspired news to command coverage by the media.

No less impressive were administration attempts to extend its informational reach abroad. During 1981 the administration prepared a slick report on Soviet military strength that was destined, Defense Department officials hoped, "for every coffee table in America." It is doubtful that the document became a conversation piece at American coffee klatches or dinner tables, but foreign observers noted that the book appeared in large quantities throughout Western Europe and especially West Germany—at that moment engaged in a heated internal debate over the deployment of a new generation of American nuclear missiles on West German soil. Simultaneously, the United States Information Agency (USIA), now under the direction of Reagan's close Hollywood friend, Charles Wick, was mobilized to insure maximum European exposure for the President's reply to Soviet arms control proposals for Europe. The USIA purchased time on European television, and the speech was timed to be broadcast live at dinner time in Western Europe. Finally, in early 1982, the USIA mounted a star-studded spectacular including Hollywood luminaries such as Charlton Heston and Frank Sinatra designed to dramatize American backing of the Polish people in the face of the imposition of martial law by the Polish regime during the winter of 1981–1982. The show was not only beamed to Western and Eastern Europe but was also made available for broadcast in the United States. Of course, the USIA operations abroad were not in themselves unusual. However, the fact that they were also employed within the United States was extraordinary. This represented only the second time in the history of the American propaganda agency that one of its productions had been broadcast in the United States, the first being the United States Information Agency mid-1960s film on the assassination of President John F. Kennedy.

The Media: A Countervailing Force?

The vigorous attempts by a succession of administrations to seize control of the flow of information on foreign policy may, however, have had effects contrary to presidential intentions. Thus there may now be a more aggressive and skeptical media than at any time since the end of World War II. The revelations of the Pentagon Papers and Watergate have not only produced more suspicion of information sponsored and promoted by the government, but also have contributed to journalists' assuming a more adversarial relationship to government. It was aggressive investigative reporting that led to Watergate and the fall of the Nixon administration. The decision to publish the purloined Pentagon Papers was hardly the act of a cowed and controlled media. Throughout the Carter administration, the press maintained a merciless accounting of the administration's meandering and at times contradictory policy path. Television and print media proved to be both provocateur and communicator of the personal and policy disputes within the administration. Furthermore, the Reagan administration's El Salvador White Paper received immediate, critical scrutiny, and as the administration's economic and foreign policies emerged from the postelection honeymoon period, press commentary became more pointed. Early references to the President's easy amiability were increasingly replaced by speculation that he lacked a grasp of the substance of policy. By early 1982, reporters and columnists gleefully displayed and corrected Reagan's frequent misstatements of fact and history. Clearly the media of the 1980s was not prepared to confine its reportorial role to that of communicator and interpreter of official policy positions, as had often been the case during the 1940s, 1950s, and 1960s. The reportorial model for the late 1970s and 1980s seemed less the intimacy with policy makers of a Reston and more the sometimes sensational investigatory style of Woodward and Bernstein. Rather than interview the Secretary of State at year's end,[10] journalists obtained the notes of participants in staff meetings with the Secretary and published them.[11]

The questions of whether the balance between presidential power and the press is appropriate or whether the media use their power responsibly are probably beyond definitive resolution. Journalists, outside observers, and, of course, Presidents have periodically attacked the media for an antigovernment bias, especially in their coverage of events in Third World conflicts. The tendency, it is charged, is to romanticize the insurgent and discount information provided by governmental authorities. Defenders of the foreign affairs journalism of the 1970s and 1980s maintain, in contrast, that most reporters get most of their information from government sources and rarely get the opportunity to contact guerillas or antigovernment forces. Indeed, it is argued, such attacks on the coverage of foreign affairs is sometimes part of the United States government's attempt to discredit the source of information that casts doubt on the official rationale for U.S. policy, as in the case of the media's coverage of growing American involvement in Central America in the early 1980s.[12]

As with so many other questions of the proper balance of institutional power, judgments are frequently more a reflection of policy preferences than of calculations of institutional weights. Thus when an administration pursues policies contrary to those of the observer, media aggressiveness is considered responsible. When, however, an assertive media proves an obstacle to a presidential initiative in accord with one's predispositions, the institutional relationship between media and officialdom is judged out of balance.

No less perplexing is the problem of the media's responsibilities to communicate the complex range of choice that exists on many foreign policy questions. The task of laying out the continuum of options on questions such as a new strategic missile system, elaborating the consequences of alternative policies concerning trade, or explaining the often esoteric implications of international monetary policy is extraordinarily difficult. Although elite media such as the *New York Times,* the *Washington Post,* or the *Wall Street Journal,* and the commercial TV networks' "White Papers" or special reports, and public television news programming such as the McNeil/Lehrer Report regularly shoulder the burden, it is debatable whether their often brilliant efforts reach mass publics. Moreover, when those media that do command a mass audience choose to focus on personalities and not policy, the role of the media as necessary interlocutor between people and policy maker becomes even more problematical. Insofar as the image of public affairs communicated to mass publics is but sound and fury, a mere clash of ego and ambition, a dramatic swirl of events and spectacle, is it surprising that the publics' substantive grasp seems frequently weak and underdeveloped? And if the policy maker's cynicism concerning the public's capacity for self-government is thereby confirmed, can it not be said that the messenger who brings the bad news is, in this instance at least, partially to blame?

The President retains significant advantages. Because the Executive is the source of much information in foreign affairs, one usually needs to go to the source itself to test the information's validity.

Besides the difficulty of asking the Executive to present information that would disprove its own case, there is usually a presumption that what is presented is true, if not always complete. To catch mendacity from a sea of usually true information takes a skilled angler indeed.

On the other hand, there is evidence that media coverage of foreign affairs can and does influence public opinion in directions contrary to official policy. Thus during the Vietnam era, those with greatest exposure to mass media were most likely to turn against government policy supporting the war. Similarly, analysis of media coverage of the decisive Tet offensive in February 1968 portraying the offensive as a political defeat for the United States "had a massive psychological effect on the American public."[13] Finally, as the Reagan administration sought to build support for its policies in El Salvador it was faced with press and television coverage that challenged the administration's relatively benign interpretation of the El Salvadoran government's human rights record and forceful repression of dissent. In fact, as the rhetoric of the Reagan administration escalated, mail to the State Department and White House increased and public sentiment turned against U.S. policy by margins of between 10 and 20 to 1.[14]

Predictably, policy makers attribute such results to biased reporting from the field, and no less surprisingly, representatives of the media assert that this complaint is little more than an attempt to kill the bearer of bad news. At a minimum, however, it can be said that the media can serve as a second voice in interpreting what is significant in international affairs even as it acts as a conduit for the government's version of reality and the proper response to it. It is not surprising that there is tension between the two roles or that the policy maker prefers a conduit to a critic. What is disturbing are the lengths to which Presidents have been prepared to go in their attempts to constrain an ostensibly free press and opposition to their policies.

AN UNCERTAIN BALANCE

Keeping the public attuned to policy imperatives as perceived by the President has led some administrations to take vigorous efforts—both legal and extralegal—to control the press and media. During the

1970s when these efforts reached a peak, the media responded with perhaps its most aggressive posture vis-a-vis the presidency since the onset of the cold war. Nonetheless, as the relationship entered the 1980s the problem of the proper balance between the needs of the President as leader of the policy making establishment versus the rights of the press and people to information about their government's most consequential decisions remained uncertain.

The Imperial Presidency in Court

Undoubtedly the Nixon administration went farther than its predecessors or successors in attempting to gain and maintain control of the relationship between the presidency and the press. In addition to seeking legal justification for its position, the Nixon administration tapped the phones of prominent journalists, burglarized their files, conceived plans to burglarize and even firebomb presumed repositories of information and documents leaked to the press, as well as sought to intimidate the corporate leadership of leading newspapers and other media. These were extraordinary, even bizarre acts. However, they were conceived and justified within a framework and conception of presidential need with which virtually every President during the post–World War II era could associate himself. This rationalization of presidential control of information took shape in litigation throughout the 1970s.

The precipitating event in this chain of court cases was the leak by former DOD official Daniel Ellsberg to the *New York Times* and *Washington Post* of the secret history of the Vietnam War prepared by the McNamara Defense Department. These Pentagon Papers revealed little that was not already well known, for almost all the basic information contained in the papers had always been in the public domain. [15] But the Nixon administration obtained a temporary restraining order blocking further publication of the Pentagon Papers. When appeal to the espionage laws was rejected by the courts, the administration argued that it possessed an inherent power to exercise prior restraint over the release of materials that might threaten the national security. But in the 1971 case of *New York Times Co. v. U.S.*, the Supreme Court denied the constitutionality of any such generalized claim, though it recognized that if an explicit congressional mandate was provided and/or the Executive could demonstrate to the Court that the release of information would in Justice Brennan's words, "inevitably, directly and immediately" cause harm equivalent to that of wartime disclosure, then prior restraint might be imposed.[16]

In 1972 the government successfully enjoined a former CIA employee, Victor Marchetti, from publishing a completed manuscript on the operations of the agency that contained materials that the CIA claimed would damage the agency and the national security if published. The basis of the government's restraint on Marchetti was the contractual arrangement between government employees and the government, which provides the government with the authority to review and censor any material subsequently published by the employee even if the individual has left government service. Although such an arrangement constitutes a waiver of the employee's First Amendment rights, lower federal courts found the requirement of the waiver to be a reasonable exercise of the President's powers.[17]

In 1977 another former CIA employee, Frank Snepp, who was for 8 years a decorated operative and analyst for the CIA, published a book, *A Decent Interval*, which chronicled what Snepp believed was the unconscionable failure of Ambassador Graham Martin and Henry Kissinger to prepare for the debacle that accompanied U.S. withdrawal from Vietnam.[18] The government sued Snepp, not for disclosing classified information, but for a breach of contract in that he did not send his book to CIA censors for prior review. In the end, the Supreme Court found that Snepp had breached his oath and that his contract was binding. In other words, a promise to restrict one's First Amendment rights could be enforced if exacted by the government as a precondition for employment.[19]

During the same years Snepp gained access to the public at the sacrifice of what he had earned from his book, CIA alumni known to be sympathetic with the CIA were not asked to submit their works for review. Moreover, there was suspicion that the government had gained a remarkable method for controlling criticism in the use of its employment oaths. Warrant for this fear lay in the publication of Henry Kissinger's memoirs, *The White House Years*, which did, avowedly, deal with matters of great sensitivity.

Kissinger worked from materials that he removed from the State

Department on his departure from government. He asserted that arrangements had been "worked out"[20] with the office of Zbigniew Brzezinski concerning the use of classified materials and that these materials were then donated to the Library of Congress under a 20 year secrecy stipulation. However, in litigation resulting from an attempt by a group of scholars and journalists to gain access to Kissinger's papers under the Freedom of Information Act, Brzezinski's office revealed that Kissinger's assertion concerning clearance of the classified materials "vastly overstates at least by implication, the degree of classification review to which the book was subjected by Brzezinski's office."[21]

The contrast between the fates of Snepp and Kissinger is stark. Nobody even alleged—although it was vaguely hinted—that government secrets had been divulged by Snepp. On the other hand, Kissinger's memoirs are widely considered the most revealing and intimate portraits of individuals and events ever published by a living statesman so recently retired from office. Yet only a fraction of the material was reviewed by current government officers.[22] Like CIA officers such as Snepp, all State Department officers are upon retirement requested to sign an affirmation that they no longer possess "classified or administratively controlled information furnished to [them] during the course of such employment."[23] But the government did not press any breach of contract even though the National Archivist concluded that about 90 percent of Kissinger's transcripts had the character of official records and should be returned to government control instead of remaining subject to Kissinger's stipulations.[24]

A suit for access to Kissinger's papers under the Freedom of Information Act was subsequently dismissed by the Supreme Court. The Court majority reasoned that because the documents had been physically removed from the control of the State Department by Kissinger, citizens could no longer sue for access to the documents now controlled by another agency. Only another government agency could now initiate a suit. Notwithstanding the fact that the scholars and journalists could not have known of the transfer, they had pressed their suit too late.[25] If this decision and practice stand, an implication is that when one is highly placed and can spirit documents swiftly enough from government, what may or may not have been secrets can be controlled, even sold at profit and claimed as a tax write-off when "donated" to the archives under a secrecy rule.

In closely related attempts to place the exercise of controlling information on a constitutional footing, Presidents have claimed an inherent power of their office—executive privilege—that allows them to withhold from public scrutiny all information and communication relating to the policy formulation process. Most observers have conceded that there is some justification for the claim, in that members of an administration are not likely to give candid advice and counsel if they fear public disclosure.

Under the Nixon administration, however, the claims of executive privilege reached imperial proportions. President Nixon even extended the view that executive privilege applied to those who no longer work for the White House. Executive privilege "strongly" supported by Henry Kissinger means, as Kissinger heatedly argued, that "an appointed official has no . . . responsibility to the elective process. An appointed official has responsibility only to the immediate conduct of his affairs."[26]

As the Watergate scandal unfolded, Nixon, in his attempt to thwart release of the Watergate tapes, asserted an absolute right of executive privilege extending to even a criminal case before the courts. In the 1974 case of *U.S. v. Nixon*, the Supreme Court granted the need for some measure of "protection of communications between high government officials and those who advise and assist them in the performance of their manifold duties."[27] However, the Court rejected the President's claim that this privilege was absolute and constitutionally grounded under the doctrine of separation of powers. At least with respect to a criminal trial, "the generalized interest in confidentiality . . . cannot prevail over the fundamental demands of due process of law in the fair administration of criminal justice. The generalized assertion of privilege must yield to the demonstrated, specific need for evidence in a pending criminal trial."[28]

However, the standing of the doctrine in other domains remains unclear. In cases involving the 1967 Freedom of Information Act, designed to establish a right of citizen access to information held by the Executive, the courts have proved extremely reluctant to challenge the Executive's classification prerogatives. Moreover, as post-

Vietnam concern about excessive secrecy waned, it seemed likely that Congress would move to close off even the limited access provided under the Freedom of Information Act.

The inclinations of the Reagan administration were clearly in this direction. Whereas the Carter administration had taken some steps toward limiting the authority of government officials to classify materials, Ronald Reagan brought to office with him a far more restrictive view of the role of the media and the control of information. In the spring of 1981, Reagan's attorney general announced that requests for information under the Freedom of Information Act would be examined under the narrowest terms. Instead of looking for reasons to release information—the inclination of the Carter administration—warrant would be found to keep information under government control. In October 1981, a new Freedom of Information Act was introduced that would forbid requests for documents showing illegal government activity. The draft act deleted previous stipulations that the public's interest in fullest access be a consideration in the release of information. Indeed, it would allow officials to classify documents even after they had been previously declassified. In other words, if an individual identified a document that he or she wanted access to, the document could be classified secret retroactively.

In June 1981, the administration sent to Congress a bill that would make it a crime to print the name of a current or former officer of the CIA even if the name were gleaned from previously printed sources and were already in the public domain. In September, CIA Director William Casey introduced what was to be a successful argument: that the CIA should be exempted entirely from the Freedom of Information Act. Furthermore, by the end of 1981, an Executive Order gave the CIA, for the first time, the ability to legally infiltrate domestic American organizations including universities and news media groups. Finally, in 1982, the administration sought to extend the scope of government classification and to introduce controls on the university teaching and the publication of university research deemed sensitive by the government as well as to restrict the activities of foreign graduate students studying in the United States.

What emerged from the first year of the Reagan administration, therefore, was a new mosaic of control. The new legislation and Executive Orders made lawful what had never been before for government officers. President Reagan's December 4, 1981, Executive Order, as one historian of the intelligence community, Harry Howe Ransome, wrote, departed "radically from the agency's founding principles. It is inconsistent with statutory law, ignores tradition, and will weaken the intelligence system while endangering civil liberties."[29] Ransome and former Director of Central Intelligence Stansfield Turner worried that the blurring of domestic and international intelligence would lead to bureaucratic infighting between the CIA and FBI or that the proposed changes might become a "nascent Bill of Rights" for a secret police.[30] The CIA directives, others pointed out, made existing restrictions moot because any violations would be unknown or unprovable.[31]

Many of these measures were in the form of proposals or if implemented would likely be challenged in the courts. But as the preceding survey suggests, the ultimate legal disposition of presidential claims for expanded authority in the area of information control or administrative descretion related to national security will likely remain ambiguous. Whereas the courts will usually strike down the most egregious and extreme claims and practices, they are not likely to set down explicit guidelines for the future. For almost 50 years since the *Curtiss-Wright* decision, the courts have been prepared to grant the Executive the benefit of the doubt with respect to administrative practices and discretionary claims in national security affairs. This has meant, of course, that issues have been decided on a case-by-case basis and that the relationship between the self-perceived needs of the policy maker and the rights of the people in whose name policy is made remain in a more or less undefined state. At a time when Soviet-American relations have reached one of their lowest points since the end of World War II and the rhetoric of global cold war is the only diplomatic idiom, it seems likely that these limits will be tested yet again. For it has usually been at such moments of purported and real international crisis that the most fundamental domestic rights have been redefined and elaborated.

"Enemies"

Perhaps the most troubling manifestations of these dilemmas have emerged in those instances where policy makers have come to regard the opponents of policy as enemies no longer subject to the rules of the democratic game. On occasion, officials, including Presidents, have resorted to harassment of their political opponents. This activity does not stem from any formal, constitutional grant of power, to be sure, but such power has been used. Throughout the cold war period but especially during the Vietnam War, the Federal Bureau of Investigation and other elements of the domestic and foreign intelligence establishment, systematically undertook operations to discredit and disrupt the activities and personal lives of those actively engaged in dissent from American policy. The Kennedy administration, by denying Linus Pauling a passport in the early 1960s because of his stance against nuclear weapons testing, severely limited his professional as well as political activities. But once again, these activities reached their peak during the Johnson and Nixon administrations, including turning the federal judiciary and the Department of Justice into instruments of harassment.

The Executive had only to tie up in lengthy legal wrangles the antiwar activists of the late 1960s to stifle dissent. Legal actions were taken so that protesters became inactive or discouraged and so that their following might be left without leaders and might be made wary by the example of their leaders' plight. Even if such government action were ultimately thrown out of court, it was still successful in the sense that it crippled the momentum of protest and drained financial and organizational resources.[32] Starting with the Spock case in 1968, sixty-six people were indicted under the rarely used conspiracy laws. Of the antiwar leaders who were indicted, only one ever served time in jail, and that was for smuggling a letter from prison.[33] In fact, every conspiracy charge pressed by the Nixon administration against foreign policy dissidents failed in court. But the ability to levy and prosecute such charges was a powerful and familiar means of the first-term Nixon administration to harass its critics.

Daniel Ellsberg also became the object of a federal suit over the Pentagon papers. The trial ended because of government actions that "offended justice," in the words of the judge. Efforts were made by the Nixon White House to bribe the judge with an offer to head the FBI. Further, Ellsberg's psychiatrist's office was burglarized by White House staffers to secure possibly damaging pretrial information on him. While speaking on the Capitol steps, he was even beaten by thugs dispatched by the White House. Charles Colson, former

White House Special Counsel, testified that the principal motive of Nixon in all of this was to "get out" damaging information on Ellsberg's character in order "to counter his public views."[34] Or as presidential aide Patrick Buchanan wrote to John Erlichman, "Project Ellsberg" was to demonstrate a "conspiracy" of "ex-NSC types," and "leftist writers" such as Neil Sheehan of the *New York Times*.[35] Presumably, then, if Ellsberg could, in the words of Buchanan, have his "innards cut," Ellsberg's disgrace would be shared by those with whom he was associated. One former NSC member assigned to the task, Egil Krogh, wrote to his associate David Young, "there was no apparent damage as the result of the Ellsberg disclosure"; yet it was, Colson gleefully realized, an "opportunity" to "arouse the heartland . . . with a natural villain."[36] For almost a year the FBI knew that Ellsberg was attempting to bring the Pentagon history of the war to light;[37] but the White House did not move to preempt the effort. Rather, the attempt to harass Ellsberg and the moves taken against the *Washington Post* and the *New York Times* were part of a wider undertaking of the Executive to besmirch the important loci of opposition to the American war in Indochina.

It has been argued that the cold war efforts of the Executive to silence opposition were ultimately unsuccessful and have actually resulted in an extension of civil liberties. The argument is that as courts are forced to rule on these measures and rule against them, the areas protected explicitly by case law becomes wider.[38] There is some historical merit to this view of the contracting ability of the Executive to harass. It has perhaps been worse. The "red scares" of the early twentieth century resulted in the exile and incarceration of thousands. Pacifism per se was a crime in World War I. There have been cases like Sacco and Vanzetti and the Rosenbergs—scapegoats who were found and executed. In World War II, 170,000 American-born Japanese were placed in preventive detention camps. But the Watergate memorandum released on June 27, 1973, by John Dean, entitled "How to Screw Our Political Enemies," indicates that there is little comfort to be taken in saying that it has been worse and the courts will probably find it all illegal eventually.[39] Some diseases can be survived, and one's body develops an immunity that limits the danger of contraction of the disease in the future. Surely, however, it is better not to have experienced the disease in the first place.

THE PUBLIC AND POLICY MAKING

Access to, control, and dissemination of information raises difficulties for democracy. Simply put; how can the governed give their informed consent to policies about which relevant information has been manipulated? Ironically, Nixon himself framed the problem in a speech on March 7, 1972:

> When information which properly belongs to the public is systematically withheld by those in power, the people soon become ignorant of their own affairs, distrustful of those who manage them, and—eventually—incapable of determining their own destinies.[40]

We are not arguing that all information in American society is systematically controlled by those in power. Obviously, this is not so or Richard Nixon would have served out his term in office in splendor, and books such as this could not be written. Nor are we arguing that some control of information should not be permissible in a democratic society. Few would argue that the day-to-day details of negotiations should be routinely revealed. Sources and methods of intelligence gathering should probably be restricted from public review, though some measure of congressional oversight seems in order. Similarly, military secrets about defense technologies, contingency planning, and military movements are legitimate secrets in the view of most observers. But in a democratic society the restriction and manipulation of information by those with a purported "need to know," the assertion of a vague right of prior censorship of the press concerning information in the national security domain, and an ambiguous doctrine of executive privilege contribute to a caste system, a government priesthood weighted against accountability.

And ultimately there is the danger of a spillover effect from foreign policy that touches other sectors of domestic life. Thus as the purported demands of national security escalated during the 1960s and 1970s, a series of Presidents rationalized the employment of the personnel and technical assets of the foreign intelligence establishment against citizens of the United States who disagreed with the policies of their government. Manifestations of this dilemma have become undeniable during the last two or three decades. Moreover, the courts have found no easy resolution of the problems, and there seems little prospect that in the future they will deviate from their historic inclination to support executive appeals for latitude in the formulation and conduct of foreign affairs, given the exigencies of activist world involvement.

In sum, the delicate, ambiguous, and inherently tense relationship of responsibility and accountability between leadership and citizenry that is the essence of a democratic society has become more fragile and uncertain as the United States has assumed a position of world leadership. At its best, that relationship rests, in large measure, on mutual confidence between those who make policy and those for whom it is made. But with an imbalance in the control and dissemination of information, power can go unchecked and a climate of either excessive suspicion or unwarranted trust can emerge regarding leadership isolated from the proper element of reality testing.

In the final analysis, perhaps, the people should be exposed to as much information as possible about the fundamental policies that affect their destinies, because, in the end, it is their destiny. As Edward Cahn once explained: "The people's right to obtain information does not, of course, depend on any assumed ability to understand its significance or use it wisely. Facts belong to the people simply because they relate to interests that are theirs [and a] government that is theirs."[41] Furthermore, as our earlier survey of the character of American public opinion suggested, it is not evident that the people are incapable of coming to grips with fundamental international realities. It may be convenient to believe the people benighted in foreign affairs, but even if it were so, the presumption is one that should not carry the day if Americans value their institutions.

Public censure may be harsh and sometimes unfair; public education may be burdensome. But to the extent that criticism is denied or information withheld, future opportunities and responsibilities to deal with the public forthrightly and realistically become more illusive in execution and more uncertain in their effect.

NOTES

1. Daniel Yankelovich, "Farewell to 'President Knows Best'," *Foreign Affairs* 57, no. 3 (1979): 689.
2. Ibid., p. 690. Similar conclusions were reached by Kenneth Waltz in the 1960s; see his "Electoral Punishment and Foreign Policy Crisis," in James N. Rosenau, ed., *Domestic Sources of Foreign Policy* (New York: Free Press, 1967).
3. For a review of the early literature on political socialization, see James Nathan, *International Socialization*, unpublished doctoral dissertation, Johns Hopkins University, School of Advanced International Studies, Washington, D.C., 1972. On the impact of Watergate, see F. Christopher Arterton, "The Impact of Watergate on Children's Attitudes Toward Political Authority," *Political Science Quarterly* 89, no. 2 (June 1974); and Harold M. Barger, "Images of the President and Policemen Among Black, Mexican-American and Anglo School Children: Considerations on Watergate," paper prepared for delivery, American Political Science Association, Chicago, 29 August–2 September 1974, pp. 11–12; and Yankelovich, op, cit., pp. 670–672.
4. See the following chapter for a discussion of some of these.
5. Quoted in David Weiss, *The Politics of Lying: Government Deception, Secrecy, and Power* (New York: Random House, 1973), p. 256.
6. Newton N. Minow, John Bartlow Martin, and Lee M. Mitchell, *Presidential Television, A Twentieth Century Fund Report* (New York: Basic Books, 1973), p. 56 and "Decline of the Press Conferences," *USA Today*, April 1982: 16.
7. David Halberstam, *The Best and the Brightest* (New York: Random House, 1972), pp. 533–534; and James A. Nathan and James K. Oliver, *United States Foreign Policy and World Order*, 2nd ed. (Boston: Little, Brown, 1981), chap. 9.
8. See the following chapter for further discussion.
9. *New York Times*, 23 May 1980.
10. See Reston's interviews with Haig in the *New York Times* in late 1981.
11. See Bob Woodward, "Meetings' Notes Show the Unvarnished Haig," *Washington Post*, 19 February 1982, A1, A14.
12. See the exchange on this controversy in the *McNeil/Lehrer Report*, PBS, 19 February 1982.
13. Bruce Russett and Donald Deluca, " 'Don't Tread on Me': Public Opinion and Foreign Policy in the Eighties," *Political Science Quarterly*, 96 (Fall 1981):397, citing Richard Brody and Benjamin Page, "The Impact of Events on Presidential Popularity: The Johnson and Nixon Administrations," in *Perspectives on the Presidency*, ed. Aaron Wildavsky (Boston: Little, Brown, 1975), and Peter Braestrup, *Big Story: How the American Press and Television Reported and Interpreted the Crisis of Tet 1968 in Vietnam and Washington* (Boulder, Colo.: Westview Press, 1977).
14. Robert Perry, "Reagan's Mail Shows Strong Anti-Junta Bias," AP dispatch in *Evening Journal* (Wilmington, Del.), 19 February 1982, A6.
15. Henry Fairlie, "We Knew What We Were Doing When We Went Into Vietnam," *Washington Monthly* 5, no. 3 (May 1973): 26.
16. *New York Times Co.* v. *U.S.*, 403 U.S. 713 (1971).

17. *U.S.* v. *Marchetti* 466 F.2d 1309 (1972).

18. Frank Snepp, *A Decent Interval* (New York: Random House, 1977).

19. Snepp was ordered to pay back every penny he earned from his book, which had been his sole means of livelihood for 3 years. Future works, no matter how removed from the classified world he knew—even fiction—if they were about intelligence, were mandated to the CIA for prior review. Since speedy publication is essential to anything but a celebrity author, Snepp was, in effect, condemned to an uncertain future in his new craft.

    The capability of the Executive to control information in this way was given a bizarre twist in the case of Wilbur E. Eveland, who served as CIA Director Allen Dulles's chief representative in the Middle East at the end of the 1950s. Eveland wrote a book called *Ropes of Sand* (New York: Norton, 1980). The CIA warned, using the language of the Snepp case, that Eveland "failed to live up to his fiduciary and contractual obligations" to the CIA because he did not send a copy of his book for prior review and clearance in accordance with the agreement he signed with the agency. Eveland tried to obtain a copy of the agreement but was turned down on the grounds that it was "properly classified," although he had been requesting an indication of the nature of the agreement—under the Freedom of Information Act—for 4 years. Finally, as the book was about to be published, the agency released signed contracts under two pseudonyms. The documents were of uncertain dates. But, said CIA spokesman Lavern Strong, "with or without dates, as far as we're concerned they are valid contracts." *Washington Post,* 6 April 1980.

20. From the Foreword of *The White House Years* (Boston: Little, Brown, 1980), p. xxiii.

21. Letter from Christine Dodson, National Security Council, Washington, D.C., 21 May 1980.

22. Anthony Lewis, "The Kissinger Secrets," *New York Times,* 9 June 1980.

23. Cited in U.S. Supreme Court, Nos. 78-1088 and 78-1217, October 1978 in *Henry A. Kissinger* v. *Reporter's Committee for Freedom of the Press, et al.*

24. *Kissinger* v. *Reporter's Committee.*

25. The matter is even more staggering when one considers that some of the materials for Kissinger's memoirs were drawn from conversations that were never a part of any "official record," and hence the NSC did not have the capability of reviewing Kissinger's excerpts for what they might have revealed about the rest of the context of any particular document or secrets.

    Kissinger could, if he had left these transcripts with the State Department, have retained unlimited access to them, under the department's "senior official rule." Thus it might not be an unwarranted supposition that Kissinger's essential motive for removal of the documents was to maintain exclusivity of access and prevent all access by others whom he deems, for whatever reason, unacceptable. Subsequently, arrangements were worked out that allowed for State and Justice Department review of the materials, but ultimate determination of what are "personal" as opposed to "official" documents remains in Kissinger's hands. See *Washington Post,* 16 October 1980.

26. *New York Times,* 12 June 1974.

27. *U.S.* vs. *Nixon* 481 U.S. 683 (1974).

28. Ibid.
29. H. H. Ransome, "Don't Make the CIA the KGB," *New York Times*, 24 December 1981.
30. See *Washington Post*, 19 December 1981 for Turner's concern.
31. Jack Landau of the Reporters' Committee for Freedom of the Press, "A Pattern of Censorship," *Washington Post*, 28 November 1981, p. 23.
32. In the case of the "Chicago Seven," a conspiracy case against seven antiwar leaders, most of whom had never met each other before the original indictment for conspiracy to disrupt the 1968 Democratic National Convention, the Justice Department picked an especially unsympathetic judge. The White House showed its satisfaction when the judge was granted a special reception in the White House after the last contempt citations were issued to the defendants' protesting lawyers.
    This was not the only time that White House audiences were used selectively to quell dissent. On 8 May 1970, the week after the announcement that American troops had invaded Cambodia, New York construction workers brutally beat up young war protesters. When Mayor John Lindsay angrily protested the lack of police protection for the lawfully organized antiwar protest, the construction workers rallied in support of the war. A week later a delegation of workers from the New York Building and Construction Trades Council was invited to the White House and congratulated on its peaceful demonstration. (Weis, op. cit., p. 196.)
    In other cases the administration planted agent provocateurs in antiwar groups to disrupt their activities and create suspicion and fear within the movement. Indeed, the "Camden 28" were charged with attempting to blow up a "Selective Service office with materials, funds, plans and encouragement of an FBI agent provocateur." *New York Review of Books*, 22 April 1971.
33. "CBS Evening News," 31 August 1973.
34. *New York Times*, 4 July 1974.
35. Memo from Presidential Aide Patrick Buchanan to John Erlichman, dated 8 July 1971, reprinted in *Washington Post*, 19 June 1974.
36. *Washington Post*, 19 July 1974.
37. Memo for the record by David Young, 20 July 1973, concerning meetings with Fred Buzhardt and other Defense Department officials reporting that on 27 April 1970, the head of RAND "told the FBI [Ellsberg] was copying classified material." *Washington Post*, 19 July 1974, p. A37.
38. Robert W. Tucker, *Nation or Empire: The Debate Over American Foreign Policy* (Baltimore: Johns Hopkins University Press, 1968), p. 134.
39. *New York Times*, 7 July 1973.
40. *New York times*, 8 March 1972.
41. Edward Cahn, *The Predicament of Democratic Man* (New York: Delta Books, 1962), p. 80.

Chapter 8

Private Power and American Foreign Policy

The American political system has always encompassed substantial opportunities for the exercise of private power in public affairs. The guarantee of the First Amendment that the people possess the "right . . . peaceably to assemble, and to petition the Government for a redress of grievances" has long been the basis for a significant volume of demands directed by individuals or organized groups toward the United States Government. Indeed, one of the most important analyses of the American political system written after the Second World War was developed around the central role of private associations and interest groups in American society.[1] In addition, American constitutionalism has emphasized the necessity of preserving a sizable domain of activity within which government shall not intrude. Moreover, these rights have also been extended to private associations engaged in economic activity. That is to say, corporations are, for all intents and purposes, "individuals" possessing the attendant rights of individuals under the Constitution.

Political and economic historians, especially over the last 50 years, have asserted that the government has come to exercise too much influence and control over this often ill-defined domain of private freedom. But the sheer volume of interest group activity (lobbying of Congress, presidency, courts, and bureaucracy); the development of large concentrations of private economic power such as labor unions and corporations; and the activities of multinational corporations and international financial institutions abroad are all testament to the reality and dynamism of private power in American society. In fact, during the last two decades some writers have expressed concern about the ultimate effects of the exercise of this private power on the

American political system. In the mid-1960s, Grant McConnell raised the question whether private associations of various sorts might not be assuming many of the functions of government in American society, but because of their protected and privileged constitutional status, might also be escaping accountability for their actions.[2] A decade later Samuel Huntington raised a different set of questions when he asked whether the success of interest groups in mobilizing and placing claims on public resources and institutions might be sapping needed governmental energies and reducing the governability of the American system.[3] Whereas McConnell's concerns were about the effects of private power on democracy, Huntington was concerned about its effects on the governability of the American democracy.

This chapter addresses both of these perspectives as they relate to American foreign and national security policy. It is necessary at the outset to establish a more precise basis for addressing the problem of private power and American foreign policy, because private power takes so many forms in the American political system and operates by means of different kinds of relationships to government. Having developed a framework for distinguishing the forms and activities of private power, we can turn to a survey of the variety and roles of private power in the formulation and conduct of American foreign and national security policy. Finally, we draw some conclusions concerning private power and its impact on American foreign policy making.

THE CHARACTER OF PRIVATE POWER

A major and much analyzed relationship between private power and government involves the former's trying to influence the decisions taken by public officials. This activity may take many forms, such as providing information to public officials concerning the group's interests and position on a particular issue, mobilizing political support for or opposition to policy makers who may have supported or opposed the group's position, or, in extreme cases, providing financial inducements—bribes—to public officials. These forms of activity are widely characterized as lobbying or interest group activity.

Numerous schemes for categorizing the types of interest groups operating in the American political system have been devised, and we return to these subsequently.[4]

For the most part the distinguishing characteristic of lobbying is that it concerns primarily the representation of its interests and demands in the policy making process. The policy making process itself, however, remains essentially beyond the ambit of the group, since in most instances members of the interest groups do not actually participate in the act of making policy.[5] But representatives of private power upon occasion establish a second kind of relationship by actually entering into the public policy making process as participants. Perhaps the most thoroughly studied example of this, an example upon which much of our attention is focused later, are the corporations that produce most of the military hardware and services purchased annually by the Department of Defense. These corporations produce goods and services for buyers other than the United States government, but the volume of their sales to the Department of Defense and other government purchasers as well as the dependence of the national security establishment upon their technical expertise and industrial capacity means that the relationship between private and government sectors becomes virtually symbiotic. Indeed, public policy making and private power are so intimately and indispensably linked that this conjoining of governmental and corporate resources is commonly referred to as the military-industrial complex.

A third significant relationship between private power and the public foreign policy making establishment involves private power acting in the international domain as a virtually autonomous actor. Most important in this regard and, once again, a phenomenon that has attracted considerable attention in recent years, is the advent of multinational corporations (MNCs) and the closely related private international financial institutions. MNCs may engage in lobbying where legislation or government regulations are likely to affect their interests and operations. MNCs may also become engaged in close relationships with the government or international organizations, as when banks coordinate lending activities with the economic assistance efforts of public agencies. However, the characteristic that sets MNCs apart from other forms of private power and its exercise is the capacity of MNCs for international action independent of government or international organization control.

In an interdependent international system, few if any actors are completely independent. However, the largest MNCs command information, communication, transportation, and financial resources comparable to and in many instances exceeding those of many nation states. Moreover, their investment and other decisions are based on a calculus of interest distinct from and often in conflict with those of even the largest national actors. Indeed, much of the recent analysis of the multinationals implicity views their international behavior as constituting at least an approximation of foreign policies of their own. Insofar as this is true, this form of private power becomes a virtual "private government."

In summary, private power can seek to influence foreign policy making, enter into a symbiotic partnership with public policy makers, or exercise power more or less independent of the state. However, the same private actor can establish several relationships with the policy making process; for example, a multinational corporation that possesses the capacity to act independently of the United States government might nonetheless lobby Congress or the executive branch concerning a piece of trade legislation or regulation that applies to international economic transactions. Also, as with most political processes the form of the relationship between private power and the public policy making process is seldom static, since the circumstances surrounding the political interplay shift and change. At the same time, however, it is possible to establish reference points to aid in understanding this dynamic process, and the three types of relationships singled out above serve as benchmarks for the following analysis.

INTEREST REPRESENTATION AND LOBBYING

Literally thousands of groups and associations exist in the United States, and hundreds of them are involved at one time or another in lobbying activities that affect foreign and national security policy. They perform functions for their membership other than lobbying, including symbolic functions (such as providing expression of a group's cultural interests and values), economic and ideological functions, and informational functions.[6] In addition they perform instrumental functions among which we might include interest and demand representation in the foreign policy making processes. The means they employ in this latter activity may run the gamut from simple articulation of the group's position to bargaining with elected policy makers, employing the threat or inducement of mobilizing financial resources or membership at election time. These groups seek, in short, to influence policy, to ensure that policy should at a maximum reflect or at a minimum not harm their interests.

Given the scope and depth of American involvement in the world it should come as no surprise that foreign policy lobbying involves a complex mix of groups, institutions, individuals, foreign governments, and even the United States government itself. Among the more important categories or examples of foreign policy lobbying are: ethnic groups; a mix of economic groups including associations of senior executives of American industry, broadly based associations as well as trade and professional associations, single industry groups, and labor; public interest and single issue groups; and foreign governments and interests.

Ethnic Groups. The ethnic and racial diversity of the United States, combined with its global involvement, ensures that many ethnically based interest groups are active at one time or another in the foreign policy arena. Associations of Italian-, Polish-, Irish-, Chinese-, and Afro-Americans, to name a few, seek to influence American foreign policy. Polish-American and other East European groups were highly visible and active during the years immediately after World War II and throughout the 1950s. Only after the division of Europe became an apparently permanent feature of the cold war terrain did this activity recede in visibility. But of all the ethnic groups the so-called Jewish lobby is widely regarded as the most important throughout the post–World War II period and especially in recent years.[7]

The number of Jews in the United States is not great, compared with other prominent ethnic groups—fewer than 6 million in contrast to more than 20 million blacks and more than 10 million Hispanics. On the other hand, Jewish voting participation is high and their concentration in urban areas in states with large electoral votes tends to magnify the group's political importance. Moreover, Israel, established at the onset of the cold war and remaining as a focus of international tension and conflict throughout the period, has served as an emotionally charged focus for the mobilization of the American Jewish community.[8] Although precise causal linkages are never easy to document, most observers of American foreign policy and domestic politics assume that American support of Israel since World War II has been largely a function of the political resources regularly mobilized by the Jewish community and political establishment.

Of the several Jewish-American organizations involved in lobbying on issues affecting Israel, the American Israel Public Affairs Committee (AIPAC) is frequently most active. Thus in 1975 when the United States sought to provide Hawk antiaircraft missiles to Jordan and again in 1978 concerning a large arms package including Saudi Arabia, Egypt, and Israel, AIPAC mobilized the Jewish community throughout the United States in an effort to reshape the arms deals in a manner more favorable to Israel. AIPAC's resources are considerable, including an extensive and sensitive network of sources within the United States government that keep AIPAC's leadership aware of issues long before they break into the public domain. On the Hawk missile sale, for example, Morris Amitay, head of AIPAC, was alerted to the deal by sources within the Defense Department even before the sale was announced to Congress. Indeed, Amitay was provided with a top secret Joint Chiefs of Staff report raising questions about the sale and used the information to prepare Congressional opposition to the arrangement. AIPAC's operation included in this instance grass roots lobbying, with the mobilization of hundreds of local Jewish communities to besiege the Congress and Department of State with calls, letters, and inquiries designed to express opposition to the sale. Other interest groups such as Americans for Democratic Action, the labor movement, and, of course, other Jewish groups were encouraged to oppose the deal.[9]

AIPAC could not block the 1978 multination arms sale, but modification of the conditions of the sale to make the arms transfer less threatening to Israel was in line with AIPAC proposals: prohibition of refueling and ground attack equipment and basing restrictions on

Saudi aircraft to make them less of a threat to Israel; limits on the ability of the Saudis to increase their aircraft inventories until the early 1980s or to transfer aircraft to another country; and, finally, assurances of increased aircraft sales to Israel. Similarly, the Hawk missiles were modified to eliminate their mobility, thereby restricting their utility to defensive missions.[10]

By 1978, however, the aggressive methods of AIPAC had begun to elicit a backlash within Congress and the Executive. Special attention was directed, for example, to AIPAC representatives participating in congressional caucuses on arms aid issues, drafting legislation, and preparing questions for use in congressional hearings. Moreover, the aggressiveness of the Jewish groups also brought forth a counterresponse from pro-Arab groups, individuals, and even Arab leaders who sought completion of the agreements. In 1975, King Hussein corresponded directly with members of Congress, and during the 1978 struggle over the package sale to Egypt and Saudi Arabia, members of Congress were visited by members of the Saudi royal family and, most effectively, by President Anwar el-Sadat of Egypt.

A second example of strong ethnic lobbying involved the reaction of the Greek-American community to the Turkish invasion of Cyprus in 1974. In this instance an American Hellenic Institute Public Affairs Committee (AHIPAC) was established to coordinate the activities of various Greek-American groups and mobilize the Greek-American community throughout the United States to support an embargo of American arms to Turkey. AHIPAC, employing many of the same grass roots techniques used by AIPAC, succeeded in getting Congress to impose the embargo over White House resistance and keep it in place until 1978. Here again, however, counterlobbying emerged and in time forced a retreat from the embargo.[11]

In neither case, therefore, can it be said that these most active of the ethnic lobbies have had unqualified success. In none of the instances examined here did the lobbies gain everything they desired. Both arms deals opposed by AIPAC went through (with modifications), and the Turkish arms embargo was eventually lifted after prolonged counterlobbying by two Presidents and other groups in and outside government. On the other hand, Jewish groups were instrumental in the passage of restrictions on trade liberalization with the Soviet Union requiring increases in Jewish immigration. And notwithstanding the eventual removal of the embargo on Turkey, AHIPAC support of Greek interests was controlling for almost 4 years.

In the final analysis, however, there is little evidence that even the qualified successes of these most active of the ethnic lobbies has been consistently replicated by other groups. Apart from the occasional visibility of some East European groups, most ethnically based lobbies are seldom active. Indeed, the largest potential ethnic or racial lobby in the United States, blacks, have traditionally shown little interest in or effect on foreign policy matters.[12]

Economic Groups. Economic groups constitute an even larger and more heterogenous set of lobbying forces that seek from time to time to influence American foreign and national security policy. It is estimated, for example, that more than 500 corporations maintain legislative liaison offices in Washington. In addition, influential groups of senior business leaders and executives, such as the 200-member Business Roundtable, have established ready access to the foreign economic policy establishment. The Chamber of Commerce and National Association of Manufacturers are perhaps the best-known business associations, with the Chamber widely regarded as the most professional and influential of the business groups. The Chamber represents tens of thousands of firms and individuals throughout the country, and its extensive network of local chapters and offices provides it with political access to virtually every congressional district in the country. Its large Washington operation insures considerable impact within Congress and the executive bureaucracy.

A second important group of economic or business lobbyists is the various single-industry groups. Four have been especially prominent during the 1970s. The fisheries and associated industries have lobbied both Congress and the Executive concerning the decade-long negotiations over the legal regime of the oceans. Of particular importance to these groups has been the status of international law relating to the coastal zone and the establishment of a 200 mile wide exclusive fisheries zone. Despite Department of State fears that establishment of such a zone by the United States would disrupt negotiations in the ongoing Law of the Sea Conference, Congress relented to the pressures of those seeking such a zone and legislatively established the 200 mile fisheries zone in 1975. It is important to note in passing that there were other segments of the American fisheries industry—such a tuna and shrimp fishermen who fish off the coasts of other countries—who were opposed to the legislation.

Another industry group concerned with the Law of the Sea negotiations is the mining companies and companies involved in the manufacture of equipment for deep seabed mining. The pressure from these groups has been for legislation to allow them to begin seabed exploration and exploitation of mineral resources notwithstanding the fact that international control of such activity has not yet been worked out in the Law of the Sea Conference. Here again the Department of State initially opposed such a legislative mandate, fearing that it would disrupt the difficult international negotiations. By the end of the decade, however, the question of international control of deep seabed mining had deadlocked, and State Department representatives began supporting such legislation, possibly as a prod to Third World countries who were demanding tight restrictions on exploitation of the seabed by the industrialized world. And with the arrival of the Reagan administration, industry pressures reportedly peaked as Reagan moved in early 1981 to reopen the entire treaty to renegotiation (and thereby possibly kill it). [13]

A third industry group of major significance is the oil industry. Whether lobbying as individual corporations or under their umbrella organization, the American Petroleum Institute—representing more than 300 oil industry corporations—this industry group has sought to advance the interests of oil-producing states in the Middle East as well as pro-Arab groups in the United States. Obviously, this stance means that the petroleum interests are frequently found in opposition to Jewish groups and, in the view of some analysts, provides an important counterweight to the influence of these groups. [14]

Finally, the arms industry comprises one of the most consequential industry lobbying forces in Washington. The scope of the American defense industry touches most congressional districts in the United States, thereby guaranteeing it a hearing in Washington. Moreover, this industry group employs literally hundreds of former Department of Defense officials and former members of Congress, most of whom are therefore well acquainted with the multiple access points to the Congress and bureaucracy. On the other hand, there is some evidence that as a lobbying force there is an important degree of incoherence in the industry's efforts. One member of Congress has noted, for example, "Nobody orchestrates because all of its members are fighting for their own piece of turf."[15] Furthermore, during the early and mid-1970s, when the defense budget was contracting, this tendency toward infighting may have increased as the turf became smaller. On the other hand, where a defense producer has significant impact on a particular congressional district or state such as Texas, Massachusetts, or southern California, Congress can prove quite responsive to pressure even when the Defense Department is equivocal in its desire for what is being produced. Thus powerful members of Congress from Texas have forced the Defense Department to purchase the A-6 aircraft in small numbers long after the department's need for the aircraft had ended. And pressure from Massachusetts legislators, including Senator Edward Kennedy and Speaker of the House Thomas O'Neill, forced the Navy to go forward with development and procurement of the F-18 fighter notwithstanding Navy doubts about its utility. The engine for the aircraft was manufactured by General Electric in the Speaker's district.

A third major economic group engaged in lobbying the government on foreign and national security policy is labor. Some fifty labor organizations operate in Washington, with the AFL/CIO long regarded as most important. With the onset of increased international economic interdependence and its sometimes disruptive effects on domestic economics, the American labor movement began to shift from its traditional internationalist position during the 1970s. For much of the period after the Second World War, most of labor could be counted on to take fairly liberal and internationalist positions on questions of trade and tariff restrictions. But the onset of intense competition and market penetration from abroad, especially in the automobile, textile, steel, and some light manufacturing industries, has led labor to take a far more protectionist posture. Thus on virtually all trade reform and expansion legislation during the 1970s, labor adopted a "fair trade" rather than "free trade" position, frequently in opposition to the Executive then engaged in trade negotiations with the Europeans and Japanese and increasingly on the opposite side from labor's traditional liberal legislative allies in the Congress. Indeed, with the onset of the 1980s, labor could be found in frequent alliance with industrial and business lobbyists seeking relief and protection from the forces of complex interdependence. Similarly, as the strategic superiority of the United States diminished during the 1970s, the traditionally activist and globalist national security posture of much of labor moved it into the camp of those who favored expanding defense budgets (hence, labor's alliance with the arms industry), opposition to the SALT agreements, and a tougher posture vis-a-vis the Soviet Union. In addition, the AFL/CIO became a dependable ally of Jewish groups such as AIPAC that seek to prevent a more evenhanded American posture in the Middle East and limit trade expansion with the Soviet Union in the absence of liberal Jewish immigration policies.

Public Interest and Single-Issue Groups. Public interest and single-issue groups have long been a part of the lobbying phenomenon. However, during the last decade the pervasiveness and intensity of activity on the part of public interest and so-called single-issue groups has been extraordinary.

Many public interest groups, like interest groups in general, are concerned primarily with domestic issues. Thus the environmental groups, organizations such as Common Cause, or the Nader groups concern themselves primarily with domestic legislation and regulations affecting their interests. Other more general public affairs groups, such as the League of Women Voters as well as some church groups and associations, frequently lobby Congress and executive agencies on issues of foreign, national security, or foreign economic policy. Similarly, there are groups such as the Foreign Policy Association and Arms Control Association, comprising civic, business, and academic leaders as well as the general public, that consistently seek to influence foreign policy decisions.

In contrast to these groups, however, are the single-issue groups. Here again, their activities may focus on exclusively domestic issues, such as abortion or gun control. In other instances foreign policy questions and debates serve as catalysts for their formation. Throughout the Vietnam War years, for example, campus-based groups sprang up to organize opposition against the war and take the message of opposition directly to Washington by means of conventional lobbying but more dramatically by means of massive demonstrations.

In the early 1970s, the rise of protectionist sentiment gave rise to the formation of the Emergency Committee for American Trade made up of business leaders committed to free trade. In the Carter years, the debate over ratification of the Panama Canal Treaties stimulated the formation of an Emergency Coalition To Save the Panama Canal, which coordinated the antiratification efforts of conservative groups such as the American Legion, Veterans of Foreign Wars, American Conservative Union, Young Americans for Freedom, and Committee for the Survival of a Free Congress. A countercoalition of interest groups took shape on the other side of the question, often with considerable White House encouragement and support.[16]

In each of these cases, as the stimulus for organization and action was removed, single-issue groups, such as those formed to oppose the Vietnam war, tended to disintegrate. "Emergency committees" of whatever source tend to vanish once the emergency is over. On the other hand, many single-issue groups are in fact coalitions of existing, well-established interest groups. Thus the raw material for subsequent alliances is always at hand. Close attention to the composition of the Emergency Coalition To Save the Panama Canal reveals a collection of conservative groups that can be found in coalition on virtually any major political, social, or economic issue whether foreign or domestic; the same can be said for "free trade" and other coalitions that form around "internationalist" positions on various issues. Furthermore, especially in the case of the conservative groups, there is considerable evidence that in addition to coalescence, there is in fact sharing and pooling of resources, especially the use of mailing lists of contributors to conservative causes. Thus a grass roots campaign can be mounted almost instantaneously on any issue that taps and depends on the same intensely ideological segment of American policy.[17]

Governments as Lobbyists.   Although not strictly examples of private power, foreign governments are active lobbyists before Congress. More than 600 agents of foreign governments are now registered as representatives of foreign governments. For the most part these are Washington lawyers hired to serve as advocates of a country's position and interests on foreign aid or trade legislation. In many instances these representatives are among the most prominent members of the Washington establishment, including former Senators such as J. William Fulbright or former high-ranking members of the executive branch. Indeed, Richard Allen, Ronald Reagan's first national security adviser, proved to be something of an embarrassment to the Reagan presidential campaign when it was revealed that he had served as a lobbyist for foreign automobile interests. In addition, foreign governments maintain offices in Washington and support trade councils designed to aid in mobilizing members of the American business community with an interest in a specific aspect of foreign trade, such as Japanese or East-West trade. Foreign governments have also contributed to American universities and research institutes in an effort to develop a sympathetic hearing within the foreign policy establishment.[18] Finally, as noted above, the last few years have seen an increasing amount of direct contact between the leadership of foreign governments and Congress.

All of this activity on the part of foreign governments falls within the bounds of normal lobbying activity by any interest group or individual seeking representation before the United States government and especially Congress. Upon occasion, however, a foreign government resorts to extraordinary and even illegal means in its attempt to gain a favorable hearing for its interests in Washington. Perhaps the most dramatic recent example of this sort of activity involved the Korean government's massive program to influence Congress and American public opinion. Throughout the 1970s, the Korean Central Intelligence Agency, working through South Korean businessman Tongsun Park and others in Washington, placed agents on the staffs of key members of Congress—including the Speaker of the House—and dispensed thousands of dollars in campaign contributions, occasional bribes, and entertainment. Also employed were trips to South Korea where members of Congress and other dignitaries would receive honorary degrees and lavish entertainment including, according to one member of Congress, "an attractive Korean woman who would be pleased to meet with the congressman on matters of mutual interest."[19] Investigation of the Korean activity revealed that over the years, some thirty-one members of Congress had received money sufficiently within the bounds of congressional rules as to avoid prosecution. In only a handful of cases were indictments brought and convictions obtained.

Lobbying and Influence

Lobbying encompasses an enormous range of activities and forms. The character of the influence resulting from these activities has, however, always been a matter of some debate among observers and participants. Most Presidents during the last decade, for example, have lamented the inordinate influence of "special interest groups." Thus President Carter hammered away at the purported pernicious influence of the petroleum industry as he fought to get his energy proposals through Congress in 1978 and 1979. On the other hand, his and other Presidents' own executive establishment has been perhaps the largest collection of lobbyists in Washington, employing all the instrumentalities we have just discussed. Thus during the Panama Canal Treaties debates, presidential emmisaries blanketed Congress, escorted members of the Senate to Panama for briefings from Panamanian officials, and mobilized a large grass roots campaign to support the treaties and to counter the activities of treaty opponents. In the SALT II treaty ratification fight, the same array of techniques was employed.

But the sheer magnitude, prestige, and intensity of activity and the resources committed to it by private power or the executive branch do not translate in any simple way into "influence." The character of the issue being lobbied, the preceived legitimacy of those lobbying, the existence of counterpressure, timing, and, especially in the foreign policy area, the context of international events surrounding lobbying can all impinge on the influence effect.

In a society in which economic interests are accorded a high degree of prominence, it should come as no surprise that individuals and interest groups with the prospect of economic gain or loss as the basis of their lobbying efforts should be accorded ongoing access, a high degree of legitimacy, and a respectful hearing. Moreover, in a political setting in which the survival of policy makers in the legislative branch as well as the presidency is a function of elections, one would expect that groups that command and can mobilize resources relevant to the electoral process (large numbers of potential voters, organizational resources, and money) are influential. But although such axioms hold much of the time, circumstances, such as a failing foreign policy in Southeast Asia, can open opportunities for groups and coalitions not normally active or influential in the policy making process.

In the final analysis, then, it must be said that the context provided by American foreign and national security policy is itself a major determinant of the form and influence of private power. Nowhere has this been more apparent than with respect to the near symbiotic relationship between government and private power within the so-called military-industrial complex.

SYMBIOTIC PUBLIC AND PRIVATE POWER: THE MILITARY-INDUSTRIAL COMPLEX

As President Eisenhower left office in 1960 he warned the nation:

> We have been compelled to create a permanent armaments industry of vast proportions. . . .
>
> This conjunction of an immense military establishment and a large arms industry is new in the American experience. The total influence—economic, political, even spiritual—is felt in every city, every statehouse, every office of the federal government. We recognize the imperative need for this development. Yet we must not fail to comprehend its grave implications. Our toil, resources, and livelihood are all involved; so is the very structure of our society.
>
> In the councils of government we must guard against the acquisition of unwarranted influence, whether sought or unsought, by the military-industrial complex. The potential for the disastrous use of misplaced power exists and will persist.[20]

Eisenhower's warning identifies the essential elements of what we might call the symbiotic linkage of governmental and private power, as well as the outline of the most prominent example of this relationship in contemporary American foreign and national security policy.

A post–World War II American foreign and national security policy that came to rely more and more on the threat or actual employment of military capability was the basis of the "imperative need for . . . development" of the military-industrial complex.[21] The threat and use of military power obviously requires a governmental military or security policy establishment. Insofar as the United States has not relied on publicly owned arsenals for the provision of materiel needed by this establishment—aircraft, ships, tanks, guns, ordnance transportation equipment, radio and other communications equipment, electronic components, parts and other accessories—corporations in the private sector have been relied upon. As these corporations come to depend on government contracts for more and more of their sales, the benefits of the linkage of public and private power become mutual. The resulting "conjunction of an immense military establishment and a large arms industry"—the military-industrial complex—is the prototype of a symbiotic relationship between public and private power.

The Arms Industry. The concentrated and relatively stable composition of the arms industry has been an outstanding and often noted characteristic of the post–World War II era. [22] By the mid-1950s the largest 100 defense contractors held more than 73 percent of the dollar value of the major contracts awarded by the United States government, with the top 25 accounting for more than 55 percent. In the mid-1960s, the top 100 held about 70 percent of the contracts, with the top 25 receiving 46 percent. By the mid-1970s, a time of falling defense spending relative to the gross national product of the country, the 100 largest contractors still received 70 percent of the contracts (about $42 billion), with the top 25 accounting for 47 percent (or about $20 billion). Moreover, the composition of this group over the last two decades, especially those in the top 25 to 50 companies, is quite stable. (See Table 8.1) There are changes in the relative position of the top companies, but only a few changes in the composition of the group as a whole. Thus 34 of the top 50 companies in the mid-1970s could be found in the top 50 at the end of the 1960s. Moreover, most of these top companies, which received about 60 percent of the contracts granted in the late 1950s, were in the same category at the end of the 1970s.

During the 1970s, as the size of the defense budget began to contract somewhat, the concentration of awards at the very top of the largest companies was noticeable. For example, at mid-decade, whereas almost 70 percent of the value of all contracts was going to 100 companies, the top 5 received over 19 percent (about $8 billion) with the bottom 75 companies receiving something over 20 percent (about $8.4 billion). The same pattern held throughout the first part of the decade.

Clearly the arms industry has a great deal at stake when the United States government formulates foreign and national security policy, and the industry is one of the largest and most active lobbyists before Congress and the executive branch national security bureaucracy. However, the industry-government linkage is far more complex and intimate than mere lobbying activity.

Table 8.1. 50 Largest Companies Receiving the Largest Dollar Volume of DOD Prime Contract Awards: 1958–1960, 1970, 1976

1976 Rank	Company	1958–1960 Rank	1970 Rank
1.	McDonnel Douglas	3	5
2.	Lockheed Aircraft	3	1
3.	Northrop	23	33
4.	General Electric	4	3
5.	United Technologies	–	–
6.	Boeing	1	12
7.	General Dynamics	2	2
8.	Grumman	17	8
9.	Litton Industries	–	9
10.	Rockwell International	5	7
11.	Hughes Aircraft	10	10
12.	Raytheon	12	18
13.	Tenneco	28	27
14.	Sperry Rand	11	15
15.	Westinghouse Electric	19	14
16.	Chrysler	18	58
17.	A.T. & T.	7	4
18.	FMC	55	41
19.	Honeywell	37	16
20.	Textron	45	13
21.	General Motors	21	17
22.	RCA	14	22
23.	LTV	25/61*	11
24.	Todd Shipyards	–	–
25.	Teledyne	59/43*	29

(continued)

Table 8.1. (continued)

1976 Rank	Company	1958–1960 Rank	1970 Rank
26. TRW		33	34
27. Ford Motor		35/36*	19
28. Standard Oil (Calif.)		29	42
29. I.T.T.		27	31
30. IBM		15	24
31. Congoleum		–	–
32. Martin Marietta		9	26
33. Exxon		24	30
34. Amerada Hess		–	–
35. Mobil		44	36
36. Fairchild Industries		52	79
37. Harsco		–	–
38. Singer		46	38
39. General Telephone and Tele.		62	49
40. Bendix		20	35
41. Texas Instruments		–	32
42. Morrison-Knudsen		65	43
43. Texaco		41	60
44. Pacific Resources		–	–
45. Reynolds (RJ) Industries		–	50
46. American Motors		–	21
47. Control Data		–	63
48. Guam Oil and Refining		–	–
49. Goodyear Tire and Rubber		40	51
50. General Tire and Rubber		22	23

*Merger

Sources: Department of Defense, Office of the Assistant Secretary of Defense (Comptroller), *100 Companies Receiving the Largest Dollar Volume of Military Prime Contract Awards, Fiscal Year 1959; Fiscal Year 1970; and Fiscal Year 1976* (Washington, D.C.: GPO, 1969; 1977).

The Conjunction of Private and Public Power. The military-industrial complex is rooted in the process whereby weapons are developed (including basic and applied research), tested, evaluated, and eventually purchased. Analysts of this process have noted that it can be divided into two phases: first, the research, development, testing, and evaluation of a weapons system; and second, the actual production and procurement of the systems for use by the military establishment.[23] In the initial phase the Department of Defense identifies a need for a weapon, undertakes some initial design, engineering, and budget development, and initiates contacts with the defense industry to develop specific proposals. Proposals are submitted, evaluated, and one or more contractors selected to undertake development of the weapons system. Upon delivery of prototypes of the weapons systems, the Defense Department tests and evaluates them and then moves the process into the second or procurement phase by selecting one of the prototypes for production.

In this model of the process one might infer the existence of an arms-length relationship between the industry and the government, but in fact there is constant interaction between the military and the companies at every step in the process. Even the identification of a security need is sometimes undertaken by the industry; many of the largest companies maintain sizable foreign and national security policy "think tanks" that constantly evaluate, either on their own or under contract from the government, the security policy—and hence the needs—of the United States. The presence of thousands of former Defense Department officials in the defense industry and years of close working relationships between the Department and the technical experts in the companies ensures that throughout the design, initial engineering, and proposal development phase of the weapons acquisition process there will be close and ongoing exchanges of information and ideas. Thus it is unlikely that there are many surprises when prototypes are produced and testing is begun.

In view of the complexity of weapons systems, this close interaction is predictable. Weapons technologies inevitably build on previously developed technologies. Moreover, the escalating performance demands placed on modern weapons systems by the Defense Department has meant that the technologies have become more and more complex. Aircraft now involve hundreds of thousands of parts, hundreds of thousands of feet of wire, thousands of resistors, capacitors, relays, and related electronic devices, all of which must operate at extremely high levels of reliability for long periods of time and under the most extreme conditions of equipment stress. Technical and training manuals involve tens of thousands of pages; the coordination and management of the entire process of research, design, testing, evaluation, and procurement involves thousands of people.

The development, production, and employment of such expensive complexity presupposes intimate, indeed integrated, working relationships among those involved in all phases of the process. At the same time the immense costs and technological complexity associated with modern weapons systems has had the effect of reducing the number of companies capable of mobilizing the necessary technological skills.[24] The defense establishment has developed a need to keep this small number of producers alive. Finally, the dependency of the national security establishment on the industry is intensified by the necessity to get the systems produced and in the hands of American forces as soon as possible in order that the "threat" be met. Thus urgency combined with dependence on a few producers compels the military to ignore rigid cost and other management considerations that otherwise might work to hold down costs and place some distance between private and public sectors in the military-industrial relationship.[25]

The Implications and Limits of Symbiosis.   In summary, what developed during the late 1950s and throughout the 1960s was what defense industry analysts Merton Peck and Frederick Scherer have called a "bilateral monopoly" between the seller (the defense industry) and the buyer (the government) that bears little or no resemblance to conventional conceptions of the marketplace; as Peck and Scherer emphasized, it is difficult for either to exist without the other.[26] In this market there is no real interaction of supply and demand. Congress sets demand through defense appropriations. The amount and type of appropriations are determined by a complex set of factors including international events, the political needs of the members of Congress making the decisions, and the lobbying of the military-industrial complex. Prices and profit are determined through negotiations between the industry and the government. Because costs associated with research, development, testing, and evaluation are beyond the resources of the supplying companies, the government—the buyer—"underwrites a sizable share of the contractor's financial investment . . . provides industrial facilities, makes advance and progress payments, and assists in strategic material acquisition."[27]

Congress also allows the Internal Revenue Service to accept defense contractor's claims for lobbying as legitimate business expenses. In one study in 1974, 10 defense contractors spent some $2 million in tax deductable lobbying. More recently, 5 companies were found to have spent $17 million on governmental relations, most of it tax deductable.[28]

Finally, in 1982 a striking example of symbiosis between a defense contractor and the government came to light. In a battle between the Boeing and Lockheed corporations for the multi-billion dollar contract for a new military cargo plane, the Air Force actively took the side of Lockheed. This became evident when a Lockheed computer printout was leaked to the press which revealed that Lockheed officials had gathered in the offices of Air Force and Defense Department officials to plot lobbying strategies to be directed at more than 250 members of Congress. Secretary of Defense Weinberger justified this activity as necessary to counter misinformation that was being put out by Lockheed's competitor and members of Congress whose districts would be harmed if the contract went to Lockheed. The effort was clearly cooperative notwithstanding the existence of a 1919 law (never enforced) which prohibits public officials from spending public money to influence legislation.[29]

Although in general the arms industry has flourished as a symbiotic partner, in those instances since the Second World War when defense spending has declined, there have been some painful adjustments, especially for smaller companies. During the early 1970s, in the backwash of the Vietnam War, declining defense budgets forced many defense industries to shift their productive focus. Thus companies specializing in large forgings and castings for heavy military equipment such as tanks were forced to spend millions of dollars to retool for civilian production. In other instances, production shifted to meet the growing demands of overseas sales of military hardware (often under U.S. government sponsorship). Most important, however, was the shift of major aircraft manufacturers such as Boeing into commercial aircraft production to replenish domestic and foreign carrier airfleets with a new generation of aircraft such as the 757 and 767 airliners. Shipyards began looking for business in the containerized cargo industry rather than depending on the U.S. Navy, and the semiconductor industry shifted its production to supply high demands in consumer markets. Shortages of trained technicians and engineers became commonplace among those companies that continued to focus on defense production, because as their contracts fell off or became less certain, workers and engineers moved elsewhere.

By late 1970s, however, the international and domestic political climate had changed once again. In the wake of the Afghanistan invasion by the Soviet Union, the declaration of the Carter Doctrine, and the election of the Reagan administration, which promised significant expansion of the defense budget beyond that called for by the Carter administration, an increase in the military-industrial complex seemed in the offing.[30]

Apart from whatever demands for even greater funding for which the industry might be positioning itself, the fact is that the essential structure and dynamics of the military-industrial relationship remained in place in the early 1980s. Government remained dependent on the industry for its weapons and other equipment, and the industry did not seem reluctant to remain dependent on government for contracts. In sum, there was mutual willingness to maintain a symbiotic relationship between public and private power that led one industry president to observe in the early 1970s: "We need a gender for our industry. At present we are neither fish nor fowl; neither private industry nor Government."[31]

"PRIVATE GOVERNMENTS" AND U.S. FOREIGN POLICY: THE MULTINATIONAL CORPORATIONS

In the last decade, students of international relations and economics focused much attention on a third category of private power which holds implications for American foreign policy: American multinational corporations (MNCs). These are not a new phenomenon; large corporations operating and owning assets in several countries are very nearly as old as the Republic.[32] But during the late 1960s and throughout the 1970s their numbers and sizes have grown, and their presence has provoked an often worried and almost always heated debate.

The size and resources commanded by the largest MNCs outstrips the wealth of all but the largest nation states. The annual sales for the largest MNC in 1978, General Motors, exceeded the gross national product of all but eighteen countries the year before; Chrysler and Ford's combined losses in 1980 exceeded the 1977 gross national products of such African countries as Ethiopia, Madagascar, Mozambique, Tanzania, Uganda, and Zaire. Indeed, the sales of Mobil Oil, fifth ranking industrial corporation in the world in 1978—a year described by *Fortune* as "rather somber"—exceeded the gross national products at mid-decade of every country in Africa, all but four in Asia, all but three in North and Central America, all but two in South America, and all but one in Oceania.[33] Raymond Vernon, a pathbreaking student of the MNC, has observed:

> they sit uncomfortably in the structure of long-established political and social institutions. They sprawl across national boundaries, linking the assets and activities of different national jurisdictions with an intimacy that seems to threaten the concept of the nation as an integral unit. Accordingly, they stir uneasy questions in the minds of men.[34]

Among the more specific questions that have been raised from various ideological perspectives are the following: Do MNCs undercut the ability of nation states to meet the needs of their citizens? Are American MNCs extensions of U.S. power and the ultimate manifestation of the liberal international order that the United States sought to construct in the years immediately after World War II?[35] Are MNCs something more than the extension of a nation's foreign policy, representing independent and near autonomous forces in the contemporary world political economy?[36] Or are MNCs weak and vulnerable entities with little overall effect on the policies of either the host state or the foreign nation in which they do business?

We need not investigate all these questions here. It is sufficient to note that most recent empirical analysis seems to support the view that American MNCs exercise a measure of decision making autonomy but that they are nonetheless constrained by United States policy interests, prevailing international political conditions, and, increasingly, by the host countries in which they operate.[37] In other words, the MNCs are not unlike other significant political economic actors in contemporary world politics. They possess interests and a demonstrable capacity to act in pursuit of those interests, but like even the largest of nations, they are constrained by the environment in which they operate. They are, of course, different from national units, since their corporate officers and administrators remain overwhelmingly American and reflect prevailing American attitudes towards international relations.[38] Even so, their loyalties often are mixed, because their interests sometimes run parallel to those of their home nationality, the United States, and in other instances diverge.

The nature of the MNCs' dependence on the United States is not obscure. The foreign policy of the United States after World War II has centered on the creation, then maintenance of a world political and economic order that would be compatible with the kinds of international economic interests pursued by MNCs. The Bretton Woods system of international economic and financial institutions and the Marshall Plan were conceived and executed in order to foster an open industrialized political economy, in which free trade, direct foreign investment, and development could prosper. Indeed, the entire economic structure was conceived as an integral part of the broader concept of containment of Soviet power. The prosperity assumed to result from such an international economy within the Western industrialized world was to remove the chaotic social and economic conditions upon which communist subversion could feed. When in the years immediately following World War II these economic approaches were perceived as inadequate by themselves to maintain the U.S. vision of world order, they were relegated to the realm of "low politics." But the political and strategic preconditions for their operation were attended to and the underlying assumptions concerning the ultimately indispensable role of the economic order remained in place.[39]

By the 1960s both the strategic and economic order were sufficiently well established that the MNCs could prosper. Longstanding opportunities for profitable extractive industry operations in the Third World were now matched by economic conditions in Europe providing incentives for an even more rapid expansion of the American MNC presence there. The establishment of a more open monetary system in Europe after 1958 combined with the tariff barriers imposed by the European Common Market made direct investment in Europe both necessary (to vault the tariff wall) and easier (full convertability of European currencies and the emergence of a transnational banking establishment made business operations within Europe more attractive). But once in place, the MNCs pursued their respective interests with mixed effects on United States foreign policy.

An important instance of MNCs pursuing their own interests occurred during the chaotic monetary crises of the early 1970s. Predictably, corporate financial managers sought to protect the financial positions of their corporations during the period of most intense monetary instability—late 1972 and especially early 1973. Thus MNCs sought to increase their holdings of the strongest currencies—German marks, Swiss francs, Dutch guilders, and Japanese yen—and unload the weakest currencies, such as the dollar. The short-term effect of this activity was undoubtedly to increase the pressure on the Nixon administration to respond to the mounting crisis. The movement by the MNCs and other holders of dollars away from the American currency and into other stronger positions tended to drive the value of the dollar down vis-a-vis other currencies. Although this contributed to a short-term strengthening of the trade position of the United States, the overall stresses introduced into the international monetary system eventually became economically and, more importantly, politically unbearable, thereby forcing the Nixon administration to take the steps that led eventually to the establishment of a more flexible and responsive international monetary system.[40]

Insofar as this shift to a more flexible international monetary system than was possible under the fixed exchange rate system of Bretton Woods is regarded as a good thing, then the MNCs pursuit of self-interest worked to the benefit of all, including the U.S. There is little evidence that the MNCs engaged in excessive speculation or profiteering during this period. Indeed, when President Nixon and his Treasury Secretary adopted a confrontationist posture during the early months of the crisis in late 1971, the MNCs added their weight to the pressure being applied by the Europeans and Henry Kissinger to resolve the crisis cooperatively lest there be irreparable harm to the alliance.[41]

The relationship of the exercise of private power to American policy goals is mixed in this case. To the extent that it was the desire of the Nixon administration to see the value of the dollar decline relative to other currencies and thereby strengthen the trade position of the United States in the early 1970s, the hedging of their financial position by the MNCs aided that policy. It is not clear, however, that this MNC activity was in any way coordinated with the United States. Moreover, when the Nixon administration pursued a policy that promised confrontation with the Europeans concerning the future of the international monetary order, many MNCs threw their weight on the side of moderation.

The attempt by the Reagan administration to halt the sale of gas pipeline equipment to the Soviet Union by American and European MNCs in the summer of 1982 underscored yet again the complex and ambiguous relationship between MNCs and American foreign policy. In this case, the Reagan administration ordered the French subsidiary of Dresser Industries, an American oil and gas technology firm, as well as foreign companies in England, Germany, and Italy which had either purchased equipment from or had constructed equipment under franchise from another American firm, General Electric, not to sell the technology to the Soviet Union under the terms of contracts negotiated by the Europeans. The French government, however, ordered the Dresser subsidiary in France—a company incorporated under the laws of France—to sell the equipment or risk nationalization by the French government. The American parent firm ordered its French subsidiary to honor its contract with the Soviet Union and follow the French government's orders. In U.S. Federal Court, Dresser challenged the legality of the U.S. government's attempt to extend American law to MNC subsidiaries operating abroad. The U.S., in turn, imposed sanctions on Dresser, ordering it not to sell any technology or information to their French subsidiary. The U.S. threatened similar sanctions against the other European firms, leading to angry denunciations from European leaders.

The legality of the American government's actions is uncertain. There seemed to be a balance of precedent for Dresser's and the Europeans' argument that the reach of American law and commercial control did not extend into the legal and commercial domain of another state. Indeed, the U.S. Supreme Court has held in the case of *Avaligno* v. *Sumitomo Shoji America* that the American subsidiaries of foreign firms (in this case Japanese) must abide by American law, in this instance affirmative action in hiring. On the other hand, legal authorities have observed that the legality of American government control on the actions of the American parent company is well founded.

No less important, however, the political ramifications of the Reagan administration's attempt to control MNCs were immediate and serious. The French, British, German, and Italian governments regarded Reagan's actions as a serious intrusion into their commercial and national interests. Their sharp orders to their own companies and the American subsidiaries operating within their countries that they ignore Reagan's demands made it clear that the consequences of MNC activities in this case extended far beyond mere commercial transactions. By the late summer of 1982, the Reagan administration seemed to grasp that nothing less than the cohesion of the NATO alliance was at stake and began to seek a diplomatic resolution of the impasse by moving to soften the sanctions and open discussions with the Europeans. By the end of 1982, the administration, bowing to European pressure and the unproductive feuding within NATO, dropped the matter. The legal questions concerning the status of the MNCs and American control remained unresolved, however.[42]

MNC activities in the Third World also vary with respect to how they have harmonized with U.S. policy. On the one hand, the presence of American MNCs engaged in extractive industries and the export of agricultural commodities throughout the Third World has long been a symbol of what many would characterize as the dark, exploitive essence of the American world order.[43] Here the MNC is viewed as an agent of American interests, imposing a political and economic order insensitive to the host country's aspirations for autonomous political and economic development. The image is seemingly confirmed by the revelations of the machinations of the International Telephone and Telegraph Company in Chile, either independently or in concert with the United States, to bring down a constitutionally elected government of that country.

American MNCs, however, proved unable to serve American interests during the oil crisis of 1973 and 1974 and subsequent OPEC price increases. In fact, even before the 1973 crisis, the oil companies offered only limited resistance to OPEC's insistence that the oil companies join the producing companies on the price escalator. Insofar as the prices charged by the producing countries to the oil companies could be passed on to industrialized and developing world consumers, the oil companies could not lose. In time, of course, the companies would have their controlling interests in the production of the oil taken over by the producing countries. Nonetheless, they have maintained their distribution and marketing systems, the refining capacity necessary to the delivery of petroleum products, and high profit levels.

The MNC-OPEC relationship is likely to be the model for future MNC operations in the Third World rather than the conventional neoimperialist relationship.[44] As Third World countries become more sophisticated in their response to the MNC presence, and as MNCs seek to protect their base of operations and economic opportunities in Third World and even in industrialized countries, MNCs are seen as becoming more and more accommodating to host-country demands. For example, there need not be any inherent incompatibility between host-country desires to export goods and services to the rest of the world and the MNC desire to take advantage of lower labor costs abroad. The negative economic effects of such an arrangement are likely to show up in the United States and other industrialized countries that become the object of these lower-cost imports and suffer the political and economic disruptions from any labor displacement that might occur.

Thus the MNC emerges as perhaps the most complex of the concentrations of private power examined in this chapter. In the broadest sense, the MNC can act as a private government with interests of its own and the resources to pursue them. On the other hand, its very existence and its ability to operate with such flexibility depends upon a political and strategic order largely created and sustained by American power during a time when the United States possessed clear and unchallenged economic and military hegemony throughout most of the international system. As the military and economic hegemony of the United States recedes, the MNCs pursuit of their interests probably will more frequently diverge from those of the United States.

> For example, a radio announcement of King Faisal's decision to impose an oil embargo on the United States was enough to propel Frank

Jungers, chairman and chief executive officer of Aramco, to order a cutback larger than the percentage demanded by Faisal, just for good measure. "The important thing," according to Jungers, "was to give the immediate image of being *with* the government, not trying to fight it."[45]

PRIVATE POWER AND THE POLICY PROCESS

A phenomenon displaying as many dimensions as private power is not one about which simple conclusions can be drawn. Rather, we have emphasized in this survey the range of forms that private power can take and the relationships that may exist between private and public power in the foreign policy making processes. As with much else in the American policy making system, one's judgments concerning these relationships are frequently colored by judgments concerning the policy outcomes resulting from the relationships. Thus MNCs could become a cause of alarm when they pursued their interests in conjunction with OPEC in 1973–1974, but other MNCs—in this case multinational financial institutions—have been applauded for their capacity and willingness to manage the massive financial consequences of the oil crisis. "Special interest groups" are roundly condemned when they block comprehensive energy legislation or pursue higher defense spending, but the same behavior is acceptable when one's own interests are "represented," such as opposition to or support for the Panama Canal Treaties or the Vietman War.

Nonetheless, those who have ventured an assessment of the effects of the exercise of private power during the last decade have tended to draw essentially negative conclusions. The most serious problem resulting from such activity is not so much related to the policy outcomes pursued by private power but instead, the effect that the upsurge in private activity has had on the governability of American democracy and, hence, the efficacy of American foreign policy. That is to say, the exercise of private power, whatever its specific form of policy objectives, can be seen as exacerbating the inherent fragmentation of the American policy making process as well as increasing the claims on the considerable but, nonetheless, finite resources available for the pursuit of the national interest.[46] The upshot, it is argued, has been an undermining of authority and the onset of a kind of "democratic distemper" in which demands escalate and governmental effectiveness declines.

> Conflicting goals and specialized interests crowd one in upon another, with executives, cabinets, parliaments, and bureaucrats lacking the criteria to discriminate among them. The system becomes one of anomic democracy, in which democratic politics becomes more an arena for the assertion of conflicting interests than a process for the building of common purpose.[47]

But there is an additional dimension of the problem: the dilemmas posed by private power also extend to sharing policy making power or, in the case of MNCs, some degree of independent policy making capability. First, the fragmentation of the American policy making process is compounded. Centers of private power existing in symbiotic relationships with the government as well as independent sources of private power extend and complicate the policy making process. The already complex process of organizing and mobilizing constitutionally decreed shared power within the government takes on an added dimension of complexity when the mobilization must now encompass relevant policy making centers outside the formal policy making process. Second, the existence of these concentrations of power that constrain the policy making process and its outcomes recalls the problems of accountability raised by these conditions. Institutional complexity and shared constitutional power were designed into the policy making process to insure a measure of accountability within government. But when the locus of the policy process becomes situated in a gray netherworld between, for example, Congress, the executive national security establishment, and the industrial centers that provide the material wherewithal to meet security needs, accountability becomes more problematical. Similarly when actors such as MNCs and conditions beyond the control of national authorities can constrain national policy making, democratic policy making is itself constrained.[48]

In the American political system multiple centers of public policy making provide mutliple points of access for interest groups. Moreover, the underlying assumptions of the American constitutional design and political culture have encouraged the development and concentration of private power and activism, especially economic power. Accordingly, one should not be surprised when concentrations of such power emerge and are brought to bear on public policy making. Such behavior is quite consistent with American tradition; on the other hand, such power and its exercise can constrain and limit governmental action.

American foreign and national security policy itself compounds the dilemmas. Post–World War II dependence on the instrumentalities of force has necessitated the development and maintenance of a large industrial infrastructure to supply the necessary weapons systems. The resulting military-industrial complex (in which we find public and private power existing in a near symbiotic relationship) has provided a strong defense. But as President Eisenhower warned, this conjunction of industry and government poses serious questions concerning the efficiency and accountability of the process. Since the policy assumptions that have given rise to the military-industrial complex are not likely to be modified in the near future, there remains the necessity of maintaining some form of arms production and acquisition process. Some have suggested that the ostensibly private sector of the complex simply be nationalized in recognition of the fact that they no longer conform in any way to our traditional conceptions of private enterprise.[49] Such a step would not be without precedent—as in much of the railroad system. But to propose a nationalized arms industry is to advocate the changing of deeply and intensely held attitudes towards the relationship of public and private power.

Finally, a foreign policy that has encouraged the growth and activities of private actors in the international political economy has simultaneously encouraged the development of at least some constraints on that foreign policy. An expanding network of governmental and private economic transactions was regarded as an essential element of postwar containment and order. On the other hand, this network of transactions was undertaken in part by MNCs and private financial institutions that had interests and capabilities of their own. In this respect they were private governments that have taken advantage of the framework of political and economic order established and maintained by American power, and now possess a kind of autonomy that, when exercised, can constrain American foreign policy formulation and latitude. Of all of the dilemmas posed by the interaction of public and private power in the foreign policy realm, this one is most wanting of simple remedy.

NOTES

1. David B. Truman, *The Governmental Process: Political Interests and Public Opinion* (New York: Knopf, 1951).
2. Grant McConnell, *Private Power and American Democracy* (New York: Vintage, 1966).
3. Samuel Huntington, "The Governability of Democracies: USA," in Michael Crozier, Samuel Huntington, and Joji Watanuki, *The Governability of Democracies* (Trilateral Commission, May 1975). Huntington's argument was also published as "The Democratic Distemper," in Nathan Glazer and Irving Kristol, eds., *The American Commonwealth* (New York: Basic Books, 1976).
4. See for example, Norman J. Ornstein and Shirley Elder, *Interest Groups, Lobbying and Policymaking* (Washington, D.C.: Congressional Quarterly Press, 1978), esp. pp. 35–53. In addition see Truman, op. cit., pp. 111–155.
5. Qualification and a blurring of the edges of this category are necessary, however, for in some instances the "information" provided by interest groups may include actual language for legislation or regulations affecting the group's interests. Indeed, there are cases in which lobbyists or representatives of interest groups have been taken into the legislation drafting process itself. When drafting complex tax and tariff legislation, for example, it is not uncommon for lobbyists for affected industries to actually take part in the deliberations of congressional committees as they develop legislative language. John Manley, *The Politics of Finance* (Boston: Little, Brown, 1970).
6. For a discussion of these functions, see Ornstein and Elder, op. cit., pp. 28–34, and Robert H. Salisbury, "An Exchange Theory of Interest Groups," *Midwest Journal of Political Science* 13, no. 1 (February 1969): 16.
7. This analysis is based on the excellent and extensive survey of lobbying in Congress undertaken by Thomas M. Frank and Edward Weisband in *Foreign Policy and Congress* (New York: Oxford University Press, 1979), pp. 165–209.
8. See *The Washington Lobby* (Washington, D.C.: Congressional Quarterly, Inc., 1979) and Stephen D. Issacs, *Jews and American Politics* (New York: Doubleday, 1974).
9. Frank and Weisband, op. cit., pp. 186–190.
10. Ibid., pp. 102–103 and 108–109.
11. Ibid., pp. 191–193.
12. See Philip V. White's report on a pair of round tables on black and foreign affairs convened by the Joint Center for Political Studies, "Blacks and International Relations," *Focus* 9, no. 1 (January 1981): 3.

13. See *New York Times*, 9 March 1981; and Barry Schweid, "Firing of Sea-riches Mediator Bares Rift," *Wilmington Morning News*, 10 March 1981, p. A2.
14. Frank and Weisband, op. cit., p. 196. For a general overview of the oil industry and its operation, see John M. Blair, *The Control of Oil* (New York: Vintage Books, 1976).
15. Les Aspin, *New York Times*, 10 October 1977.
16. For examples see Frank and Weisband, op. cit., p. 198.
17. For the use of the resources in the Panama Canal Treaties case, see William Languette, "The Panama Canal Treaties: Playing in Peoria and the Senate," *National Journal*, October 8, 1977, p. 1560.
18. See *New York Times*, 30 April 1978.
19. *Washington Post*, 8 June 1976.
20. Dwight D. Eisenhower, *Waging Peace* (Garden City, N.Y.: Doubleday, 1965), p. 616.
21. On this point see Richard Barnet, *The Economy of Death* (New York: Athenaeum, 1969), pp. 112FF.
22. Perhaps the best single analysis of the military-industrial complex in the 1970s is J. Ronald Fox, *Arming America: How the U.S. Buys Weapons* (Boston: Division of Reasearch, Harvard Business School, 1974). For a comparable analysis of the 1950s and 1960s, see Merton J. Peck and Frederick M. Scherer, *The Weapons Acquisition Process: An Economic Analysis* (Boston: Division of Research, Harvard Business School, 1962). For the data presented in these paragraphs, see Fox, p. 43 and Department of Defense, Office of the Assistant Secretary of Defense (Comptroller), *100 Companies Receiving the Largest Dollar Volume of Military Prime Contracts, Fiscal Year 1976* (Washington, D.C.: GPO, 1977), p. 1.
23. Fox, op. cit., pp. 15–24.
24. Thus a main battle tank that could be produced for about $125,000 in the 1940s now costs the U.S. Army well in excess of $1,000,000. The first mass-produced jet fighter aircraft, the F-86, cost about $400,000 apiece; the F-15 and F-14 now cost the Air Force and Navy tens of millions of dollars each.
25. For a detailed discussion of these and other considerations, see Fox, op. cit.
26. Peck and Scherer, op. cit., p. 60.
27. Fox, op. cit., p. 38.
28. David Prior, "The Lobby Industry: A Growing Concern," *USA Today*, July 1982: 14–15.
29. "Turbulent Flight for the C-5B," *Time*, 2 August, 1982: 14.
30. However, even as the prospect of more spending emerged, warnings were issued from the industrial sector that rearmament could not occur rapidly. The preceding years of drought, it was claimed, had very nearly killed off the industrial partner in the military-industrial relationship. For a survey of these developments see "The Defense Production Gap: Why the U.S. Can't Rearm Fast," *Business Week*, 4 February 1980, pp. 80–86.
31. Jackson R. McGowan, president of the Douglas Aircraft Division of the McDonnell Douglas Corporation, in the *Los Angeles Times*, 1 October 1971, as quoted by Fox, op. cit., p. 68.

32. For historical analysis of the multinational corporation, see Mira Wilkins, *The Emergence of Multinational Enterprise: American Business Abroad From the Colonial Era to 1914* (Cambridge, Mass.: Harvard University Press, 1970) and idem, *The Maturing of Multinational Enterprise: American Business Abroad From 1914 to 1970* (Cambridge, Mass.: Harvard University Press, 1974).

33. *Fortune World Business Directory, 1979,* p. 22; *World Bank Atlas, 1977;* and *Statistical Abstract of the U.S., 1981,* p. 895.

34. Raymond Vernon, *Sovereignty at Bay: The Multinational Spread of U.S. Enterprise* (New York: Basic Books, 1971), p. 5.

35. For analysis from the left that views the MNCs as neoimperialist agents of an essentially American world order, see Gabriel Kolko, *The Politics of War: The World and United States Foreign Policy, 1943–1945* (New York: Random House, 1969); Joyce Kolko and Gabriel Kolko, *The Limits of Power: The World and United States Foreign Policy, 1945–1954* (New York: Harper and Row, 1970); Harry Magdoff, *The Age of Imperialism: The Economics of U.S. Foreign Policy* (New York: Monthly Review Press, 1969). For perhaps the most subtle analysis from this perspective, see Stephen Hymer, "The Multinational Corporation and the Law of Uneven Development," in Jagdish N. Bhagwati, ed., *Economics and World Order: From the 1970s to the 1980s* (New York: Macmillan, 1972). For a counteranalysis that nonetheless links the MNCs to the prevailing political order, see Robert Gilpin, *U.S. Power and the Multinational Corporation: The Political Economy of Foreign Direct Investment* (New York: Basic Books, 1975). See also Gilpin, *The Multinational Corporation and the National Interest,* prepared for the Senate Committee on Labor and Public Welfare, 93rd Congress, 1st Session, 1973.

36. For this view see Vernon, op. cit.; and Richard Barnet and Ronald E. Muller, *Global Reach: The Power of Multinational Corporations* (New York: Simon and Schuster, 1974).

37. See C. Fred Bergsten, Thomas Horst, and Theodore H. Moran, *American Multinationals and American Interests* (Washington, D.C.: The Brookings Institution, 1978).

38. On the "American" character of American MNCs, see Kenneth Simmonds, "Multinational? Well Not Quite," *Columbia Journal of World Business* (Fall 1966). See also, Vernon, op. cit., p. 146.

39. For detailed exposition and elaboration of this thesis, see James A. Nathan and James K. Oliver, *United States Foreign Policy and World Order,* 2nd ed. (Boston: Little, Brown, 1981).

40. For an analysis of the behavior of American MNCs during the monetary crises, see *Multinational Corporations in the Dollar-Devaluation Crisis: Report on a Questionnaire,* prepared by the Staff of the Subcommittee on Multinational Corporations of the Senate Foreign Relations Committee, 94th Congress, 1st Session, 1975. See also Sidney M. Robbins and Robert B. Stobaugh, *Money in the Multinational Enterprise: A Study of Financial Management* (New York: Basic Books, 1973).

41. Bergsten, Horst, and Moran, op. cit., pp. 289–290.

42. For a discussion of the legal dimensions of the pipeline case see Leslie Gelb, "Pipeline: An Impasse With No End in Sight," *New York Times*, 31 August 1982, p. D1. On the economics of the deal see Steve Mufson, "Anatomy of Continuing Soviet Pipeline Controversy," *Wall Street Journal*, 31 August 1982, p. 29.
43. See footnote 33.
44. Bergsten, Horst, and Moran, op. cit., pp. 335–353.
45. Quoted in ibid., footnote 74, p. 352, and drawn from Allan T. Demarree, "Aramco is a Lesson in the Management of Chaos," *Fortune* 89 (February 1974): 58–65.
46. Huntington, op. cit., p. 21.
47. Ibid., p. 5.
48. For a useful discussion of this aspect of "interdependence," see Karl Kaiser, "Transnational Relations as a Threat to the Democratic Process," *International Organization* 25, no. 3 (Summer 1971): 706–720.
49. John Kenneth Galbraith, *How to Control the Military* (Garden City, N.Y.: Doubleday, 1969).

Chapter 9
Foreign Policy Making and American Democracy

Assessments of the domestic environment and institutions that shape the American approach toward international affairs frequently echo de Tocqueville's conclusion that "as for myself, I do not hesitate to say that it is especially in the conduct of their foreign relations that democracies appear to me decidedly inferior to other governments." De Tocqueville continued:

> Foreign politics demand scarcely any of those qualities which are peculiar to a democracy; they require, on the contrary, the perfect use of almost all those in which it is deficient. . . . [A] democracy can only with great difficulty regulate the details of an important undertaking, persevere in a fixed design, and work out its execution in spite of serious obstacles. It cannot combine its measures with secrecy or await their consequences with patience.[1]

There is ample evidence that policy makers responsible for the formulation and conduct of foreign and national security have often been as troubled by these domestic environmental and institutional limits as they have with the foreign objects and international conditions that are presumably the essence of foreign and national security policies. Indeed, one could very nearly write a history of American foreign and national security policy after World War II solely from the perspective of policy makers straining against the limits imposed by the American cultural, constitutional, institutional, and political milieu. In this book we have surveyed the many elements of this domestic framework. Let us, in this conclusion,[2] review the main themes developed above and offer some closing observations concerning both the obstacles and opportunities presented by the American foreign and national security policy making process.

CONSTRAINTS AND LIMITS

Whether during the late 1940s, the 1950s, or the early 1960s, when the apparent combination of international anarchy and strong ideologically antagonistic enemies armed with nuclear weapons dominated the American world view, or during the late 1960s and the 1970s, when political economics and economic power perplexed the policy establishment, a set of images and concerns about the American policy making and domestic political milieu were in evidence. The fragmented policy making and decisional processes as well as the generally uninformed and unpredictable character of a democratic society were liabilities in the planning and conduct of foreign and national security policy. The implication of this for many observers of the national security machinery is that such a system is inefficient, even dangerous within the contemporary international system. For a policy making system of fragmented and diffused power would seem to frustrate the needs of a state that would operate in, or impose order upon the international system. Accordingly, the policy making institutions and processes had to be somehow "protected" from the "excesses of democracy" and the institutions and processes themselves centralized and "rationalized" so as to permit flexibility and responsiveness in dealing with a dangerous and complex international environment.

Constitutional Constraints.   Not the least of the obstacles to such a transformation is the basic constitutional framework of the United States. The Constitution militates against coherence and efficiency. From the very outset, an unresolved tension has lain at the nexus of the constitutionally prescribed foreign and national security policy making authority. On the one hand there is Alexander Hamilton's assertion:

> The authorities essential to the common defense are these: to raise armies; to build and equip fleets; to prescribe rules for the government of both; to direct their operations; to provide for their support. These powers ought to exist without limitation, *because it is impossible to foresee or to define the extent and variety of national exigencies, and the correspondent extent and variety of the means which may be necessary to satisfy them.* The circumstances that endanger the safety

of nations are infinite, and for this reason no constitutional shackles can wisely be imposed on the power to which the care of it is committed. The power ought to be coextensive with all the possible combinations of such circumstances; and ought to be under the direction of the same councils which are appointed to preside over the common defense.[3]

In contrast, however, there was the statement of James Madison:

In time of *actual* war, great discretionary powers are constantly given to the Executive Magistrate. Constant apprehension of war, has the same tendency to render the head too large for the body. A standing military force, with an overgrown Executive will not long be safe companions to liberty. The means of defense against foreign danger, have been always the instruments of tyranny at home.[4]

Madison's fear of tyranny proved the stronger force in the construction of the constitutional design. While accepting Hamilton's concern that the exigencies of the common defense demanded centralization of decisional authority in the national government, that authority was itself subject to the now familiar Madisonian approach of "so contriving the interior structure of the government as that its several constituent parts may, by their mutual relations, be the means of keeping each other in their proper places."[5] Thus decisional power was fragmented and processes established that would, it was hoped, at least minimize the possibility of preponderant decisional authority and responsibility accruing to any single individual or institution. "In republican government," Madison asserted, "the legislative authority necessarily predominates."[6] But Hamilton's arguments were not without force. Accordingly, a unitary Commander-in-Chief was established to whom was given treaty making and other diplomatic functions, but the power to declare war, the authority to raise and maintain armies and navies, and the power to ratify treaties were vested in Congress. It was not an especially neat structure, but the pattern of overlapping, shared, and even conflicting powers present in the system was deemed a necessary price to pay to protect the transcendent value of nontyrannical government. This position was reaffirmed by the twentieth-century jurist, Justice Louis Brandeis:

The doctrine of separation of powers was adopted by the Convention of 1787, not to promote efficiency but to preclude the exercise of arbitrary power. The purpose was, not to avoid friction, but, by means of the inevitable friction incident to the distribution of the governmental powers among three departments, to save the people from autocracy.[7]

Viewed from this perspective, these policy making inefficiencies are by no means irrational.

But if the problems presented by the original constitutional design could be rationalized in terms of transcendent principles of political liberty, subsequent developments seemed to demand structural modifications. Once committed to the course of global activism in an international context of ambiguous cold war, the mobilization and deployment of resources, as well as the permanent possibility of nuclear war, led inexorably to modification of constitutional interpretation. By the 1960s there had been a near transformation of the executive-legislative relationship.

Under the constitutional design, substantial foreign policy power was given to Congress with the expectation that it would exercise those powers with responsibility to a vision larger than the individual member's political survival. Unfortunately, critics have asserted, the reality has been too frequently contrary to the constitutional theory. Congress, it has been argued, became preoccupied with the persistent press of reelection and hampered by a complex and cumbersome internal structure. Nowhere was de Tocqueville's critique of democracy more appropriate than with respect to Congress.

The exigencies of mid-century recalled the Hamiltonian argument and his "axioms as simple as they are universal; the *means* ought to be proportioned to the *end;* the persons from whose agency the attainment of any *end* is expected ought to possess the *means* by which it is attained."[8] The end of global management required, it seemed, an energetic executive, and thus throughout the 1950s and 1960s Congress granted authority and instrumentalities to a succession of Presidents.

But if events and circumstances had seemed to resolve the constitutional tension in favor of the presidency by the 1960s, the fate of the policy response to those circumstances once again called forth the constitutional constraints. As America's Vietnam involvement accrued more and more costs, popular and congressional reaction turned negative. Presidents Johnson and Nixon resorted to increasingly blatant assertions of presidential prerogative, thereby forcing the issue of the fundamental imbalance that had developed between the presidency on the one hand and Congress on the other. Thus by the 1970s, it had become commonplace to speak of an "imperial Presidency"[9] with powers greater than those of history's great autocrats.[10]

As the excesses of the Nixon presidency became more manifest and culminated in the Watergate scandal, attention concentrated on the swollen institution and powers of the office. By the middle and late 1970s, some scholars had begun openly asking whether the kind of presidency seemingly demanded by American foreign policy was compatible with traditional American freedoms. The resort to secrecy, control and manipulation of information, deceit, and spying on and interference with the legitimate exercise of the political rights of American citizens was deemed by some to have become an inherent and ongoing necessity of a national security bureaucracy increasingly out of and perhaps beyond control.[11] The Madisonian fears now seemed more compelling.

Paralleling these concerns about the dangers and even pathologies of the cold war presidency was a renewed interest in what was taken to be a renascence of Congress. Congress had emerged as a focal point of organized and effective political opposition to the Vietnam War and the claims of presidential power advanced by the Johnson and especially the Nixon administrations. Accordingly, interest in the capacity of the institution for "congressional government" surged. It was clear that the congressional reaction to the war and the Nixon administration had contributed to significant internal reforms within Congress and the assertion of new powers such as the legislative or congressional veto. On the other hand, it was not self-evident that Congress had succeeded by the end of the 1970s in establishing a means whereby the legislature could become a full and responsible partner in the policy planning and formulation phase of American foreign policy making. Rather, Congress remained an essentially reactive participant in the process; policy initiative could be exercised by Congress only spasmodically. Indeed, to the extent that Congress had become more effective as a check on presidential power and initiative, concern began to mount by the end of the decade that the American system was becoming bogged down in institutional deadlock and political stalemate and therefore incapable of exercising world leadership. [12] Moreover, with the advent, in the 1980 election, of what could be an extended period of Republican control of the Senate, the role of a politically divided Congress seemed even more problematical. The resurgence of intense anti-Soviet feeling raised the possibility of a return to the kind of diminished congressional role typical of the 1950s and 1960s.

Nonetheless, on the threshold of the 1980s, the constitutional constraints of 200 years ago retain their force. For the small isolated nation that constructed the Constitution, institutional deadlock and political stalemate were desirable outcomes. World leadership was explicitly abjured by Washington in part out of a fear of what such a role would do to the constitutional design and the values it was to protect. For the framers of the constitutional constraints, structural tension and policy making complexity were necessary, even elegant, accouterments of a republican form of government. For late twentieth century American foreign and national security policymakers, such accouterments have also taken on the attributes of seemingly intractible impediments to the planning and implementation of policy.

Bureaucratic Constraints. Constitutional constraints are givens in the policy making environment. They have come to be viewed as constraints, in no small measure because the institutional framework has been called upon to serve a perceived national interest far beyond anything imagined in the eighteenth century. On the other hand, there are other institutional constraints present in the American system that have resulted precisely from the effort to augment the constitutional structure to deal with the demands of a foreign policy predicated on the construction and maintenance of world order. Specifically, the implementation of a foreign and national security policy as multifaceted as containment had become by the early 1950s, required thousands and eventually tens of thousands of people organized around the planning and administration of the programs designed to mobilize the money, people, information, and technology necessary for the establishment and maintenance of world order. In a word, a large and growing bureaucracy, a foreign and national security policy establishment has developed. And though it was originally established to facilitate the planning and implementing of national security and foreign policy, its very size and diversity, and their effects on policy making processes, have come to be viewed as constraints as important as the constitutional structure itself. The fragmentation of a now enormous foreign policy establishment is therefore, a legitimate source of concern. For it pushes the inherent and constitutionally mandated fragmentation of the American government and policy making processes to a point where it is fair to ask whether the difficulties of policy formulation and administration in such a complex bureaucratic milieu may not undermine the very national interests and security that the bureaucracies are purportedly serving. Might not the ponderous process of coordinating these many departments, agencies, and bureaus move too slowly and produce an ultimately inadequate compromise of many departments' interests rather than a foreign policy that serves the interests of the American people? Or, failing such compromise and coordination, might not so many actors promoting so many and often such conflicting perceptions of the national interest contribute to a chaotic congeries of foreign policies that work at cross-purposes?

The National Security Act of 1947 anticipated this problem of a growing national security policy bureaucracy to a certain extent. The National Security Council was to be a means for coordinating the activities of the various departments and agencies. But by the late 1960s, the NSC and especially the security adviser had become a powerful locus of national security advice and formulation. Indeed, many critics contended that the Special Assistant for National Security Affairs and the NSC staff had become the center of an inordinant and dangerous concentration of policy making power within the White House. Thus critics of American foreign policy and policy making could contend that even as the growth of the foreign policy bureaucracy constituted an excessive and dangerous caricature of the Madisonian separation of power, the attempt to counter organizational and administrative disarray had produced an excessive and dangerous centralization of power.

Yet, to steer events by the customary repertory of coercive devices, even in a new international environment and in a domestic context of circumscribed options, would be still conceivable if the

United States were governed as it was for most of the cold war. As the Trilateral Commission Report authored by Samuel Huntington noted, "to the extent that the United States was governed by anyone during the decade after WW II, it was governed by the President acting with the support and cooperation of the individuals and groups in the Executive Office, the federal bureaucracy, banks, law firms, foundations, and media, which constitute the private establishment."[13] To confine the elements of the policy making group to a fairly small and identifiable number of individuals led by the Executive did help overcome some of the inherent limitations of "a government of separated institutions sharing power."[14] But in the wake of Vietnam and Watergate in the late sixties and early seventies, there were many who questioned, as Professor Huntington explained it, "the legitimacy of hierarchy, coercion, discipline, secrecy and deception—all of which are, in some measure, inescapable attributes of the process of government."[15] And they all, Huntington might also have concluded, logically proceed from executive power.

The late 1970s, however, saw a great turnaround in domestic opinion and in policy circles toward the issue of Soviet power and the need for greater preparedness. By 1980, the new strategic consensus was well buttressed and even, as Zbigniew Brzezinski pridefully told reporters on the eve of the Reagan transition, once again "fashionable."[16] But the global vision that has been the hallmark of the cold war is always subject to bureaucratic fragmentation. Hence, the need for executive control. As Brzezinski explained neatly, and in the case of the Reagan administration, prophetically:

> I think everyone feels that he is for the U.S. national interest, except how that interest is perceived and defined gets very much influenced by narrow institutional interests. The typical response of the Defense Department to a problem is to try and obtain an increase in the defense budget, while at the same time often being very reluctant to use force once that budget is increased. The institutional response of State is to rely on diplomacy and to be rather skeptical of the use of power even for demonstration purposes.
>
> That is why, ultimately, the president does need some sort of a coordinating framework or organ within which a broader vision is generated. This is one reason why, over the years, a presidential office for national security affairs emerged.

It is not because of the personal talents or pecularities of individuals who have held that position . . . [Rather, the office emerged because of] the logic of America's engagement in the world and the president's need for a perspective that integrates the different institutional divisions.[17]

The Reagan administration flirted briefly with breaking the pattern of more than 20 years of bureaucratic political development by reducing the stature of the security adviser. Even so, however ill-defined, the administrative hierarchy that remained was centered in the personal staff of the President, ostensibly under his direct control. A year of national security and foreign affairs disarray, bickering, and administrative disorder rivaling that of the Carter administration, called forth a major reorganization in early 1982. Once again, the position of security adviser was elevated to primacy in the coordination of the national security bureaucracy. Nonetheless, public disagreement persisted between the Departments of State and Defense, and the observer of these struggles within a supposedly ideologically homogenous administration was left to wonder if bureaucratic fragmentation and struggle was not an inevitable and irremediable concomitant of a globalist and activist foreign policy.

Democracy as a Constraint.   But the dilemmas of foreign policy formulation, planning, and management in the American political system are more complex yet, for the American system has during the 2 centuries of its existence developed into a far more democratic system than the original designers of the Constitution foresaw. Thus with expansion of voting to a larger electorate and with the number, range, and access of organized interest groups also expanding, the problems of contemporary policy makers have become even more complicated. The nature of the electorate to whom policy makers are accountable is frequently cited as the essence of the problem. Thus one student of the American political system, having evaluated research findings on public opinion and attitudes, concludes:

> The masses are incompetent in the tasks of government. They have neither the time, intelligence, information, skills, nor knowledge to direct the course of a nation. . . . Governing a nation is a task which is too vital, too complex, and too difficult to be left to the masses.[18]

Furthermore, some claim that in no area of public policy are most Americans so ill-informed and unconcerned as in foreign policy:

> The "ordinary citizen" does not seem to have enough information at his command to play even his limited public part with full efficiency. Public opinion polls reveal a startling lack of knowledge about such important matters as the United Nations, NATO, the nature of Communism, and so on. Without basic data, it is a near-impossibility for individuals to make intelligent decisions—or even any decisions at all.[19]

This combination of an uneven public awareness of foreign affairs and the frequently disruptive nature of the American electoral process has contributed to a certain uneasiness on the part of some concerning the relationship of democratic processes and foreign policy making. George Kennan reflected this ambivalence when he lamented that "it is sometimes easier for a strong and authoritative government to shape its external conduct in an enlightened manner, when the spirit so moves it, than it is for a democratic government locked in the throes of domestic political conflict."[20]

Finally, another group of observers, taking note of the collapse during the 1970s of whatever foreign policy consensus might have existed during the cold war years, has emphasized yet another difficulty posed by democracy. American constitutional theory always presupposed limited government so as to protect and allow for the development and exercise of substantial private initiative and freedom, especially with respect to economic activity. As a result, concentrations of private nongovernmental power have always been an important part of the American system. But by the late 1950s and 1960s, the American system underwent a veritable explosion of political and economic organization as various groups sought to emulate the success of the labor and civil rights movements. Moreover, the articulation and expression of demands became increasingly direct and intensely focused on Congress and the presidency. The traditional intermediary role played by the political parties was in some measure short-circuited as political, economic, social, and environmental activists exploited the immediate and pervasive presence of modern media such as television to bring their demands and political pressures to bear on the governmental system.

The pervasiveness of contemporary electronic and print media have had additional effects beyond serving as a ready means for more highly mobilized activists to gain a hearing. More subtle but no less important consequences flow from the pervasiveness of media, in that the public is now exposed to numerous alternative views of international reality other than those traditionally provided by policy making elites. Moreover, the aggressiveness of the media now makes it more difficult for the government to maintain a public posture of consistency. Leaking to the media becomes virtually endemic, and the government quicky loses its monopoly on information and hence the command of the loyalties of the public. Under such circumstances the legitimacy of governmental policy is easily challenged, and with the challenge goes an undermining of authority and the erosion of policy coherence.

Perhaps nowhere were the consequences of this combination of higher public mobilization and media impact more apparent than during the late 1960s and throughout the 1970s. First with respect to Vietnam but then concerning a volatile mix of single issue campaigns, the governmental structure yielded wherever the pressure became most intense. But as Samuel Huntington has argued in one of the seminal analyses of the phenomenon, such a response was ultimately inadequate:

> Polarization over issues generated distrust about government, as those who had strong positions on issues became dissatisfied with the ambivalent, compromising policies of government. Political leaders, in effect, alienated more and more people by attempting to please them through time-honored traditional politics of compromise.[21]

By the 1970s, therefore, some observers felt that the ultimate and dangerous democratic character of the American system was manifest. The result, they asserted, was democratic excess in which the American political system had degenerated to little more than an arena in which intensely felt but conflicting demands contended, but out of which the common purpose necessary to successful foreign policy had not, indeed could not, emerge. The failure of Vietnam, the sordid spectacle of Watergate, and the seeming inability of government to protect and cushion people against the shocks of economic interdependence in the form of high energy prices and foreign competition combined to undermine the legitimacy of political institutions and the authority of the formal and informal policy establishment. The upshot was a "zero-sum society" in which no one was willing to pay the social and economic price of adjustment required by the international position in which the United States found itself. Furthermore, the scale of political, economic, and social organization combined with the fragmented character of the American governmental system made it extraordinarily difficult to apportion the costs and shift the burdens of adjustment with the decisiveness and speed that international circumstances seemed to demand.[22] There was, in short, a "democratic distemper"[23]—the fulfillment of de Tocqueville's gloomy prognosis.

A DECIDEDLY INFERIOR FORM?

These are in no sense trivial issues and problems. Insofar as the United States remained at the time of de Tocqueville's visit in the early nineteenth century an essentially agrarian nation on the periphery of the world and international relations, his concerns about the prospects for democracy in America and the world were largely theoretical. Now, however, the global entanglements and aspirations of the United States far exceed those of even the greatest of powers of the previous century. At the same time, American democracy is, if anything, more extensive than then if measured by such indexes as the scope of the potential electorate and the availability of participatory opportunities. Thus de Tocqueville's concerns about the capacities and ultimate viability of American democracy have, today, an immediacy and relevance far beyond his speculation on the future of the young Republic.

Fragmentation and Coherence. In the United States, sovereignty is constitutionally defined as "popular." It "belongs" to the people and is institutionally manifested in three branches of government and the Constitution itself. When foreigners deal with the American system, there is always perplexity regarding the decisional processes. Even the strongest of Presidents is constrained by the formal and informal routines of bureaucrats, legislators, the courts, not to speak of the press, lobbyists, and special interest groups. The peculiar "defects" of the American Constitution, which institutionalizes pluralism, have always seemed to mean that the United States would be at a disadvantage in diplomatic and military enterprises. Other states had a sovereign. When the old states of Europe dealt with one another, they could be reasonably sure who spoke authoritatively and who did not. Today, when the United States deals with authoritarian regimes or democracies, not a few analysts have many problems discovering what weight to assign to the public statements of official and private interests. Foreigners might find this process at least as baffling when they try to tune themselves to the potential cacophony of voices and process of American policy.

No one wonders why there is an urge to clarify it all and to make policy more malleable. This urge is shared by policy planners, pundits, Presidents, and Congress alike. And it is probably most true of the Executive. As former Senate and White House aid George Reedy testified:

> In observing the two major divisions of the government, the legislative and the executive, one of the principal differences is that within the executive branch, there exists a virtual horror of public debate on issues. . . . I think it's [due to] a feeling . . . that if the public debates these issues they think the debate is going to make government impossible.[24]

To many observers, the policy making fragmentation of American institutions and processes not only begets incoherence at home and abroad, it is symptomatic of a larger disorder: a kind of immaturity in the exercise of power. As Hans Morgenthau once wrote:

> Nations with a long experience in the conduct of foreign policy and a vivid awareness of its vital importance . . . have developed constitutional devices and political practices which tend to minimize the dangers . . . inherent in the democratic conduct of foreign policy. . . . [In Great Britain, for instance] [t]he collective parliamentary responsibility of the cabinet compels the government to speak in foreign affairs with one voice, so that there can be no doubt, either at home or abroad, about the government's foreign policy at a particular moment.[25]

It is hard, however, to demonstrate empirically that other significant actors in international politics have much of an advantage at home or abroad save, perhaps, in their capacity to dissimulate with more ease. The other great protagonist of world politics in the late twentieth century, the Soviet Union, is certainly no less beset by social, racial, and ethnic tensions than the United States. Contemporary analysis of the Soviet state portrays anything but a monolithic entity lacking in interest groups and complex (and for Soviet authorities frustratingly unresponsive) "bureaucratic politics."[26] Resource constraints are as prevalent and perhaps more limiting within the Soviet economic context.[27] And it is by no means frivolous to query the future of the Soviet state as it confronts yet another traumatic leadership turnover at the top,[28] which in this case, will be a generational turnover as well.

All modern societies of any scale have vested interests that contribute to policy in not wholly predictable fashion. The most prescient and well-informed observers of Soviet policy are constantly attempting to sort out who is "in" and who is "out" at a given moment. The means of doing this is as much a process of divination akin to tea leaf reading as it is a truly scientific analysis of formal authority relationships. Thus the best of these analysts did not see that it was Brezhnev who was beginning to triumph in the struggle after the ouster of Khrushchev.[29] Apparently as surprised and confused as both the Soviet people and the U.S. government over Khrushchev's fall from power, was Khrushchev himself. And who, if not him, should have been an adept "Kremlinologist?"

Authoritarian and totalitarian systems may have about them an air of coherence and stability stemming from concentration of power in the hands of an individual or small group of individuals. But in them the transfer of power has proved sometimes tumultuous, with resultant long and unpredictable periods during which leadership and policy are in disarray. Thus in the wake of Stalin's death, literally years passed—virtually two-thirds of the Eisenhower administration—before Khrushchev consolidated his position. If after finally consolidating control, the regime is long-lived (an uncertain prospect in itself), its policy, though perhaps consistent, is nonetheless bounded by the creativity and virtuosity of those in control.

Thus it would seem an error to equate coherence with diplomatic success or even greater prospect of success. The presumed coherence of Soviet policy proved no guarantee of success in Egypt in the late 1960s and early 1970s. Persistence and coherence undoubtedly facilitate the undertaking of a singular though impressive task, such as the single-minded Soviet pursuit of strategic parity with the United States and the capacity to challenge the global reach of American conventional power. But these characteristics of Soviet policy did not serve them especially well in the Middle Eastern diplomatic milieu of the 1970s and early 1980s; nor guarantee wisdom in dealing with indigenous instability on their periphery in Afghanistan or within their empire in Eastern Europe; nor escape the difficulties ensuing from the momentous rupture of their relations with communist China. And in the final analysis, Soviet national economic autarchy, although it may have cushioned the Soviet Union from the shocks of complex interdependence, has also consigned the Soviet Union to the sidelines as the rest of the world, and especially the United States, wrestles with the future of the global political and economic order.

Institutional fragmentation need not require an incoherent foreign policy. The post–World War II course of American policy suggests that to the contrary, once the American system is mobilized within a particular policy consensus, it is quite capable of setting and pursuing a foreign policy of some consistency. Thus from 1947 until the end of the 1960s, American policy pursued objectives first defined by Harry Truman and Dean Acheson. Debates were largely confined to the question of the appropriate means to be employed by the United States as it sought to construct and then maintain a world order consistent with its world view. The process of fashioning the consensus and setting the course was not without difficulty. The period between Truman's speech to Congress in March 1947 and the end of the Korean War was by no means placid. But once institutionalized in the early Eisenhower administration, the policy of containment remained remarkably stable for the next twenty years.

Indeed, policy consistency built on the smothering of the inherently conflictual institutional relationships of the American system contributed by the late 1960s and early 1970s to the collapse of policy consensus in the 1970s. The coherence of bipartisanship led ultimately to a complacency in Congress and an atrophying of its role in policy formulation. It is not to ignore the difficulties and problems involved in maintaining a creative congressional role in foreign policy formulation, that we suggest that American policy suffered ultimate disaster in Southeast Asia in part *because* Congress foreswore an active role under the presumed exigencies of the cold war in the 1950s. Moreover, the subsequent confusion and even occasional wrongheadedness attendant to the reassertion of the congressional role in the 1970s is not in itself proof of a failing and paralyzed system. Rather, it suggests the necessity of consistent attention within Congress to its constitutionally mandated role in the policy making process. That role does not extend far, if at all, into the realm of the conduct of diplomacy and foreign policy. And the attempt by Congress to develop mechanisms that facilitate congressional involvement in the conduct of policy are potentially mischievous. More important, they detract from the task—constitutionally mandated—of insisting upon and institutionalizing a role in the process of shaping policy objectives and the popular consensus necessary to their achievement. Nor can it be said that the means necessary for the effort are not available. It was, after all, no coincidence that the men who framed the Constitution placed the budgetary process, the power to declare war, important treaty powers, and the power to give advice and consent concerning the most important foreign and national security officers in Congress.

Bureaucracy and Diplomacy. It is of course, heretical to suggest that bureaucracies are anything less than the source of evil in the modern nation-state. For a decade or more, presidential candidates of both parties have been promising "to get Washington off the people's back." To argue against oppressive and overadministered government is one thing. To argue against governmental services rationally apportioned is another. The modern bureaucratic state is, after all, an advance from the rule of the shaman, mystic, animist, or Messiah. Thus Americans cursed the "irrationality" and "anarchy" of an Iranian nation in the grip of Islamic revolution and an ayatollah who counseled chiefly with God. Here, if ever, was consistency and coherence in the form of one man; but where, it was indignantly demanded throughout 1980, was the Iranian government?

Bureaucracy, at least, follows public rules and a generally public, knowable agenda. Hence, it can be sued, contained, or opposed on rational or legal grounds. The political world of the bureaucracy is permeable; the personal office of the President less so. The door to the Oval Office is open or shut largely at the discretion of the individual who resides therein.

A bureaucracy stores extant knowledge; it tends, however, to create new knowledge with great hesitation. This is a handicap, it is sometimes argued. After all, the world changes with great rapidity, and old answers to new challenges are needed; hence, typical bureaucratic reaction will surely be inappropriate and stale. Still, established policies have passed a certain test. A collective memory, to be sure, may mistake the future for the past. But often as not, the past and the future do resemble one another. And if there is no public agency for recalling which official policies have succeeded and which have failed, then any future innovations may well be inept. Worse, new tactics might be predictably inept and avoidable, especially if old responses are forgotten or discarded too readily.

It is true, of course, that bureaucracy tends to routinize responses and view what others see as crises as mere exaggerations of the usual. Here, too, however, bureaucracy performs a service. They do slow down reaction to events. But most novel events are not nearly as revolutionary as usually portrayed at first in any case. The usual, almost by definition, predominates over the catastrophic. By moving with caution, bureaucracies tend to let events run a natural course. We get used to them. They seem less menacing, in part, because they prove to be; in part, because they become defined as "normal"; and in part because usual routines can be brought into play. Events, like individuals defined as normal by others, tend to become subsequently normal, conforming to this public expectation.

Diplomacy is the adjustment of interests between sovereign states. Classic diplomacy views conflicts of interest as usual. International affairs are not viewed as a concatenation of crises. To the diplomat, diplomacy is a series of problems, solvable with patience and by compromise. To those who have viewed international relations as unpredictable, crisis-ridden and wholly different from normal, domestic politics, the inability of bureaucracies to create has been seen as a great debility. As Henry Kissinger disdainfully put it, "The quest for 'objectivity'—while desirable theoretically—involves

the danger . . . that an average standard of performance is established
. . . attention tends to be diverted from the act of choice . . . Decisions
can be avoided until crisis brooks no further delay."[30] If foreign
politics, however, are becoming more intertwined with domestic
politics—indeed, if international society and domestic society have
come to resemble each other[31]—this necessity for viewing statecraft
as an "act of creation" and a series of "choices" at critical junctures is as
hypothetical and unlikely as the management of any such massive,
controlled shift of public policy. The foreign policy apparatus's essential task, viewed in this light, is not crisis management, but rather the
storage of routines and information regarding the divergent interests
of states.

Finally, even if one conceives of foreign policy as the management
of a succession of crises or the employment of tactical virtuosity to
construct a new world order, the effort is for naught if the results
cannot be institutionalized. Short of a perpetually employed Metter-
nich, Bismark, or Kissinger, the task of curating their achievements
must fall to a foreign ministry. And if the achievements prove so
ephemeral that they cannot be transmitted to a foreign ministry and
institutionalized through some "average standard of performance,"
their standing as diplomatic achievements is at least arguable.

Democratic Constraints and Opportunities. In the final analysis, of
course, a democracy's foreign policy must command a degree of
public support if it is to be counted a success. But on perhaps no other
aspect of the American policy making context is there greater
ambivalence among policy elites. Leadership, we have noted, commonly views the public as narrow, ignorant, and ominous. The
upshot is that foreign policy makers feel compelled to "sell" their
policy departures for fear that they will be misunderstood and ultimately destroyed by a distracted or uncaring public.

The results are sometimes paradoxical. Thus the Truman administration, in its call to cold war, portrayed the Soviet Union as embody-
ing all that was evil and antithetical to Western civilization. Insofar as
the public responded as the Truman administration had hoped, the
President should not have been surprised that the public was uncomprehending 3 years later when he tried to rationalize a limited war
against this universal menace in Korea. The fears of an aroused and

ignorant public pursued subsequent Presidents. Eisenhower was unwilling to confront McCarthyism; Kennedy was reportedly unwilling, until after he would be reelected, to draw back from a war that he knew was beyond winning; and Johnson apparently carried with him fears that the American people would misunderstand any effort on his part to exit Vietnam with anything less than victory. And finally, Nixon, when he sought to construct a new and fairly limited strategic relationship with the Soviet Union, was forced to try to reverse this portrayal of the international system and especially the Soviet Union. Accordingly, detente was advanced as a breakthrough and a transformation of relations with a now reasonable and civilized Soviet Union. When the deep underlying conflicts in interest between the United States and the Soviet Union persisted, public skepticism about detente emerged and constrained and finally frustrated Jimmy Carter's effort to bring to fruition the SALT process set in motion by his predecessors. Indeed, he found himself shrilly scolding the Soviets for a military presence in Cuba that was almost 2 decades old in a vain attempt to save the SALT treaty by countering a public image that he was not tough enough on the Russians.

But were all these difficulties and constraints imposed by the public? Daniel Yankelovich, after some 25 years of polling the American people on their public policy attitudes, suggests a complex answer:

> In its statements to the American public, the U.S. leadership blows hot and cold. The tone is rarely balanced, ambiguities are played down, subtlety is sacrificed to overstatement. Some (perhaps all) . . . government statements harbor the assumption that the public is simpleminded, capable of holding only one extreme alternative in mind at a time—black *or* white, for *or* against, friend *or* foe. As policy needs dictate, the appropriate switch is thrown in an attempt to elicit the appropriate single-dimensioned response.[32]

To some extent, therefore, policy makers get the public opinion and, therefore, the constraints that they deserve. But it need not be that way, for as we have suggested, this view of a dark, sullen public is overdrawn.

It would be fatuous to argue that more than some small fraction of the public is fully informed and consistent in its foreign policy opinions. "But," as Yankelovich argues, "this should not be interpreted as meaning that the publc has no rational means of arriving at judgments on pressing issues in the foreign policy field. There is a definite 'public mind' at work—a special way in which the American people view the role of the United States in the foreign policy field."[33] Poll data are always controversial as to their meaning, but Yankelovich and others[34] have concluded that Americans, *in the face of a full debate* on complex issues, are quite capable of forming and articulating informed judgments as to their interests and the national interest. But if full debate of foreign policy assumptions, objectives, or alternative means (as distinct from the technical parameters of warheads, for example) is the exception rather than the rule, is it reasonable not to expect the public to hold overly simple and sometimes unstable or inconsistent opinions?

There was reason to believe in the mid 1970s that the public was "balancing the moral and the practical, calibrating the appropriate degree of involvement" as it attempted to come to grips with the implications of a heightened degree of activism on the part of the United States even as it retained the memory of the Vietnam experience and confronted the 1980s.[35] And surely it was not coincidental that these findings were drawn from an environment within which foreign policy makers and opinion leaders were compelled by public skepticism and their own uncertainty to articulate and debate these questions more openly than at perhaps any other time since the end of the Second World War. That experience has undoubtedly been an uncomfortable one for all concerned, especially policy makers and potential policy makers who in times past could claim a kind of privileged sanctuary from debate. But the failures of policy and the collapse of consensus within the policy elite itself, for the time being at least, contributed to circumstances in which debate was inevitable. The 1980s may witness the emergence of a new consensus and a corollary decline in the cacophony of voices, for once again policy elites assert the presence of foreign menace. It is not self-evident, however, that the quiet will attest to American democracy operating most efficiently. Indeed, if, as seems to have been the case throughout the period since World War II, a viable foreign policy must proceed within the context of a deep and legitimate domestic consensus, then debate remains essential.

In the final analysis, therefore, the assertion that democracy in America is a decidedly inferior form of government for undertaking foreign policy may be more a comment on the foreign policy than on the governmental form. A foreign policy requiring the permanent mobilization of the American political economy in the efficient global application of force and the threat of force including the resort to nuclear war, may indeed be beyond the capacity of American democracy and government traditionally defined. But then, there is reason to believe that such a policy is neither any longer appropriate to the world politics of the late twentieth century, nor capable of commanding the sustained support of the American people. An interdependent world of many nuclear powers, environmental fragility, crushing poverty for its less-developed countries, and uncertain economic prospects for its most-developed countries may require a considerable measure of mutual sensitivity and responsiveness within a framework of legitimate institutional and *ad hoc* arrangements for managing and resolving conflict, if it is to survive into the twenty-first century. The democratic experience, insofar as it encompasses the development and operation of such political forms, would certainly seem to speak to such a need. At a minimum, the American people seem unlikely to develop and sustain a creative and positive response to such a world unless they and their leadership are true to the wisdom of that democratic experience.

NOTES

1. Alexis de Tocqueville, *Democracy in America*, vol. 1 (New York: Vintage Books, 1945), p. 243.
2. For a review of American policy after World War II that emphasizes (though in balance with other factors) the role of domestic forces and constraints see, James A. Nathan and James K. Oliver, *United States Foreign Policy and World Order*, 2nd ed. (Boston: Little, Brown, 1981). An earlier version of the first part of this chapter was presented before the 1980–81 Dinner Seminar Series on National Security Affairs of the National Security Affairs Institute of the National Defense University, Washington, D.C. and published in Philip S. Kronenberg, ed., *Planning U.S. Security* (Washington, D.C.: National Defense University, 1981).
3. Alexander Hamilton, "Federalist Paper No. 24," in *The Federalist Papers* (New York: New American Library, 1961), p. 153 (emphasis in the original).

4. James Madison, *Notes of Debates in the Federal Convention of 1787* (New York: Norton, 1969), p. 214 (emphasis added).

5. Madison, "Federalist Paper No. 51," *The Federalist Papers*, p. 320.

6. Ibid., p. 322.

7. *Meyers* v. *United States*, 272 U.S. 293 (1926), Justice Brandeis dissenting.

8. Hamilton, op. cit., p. 153.

9. Arthur M. Schlesinger, Jr., *The Imperial Presidency* (Boston: Houghton Mifflin, 1973).

10. See Clinton Rossitor, *The American Presidency*, 2nd ed. (New York: Harcourt, Brace, Jovanovich, 1960), p. 30.

11. For an expression and elaboration of the latter view see, Morton Halperin, et al., *The Lawless State: The Crimes of the Intelligence Agencies* (New York: Penguin, 1976) and Halperin and Daniel Hoffman, *Freedom vs. National Security: Secrecy and Surveillance* (New York: Chelsea House, 1977). See also Frank J. Bonner, *The Age of Surveillance: The Aims and Methods of America's Political Intelligence System* (New York: Knopf, 1980). For a discussion of the development of the presidency during the late 1960s and early 1970s in addition to that presented by Schlesinger, see Thomas Cronin, *The State of the Presidency*, 2nd ed. (Boston: Little, Brown, 1980) and Cronin, *The Presidency Reappraised* (New York: Praeger, 1977).

12. Perhaps the most comprehensive reviews of Congress and foreign policy during the 1970s are Alton Frye, *A Responsible Congress* (New York: McGraw-Hill, 1975) and Thomas M. Frank and Edward Weisband, *Foreign Policy by Congress* (New York: Oxford University Press, 1979); see also, Cecil V. Crabb, Jr. and Pat M. Holt, *Invitation to Struggle: Congress, the President and Foreign Policy* (Washington, D.C.: Congressional Quarterly Press, 1980).

13. Michael J. Crozier, Samuel P. Huntington, Joji Watanuki, *The Crisis of Democracy: Report on the Governability of Democracies to the Trilateral Commission, Paper 8* (New York: New York University Press, 1975), p. 93.

14. Richard E. Neustadt, *Presidential Power* (New York: Wiley, 1960), p. 33.

15. Crozier, et al., op. cit., p. 93.

16. *Washington Post*, 30 November 1980, p. A12.

17. Ibid., p. A13.

18. Thomas R. Dye, "What to Do About the Establishment: Prescription for Elites," in Thomas R. Dye and L. Harmon Zeigler, *The Irony of Democracy: An Uncommon Introduction to American Politics*, 2nd ed. (Belmont, Calif.: Duxbury Press, 1972), p. 365.

19. Charles O. Lerche, Jr., *Foreign Policy of the American People*, 3rd ed. (Englewood Cliffs, N.J.: Prentice-Hall, 1967), p. 120.

20. George F. Kennan, *The Realities of American Foreign Policy* (Princeton, N.J.: Princeton University Press, 1954), p. 44.

21. Samuel P. Huntington in his contribution to the Trilateral Commission's report, *The Governability of Democracies*, p. 21.

22. See Lester Thurow's analysis of the economic implications of this situation in *The Zero-Sum Society* (New York: Basic Books, 1980).

23. Huntington, op. cit., passim.
24. Hearing before the Subcommittee on the Separation of Powers of the Committee on the Judiciary, U.S. Senate, 2nd Congress, 1st Session on *Executive Privilege: The Withholding of Information by the Executive* (Washington, D.C., U.S. G.P.O. 1971), pp. 455–456.
25. H. J. Morganthau, "The American Tradition in Foreign Policy" in Ray C. Macridis, ed., *Foreign Policy in World Politics*, 3rd ed. (Englewood Cliffs, N.J.: Prentice-Hall, 1967), p. 261.
26. On Soviet ethnic and racial problems see Helene Carrere d'Encausse, *Decline of an Empire: The Soviet Socialist Republics in Revolt* (New York: Newsweek Books, 1980). On the contemporary Soviet system: Seweryn Bialer, *Stalin's Successors: Leadership, Stability and Change in the Soviet Union* (New York: Cambridge University Press, 1980).
27. U.S., Congress, Joint Economic Committee, *Soviet Economy in a New Perspective: A Compendium of Papers*, 94th Congress, 2nd Session, 1976.
28. Jerry F. Hough, *Soviet Leadership in Transition* (Washington, D.C.: Brookings Institution, 1980).
29. Michael Tatu, *Power in the Kremlin*, trans. Helen Katel (New York: Viking Press, 1969), p. 519.
30. Henry A. Kissinger, *American Foreign Policy*, expanded edition (New York: Norton, 1974), p. 18.
31. For one of the best discussions of the similarities between domestic and international politics see Edward L. Morse, *The Transformation and Modernization of International Politics*, (New York: The Free Press, Macmillan, 1977). For a denial of this line of analysis, see Robert Tucker, *The Inequality of Nations* (New York: Basic Books, 1977).
32. Daniel Yankelovich, "Farewell to 'President Knows Best'," *Foreign Affairs* 57, no. 3 (1979): 687–688.
33. Ibid., p. 688.
34. See U.S. Congress, Hearings before the Senate Committee on Foreign Relations, *Foreign Policy Choices for the Seventies and Eighties*, 94th Congress, 1st and 2nd Session, 1975–1976.
35. Yankelovich, op. cit., p. 689.

Index